fat envelope frenzy

fat envelope frenzy

· · ·

One Year, Five Promising Students, and the Pursuit of the Ivy League Prize

JOIE JAGER-HYMAN

HARPER

NEW YORK · LONDON · TORONTO · SYDNEY

HARPER

HarperCollins books may be purchased for educational, business, or sales promotional use. For information please write: Special Markets Department, HarperCollins Publishers, 10 East 53rd Street, New York, NY 10022.

FIRST EDITION

Designed by Laura Kaeppel

Library of Congress Cataloging-in-Publication Data is available upon request.

ISBN: 978-0-06-125716-2

08 09 10 11 12 OV/RRD 10 9 8 7 6 5 4 3 2 1

This book is dedicated to my parents,
Wende and Arnold,
who always lead by example,

•

and my husband, Josh,
whose presence in my life
has been my greatest joy,

•

and in loving memory of
Christopher John Pearson,
who I miss very much.

· CONTENTS ·

· INTRODUCTION ·

My absolute favorite movie about the Harvard experience is 1973's *The Paper Chase*. The film tells the story of Professor Kingsfield, the commanding legal scholar, and his relationship with the green gang of first-year law students who enter his lecture hall each September. For the most part, the cast consists of archetypal characters—the insecure know-it-alls; the hard workers who can't make the grade; the privileged cruisers with cushy jobs waiting for them on the other end; and the needle-in-the-haystack really smart guy who made it to Harvard without connections or pedigree. In this case, the really smart guy's name is Hart (all the fellas go by their last names).

About halfway through the movie, Hart, who simultaneously adores and abhors the icy Kingsfield, learns that the Harvard Law School library keeps an off-limits archive of the handwritten class notes that their professors took when they themselves were law students. Fueled by his obsession with Kingsfield, Hart decides to risk his academic standing and future career by convincing one of his classmates to help him break into the annals. Hart believes that if he could just access the professor's old notes, perhaps he could penetrate his mind as well.

The screen is dark except for the beam of a flashlight illuminating the wire cages of paper, scanning the stacks. Soon, Hart discovers Kingsfield's dusty notebooks. He freezes and stands there slack-jawed, like he has just discovered the Holy Grail. "This is it," Hart says to his colleague. "This is the ageless passage of wisdom."

The idea that wisdom is somehow caged or exclusive is the central and brutal irony of Harvard's status as an American icon. Like so many students, Hart fetishizes Harvard. He has already been accepted to Harvard Law School—he is an "insider"—yet he strives for some wisdom or understanding that is out of his reach. Such is an environment where achievement will always be elusive and real success is impossible. At its worst, it is the resurrection of a modern-day golden calf.

Nowhere else is this phenomenon more pronounced than in the selective college admissions process, the gatekeeping mechanism that has so many otherwise rational, accomplished individuals experiencing unrivaled anxiety and panic. It doesn't help that it is harder today than ever before to get into a selective college. Harvard College turned down almost 21,000 candidates—including thousands of valedictorians and students with perfect SAT scores—in 2006–2007. That same school year, Columbia University denied admission to about 16,500 high-achievers. And Stanford University sent out approximately 21,500 rejection letters to ambitious applicants across the globe.

With competition at an all-time high, grooming for a spot at a top college has become a full-time job for scores of Ivy League hopefuls, who literally spend years studying for the SAT, loading up on Advanced Placement courses, and accumulating brag-worthy rosters of extracurricular activities. Across the nation, dinner table discussions are dominated by college talk, and some parents will stop at nothing to give their child every advantage. They hire high-priced consultants to help with educational decisions, from choosing the "best" nursery school to the "best" academic enrichment programs to the "best" internships, community service activities, and sports programs.

Too many communities are enmeshed in a collective obsession with achievement and accomplishment. And almost everyone involved—even admissions officers and college presidents—at some point feels victimized by the admissions process. We are in the midst of a cultural craze. I call it the Fat Envelope Frenzy.

The Fat Envelope Frenzy is somewhat predicated on the myth that college admission is contingent solely on merit. In reality, colleges often use their admissions policies to accommodate numerous stakeholders and accomplish various goals that are not always aligned. Prestigious colleges strive to attain diverse student bodies, while favoring the children of alumni and generous donors. They want all-star football teams and several Rhodes Scholars in each class. They recruit low-income students, but tie their admissions policies to performance on the SAT, which gives a well-known advantage to high-income students who are able to enroll in test-prep classes and gain access to pricey private tutors. Simply put, college admissions policies are confusing because colleges are confused. American higher education does not have a single, clear mission.

Seven years ago, I accepted a position as Assistant Director of Admissions at my alma mater, Dartmouth College. I was hired to give on-campus information sessions, recruit students by traveling to high schools and college fairs, interview dozens of applicants, and read and evaluate thousands of applications. For the most part, the students I met were delightful, accomplished young men and women. Of course, most were inevitably turned away, despite their potential and appeal. There were simply too many deserving candidates vying for a limited number of spots.

College admissions officers wear many different hats, depending on the time of year and the type of applicant with whom they are interacting. In the fall and spring, the staff hits the road for recruitment trips to give information on admissions procedures and, basically, sell the school. Part of the job includes driving up application numbers. Even the most popular universities find it essential to maintain a high degree of selectivity because external evaluators, like *U.S. News & World Report,* emphasize this in their rankings. The trick for admissions officers is to strike a balance between acknowledging the low acceptance rates at their institutions while simultaneously encouraging as many students to apply as possible. My personal strategy for mitigating these conflicting objectives was to distance myself from the students I met. I would go so far as to cut them off or redirect the conversation if they started telling me about their academic credentials and personal accomplishments, or asking questions along the lines of "What are my chances of getting in?" If I knew nothing real about these students, I could ignore the fact that the vast majority of them (about 80 percent of Dartmouth applicants at the time) would eventually be turned away. Like the students themselves, I focused on the positive. I persuaded every high schooler I met to take a chance at applying to the Ivy League.

Everything changed once the applications were submitted in the winter. My sunny, welcoming disposition was replaced by no-nonsense assessment. It's not that I didn't like, appreciate, or respect the applicants (many of whom were more qualified than I had been when I applied). But I quickly learned that I had to evaluate each candidate based on his or her potential contribution to the school. Of course, grades, SAT scores, essays, recommendations, and extracurricular accomplishments matter, but so does satisfying trustees and/or alumni by recruiting winning athletes, admitting legacy applicants, and attracting big donors. Most admissions officers are genuinely concerned with creating opportunities for talented students from underrepresented racial and socioeconomic backgrounds. However, they are bound by competing institutional interests that limit their power to recruit students who may not have had extensive college preparation or coaching.

It can be difficult for outsiders to grasp how or why individual institutions make certain decisions about particular applicants. How could Scott not get into Brown with a 4.0 average? Why did Mary get into Yale but rejected from Cornell? Because of this, a common misunderstanding has developed. Many people now believe that the admissions decisions at Ivy League and other highly selective colleges are made at "random." On the whole, this idea could not be further from the truth, as there is a rigid system of institutional priorities that serve as guidelines for building a class. However, the process of reviewing *individual* applications is somewhat subjective.

Admissions officers hail from a variety of backgrounds, bringing their personal experiences and preferences to the table. As is human nature, we tend to like students who remind us of ourselves. It got to the point in my office where we even knew the other admissions officers' preferences—"Beth" liked the scholar/athletes; "Tom" was apt to favor the quiet intellectuals; "Cindy" was a sucker for sob stories. Most successful applicants not only have exceptional qualifications; they are also lucky enough to have their files reviewed by people who are, to some extent, already predisposed to like them.

Fortunately, the system was created with a certain degree of checks and balances. At almost every selective college, each application is evaluated by more than one admissions officer. Many colleges hold weeks' worth of committee meetings, where admissions officers collectively vote on whether or not to accept individual candidates. Even when you work in admissions, you must advocate on behalf of the students you like. And you are often outvoted. I remember pleading with my colleagues to admit many different types of students: a young woman from Jamaica who wanted to use her Ivy League education to advance women's rights in her country; a middle-class boy from Kansas City who wrote an essay about the night that his father was arrested for tax fraud when he was in seventh grade; a valedictorian from rural Vermont with poor SAT scores who always dreamed of going to Dartmouth. These committee meetings were about making tough decisions, and everyone, including my boss, was overruled on occasion. That's why it is so important to remember that individual admissions decisions are not reflections of personal worth—no matter how tempting it is for some applicants or their parents to think of them that way.

Despite the arduous process of reading tens of thousands of essays, going through piles of transcripts and test scores, and enduring intense admissions committee debates, colleges don't always make the "right" decisions. Many of society's most influential and prophetic leaders were turned down by top schools. Prominent researchers Stacy Berg Dale and Alan Krueger have even come up with a name for people who get rejected from elite colleges and go on to achieve wild success. They call this the Spielberg Effect, after—you guessed it—director Steven Spielberg, who was twice rejected from prominent film programs, both at UCLA and USC. Recently, *02138* magazine, a publication named after the Harvard zip code, ran a feature article about famous Harvard rejects, including Warren Buffett, Ted Turner, Tom Brokaw, Matt Groening, and Meredith Vieira. An institution that welcomes Ted Kaczynski (the infamous Unabomber) and rebuffs Ted Turner obviously makes mistakes.

So where do we go from here?

Here's the bad news: getting into a top college is not going to get any easier, at least not in the foreseeable future. A generation ago, the majority of Americans did not pursue higher education immediately after finishing high school. Today, more than 60 percent of high school graduates don't skip a beat before turning in their tuition checks. We are also in the midst of a demographic bulge, as the children of baby boomers—a generation known as the echo boom—come of age. About 3.2 million students graduated from high school in 2007. That's more than half a million more students than the number that graduated just a decade ago.

More kids graduating from high school and going to college means increased competition and heightened anxiety for ambitious applicants. This explains why so many students are trying to up their odds of getting into a good college by applying to more schools. According to the Higher Education Research Institute, in each year since 1999, more than 82 percent of elite institutions reported an increase in applications over the previous year. In addition to this unprecedented rise in college applications, more students are also better prepared for college than ever before. The number of students taking AP courses more than doubled in the past decade, as did the number of exams they took. All of this contributes to the fast-escalating exclusivity of top colleges and universities. Unless elite colleges decide to increase the size of their entering classes, which is unlikely because they have numerous disincentives to do so, more and more qualified applicants will continue to receive rejection letters.

Here's the good news: all of us involved in the college admissions process—parents, students, admissions officers, teachers, guidance counselors, and the media—have the power to reframe how we think about the Fat Envelope Frenzy. At its best, the selective college admissions process is a valuable educational tool. After all, we don't just send our children to school to learn to read and write. Education is about learning how to succeed in life and acquiring intellectual, analytical, and social skills. Ironically, it is often the students who are turned away from their first-choice colleges who gain the most. They are given the opportunity to demonstrate resiliency—a fundamental, and often underrated, prerequisite for achievement and success in the long-term.

Applying to college is not just about choosing a single institution, a decision that is too often based on relatively superficial variables like school colors, athletic teams, or the distance of the campus from a student's home. It's about choosing—usually for the first time—what kind of life you want to have. What are you interested in studying? Where do you want to live? What kinds of people do you want to be associated with? What are the things that really matter to you?

The truth is, the undergraduate liberal arts curriculum is virtually identical at thousands of four-year colleges across the country. Intro to Psychology or Economics 101 is pretty much the same at Harvard as it is at Hunter College. Students seek out elite universities to be surrounded by other high-achieving, ambitious students. There are scores of colleges waiting to absorb the host of super-applicants being rejected from the Ivy League. This means that formerly "second-tier" institutions are also receiving record numbers of applications and attracting student bodies with impressive credentials. As a result, they are recruiting more accomplished faculty and furnishing their campuses with Ivy League–caliber labs, dorms, and athletic facilities. These schools just keep getting better. Ironically, the Fat Envelope Frenzy actually gives kids today more options to enroll in top colleges than they had a generation ago.

No matter where they end up going to college, most kids are better off for having struggled through the admissions process. Of course, they complain. And sometimes they lose perspective. But they also take those precious first steps toward adulthood, which are more valuable than any diploma on a wall.

· AUTHOR'S NOTE ·

I left the Dartmouth Admissions Office in the summer of 2002 and enrolled at the Harvard Graduate School of Education the following fall. My professional experience in college admissions awakened me to the inequalities that permeate our educational system and just how difficult it is to level the playing field for all students. I visited privileged schools with plenty of highly motivated, intelligent, cultured, ambitious students—who could easily have skipped college altogether and headed straight for graduate school. I also visited schools where students were neither planning nor prepared to attend college. Most of them wanted to succeed and have access to opportunities but were simply cut off from the streams that channel students into higher education. The saddest part was that they didn't even know just how much they didn't know. They had no idea what they were up against when compared with the tutored prep-school kids, who had been priming for college their whole lives.

I decided to focus my academic research on policies that promote college enrollment and graduation for low-income students. However, years after I had left the Dartmouth Admissions Office, people would always ask me questions about admissions. Do colleges really read the essays? How much do SAT scores matter? What makes one student stand out from the others? I was regularly approached by overwhelmed, obsessive, and frantic parents, looking for tips or secrets about how to game the admissions system. And I met plenty of kids who seemed desperate to get into a good college. Every year, the media reported on this escalating competition and the snowballing anxiety surrounding applying to college. I kept reading about how the quest to get into a top school ruined childhoods, destroyed families, and was tearing our society apart. I couldn't help but think back to my days in the Dartmouth Admissions Office and wonder about the part I had played in what was now being depicted as an almost criminal, wicked machine.

Was the competition for a spot at a prestigious college destroying a generation of otherwise bright-eyed, hopeful students? Were students as tortured and tormented as the newspaper articles had made them out to be? What is it really like to apply to an Ivy League college today?

More than ten years after I had applied to college and five years after I had worked in admissions, I felt compelled to revisit and explore the epic journey of the college application process. The human consequence of institutional decision-making is rarely seen in all its complexity—even though these institutions could never exist without the people who buy into them.

Fat Envelope Frenzy follows five top college applicants over the course of their senior years in various high schools across the country. To document the brutal minefield of college admissions, I decided to focus on students applying to Harvard, one of the most selective colleges in the United States, as well as the place where I have been studying our education system for the past five years.

Harvard is the trendsetter of selective college admissions policies. The college pioneered the use of the SAT as the gold standard of college entrance exams, redefined the goals of affirmative action when the controversial policy was first challenged in the courts, and, most recently, was the first prominent institution to eliminate early admissions policies that favor wealthy students. With an endowment of nearly $35 billion, Harvard is the second wealthiest nonprofit organization in the country (the wealthiest is the Catholic Church, which serves far more members). Harvard is the richest, most well-known university in the world.

But this is not a book about Harvard. This is a book about gifted, determined, and capable young adults interacting with a system that will either embrace or reject them. In the pages that follow, you will read about their goals, anxieties, strategies, philosophies, and experiences. Some of them will benefit from a categorical advantage in the admissions process, like being an Olympic-level athlete or a member of a minority group that colleges seek to recruit. Others will face greater odds because of personal obstacles, poor advising, or the fact that students like them tend to be overrepresented in the applicant pool. You will also meet the people in their communities—teachers, friends, siblings, parents, and counselors—who support, guide, and influence them in their quest for a spot at our nation's top colleges.

To properly cover the variety of applicants and their experiences, I chose five students from different racial, ethnic, socioeconomic, geographic, and religious backgrounds. I used a range of sources to track down potential students, and interviewed dozens of candidates before selecting the five stories I wanted to tell. To identify interesting prospects, I spent days scanning the posts on CollegeConfidential.com, a popular discussion board Web site where thousands of applicants go for information about the admissions process. I also contacted college guidance counselors, precollege outreach programs, and Ivy League alumni associations for references. However, when all was said and done, I chose the students I was most interested in getting to know.

I took one notable risk in selecting students for this book. I decided to write only about students who, based on my academic and professional experiences, I sincerely believed had a good chance of getting in to Harvard. I did this for two reasons. The first was to illustrate the different types of students who make up a class and how various applicants are evaluated in the context of the admissions process. The second was because I did not want to exploit the young adults who have been so generous with their stories. It seemed unethical to spend a year writing about someone I knew would never make it.

To use a slightly hokey analogy, each of the students in this book represents a different slice of the American pie. But you'll notice that most of them are from immigrant backgrounds. Many people believe that the college admissions process is one of the best examples we have for the actualization of the American Dream—the idea that everyone has the opportunity to succeed through hard work and ingenuity. Many children of immigrants, people of color, Jews, Catholics, Muslims, and women, who were traditionally excluded from elite universities, now view the possibility of admission to one of these schools as their chance to gain approval from society at large. Right before she dropped me off for my first day at college, my own mother said, "I can't believe we went from Auschwitz to Dartmouth in two generations." For her, my acceptance to an Ivy League college was a clear sign of validation by an institution she considered impartial and uncorrupt.

There are some things you should know about how I researched and wrote this book. I started conducting interviews when the students were just beginning their senior years in August 2006, and I regularly tracked their progress until June 2007, when they graduated from high school. I took more than thirty trips across the country during these nine months. I also corresponded with students over e-mail and on the telephone.

Despite my background in college admissions, I did not advise these students. They wrote their own essays, selected the colleges to which they wanted to apply, and completed their applications independently. None of the students in this book hired private consultants. Their decision-making process was based on their own research and the advice they received from school counselors, teachers, and, in some cases, parents and friends.

As with any work of nonfiction, the stories you are about to read actually happened. I use real names to identify people, schools, and places (with a few exceptions, such as classmates or teammates who I did not interview but are mentioned by others in this book). However, some of the events appear out of order to facilitate the storytelling. In addition, several scenes have been re-created based on interviews. I collaborated and consulted extensively with the students, parents, friends, and other parties to re-create any event at which I was not physically present. Even so, it is important to remember that this book was written by me, based on the interviews I conducted, incidents I witnessed, observations I made, notes I took, and questions I asked.

When interacting with the students, my goal was to observe rather than advise. However, in writing this book, I often insert my own experiences, findings from academic research, advice for applicants that I have gained over the years, as well as other background information that will provide you with an understanding of how the process works. My objective is to interweave the stories of real students to show you the various forces at play in today's competitive admissions environment. What does it really take to get into a top school? And what happens to the scores of worthy wannabes who don't get picked? Read on to find out.

fat envelope
frenzy

· ONE ·

"He's quiet and, of course,
wants to be a doctor"

FELIX

Felix Zhang is wearing one of his many Harvard sweatshirts. "I've always loved the school," he says, "not just because it's Harvard, but because it has *everything* in one place." It is the third week of September. Felix and I are eating chocolate brownies in the Barnes & Noble café in Berwyn, Pennsylvania, a posh suburb fifteen miles west of Philadelphia. Berwyn is on the Main Line, a term that is shorthand for desirable real estate. Many wealthy families in the greater Philadelphia metropolitan region seek out this cluster of exclusive suburban towns in close proximity to the convenient commuter rail.

At first glance, Berwyn could easily be caricatured as the perfect place to raise a family. With large homes and manicured lawns, more than half of the residents are married with children. The town is remarkably homogenous: most residents are rich (the median family income is about $90,000 a year, almost twice as much as the average American household earns) and white (a whopping 92.26 percent). Only 2 percent of Berwynites are Asian American like Felix.

Felix embodies the term "big teddy bear." It's not just physical. Though he is broadly built with an innocent round face, the gentle teddy bear vibe actually resonates from deep within. He's friendly to everyone, the kind of kid the other kids feel safe asking for help with their homework.

Felix has been preparing to go to Harvard for sixteen years, and there's no question that he's done everything right. Going into his senior year, he has already received a perfect score of 5 on Advanced Placement tests in Physics, Calculus, American History, European History, Statistics, English Language and Composition, and Biology. He also has straight As in all of his accelerated courses and a 780 in Math, 750 in Critical Reading, and 710 on the Writing sections of the SAT.

Felix knows that it takes more than just good grades and test scores to get into Harvard, and at only sixteen years old, he is already a distinguished pianist, whose talent has taken him across the globe, from Cincinnati to China. He has been a featured soloist on National Public Radio on more than one occasion, and at the age of fourteen, he was the youngest student selected to study at the Julliard School International Summer Music Academy in Leipzig, Germany. Felix has also performed for some of the world's best musicians, including Harvard professor Robert Levin, for whom he will play in the fall. Faculty endorsements are rare in the undergraduate admissions process because very few teenagers have the capacity to make an impression on the top experts in a given field. If all goes well, a positive review from Professor Levin could distinguish Felix's application and carry considerable weight with the Harvard admissions committee.

Despite his impressive musical accomplishments, Felix is seeking an alternative professional path. "People who do music have a need to share their music," he explains. "I don't really feel that need. Even though I *love* piano, I also want to do other things." Like both of his parents, Felix plans to become a physician and has been doing research with a renowned professor at the Jefferson Medical College in Philadelphia for the past several years. Though it is not uncommon for Ivy League applicants to have some experience in academic research, Felix's work really stands out. He was even named as the lead author on a paper that the lab recently submitted to a prestigious peer-reviewed journal, a distinction that is usually reserved for hardworking graduate students or professors themselves. The study was designed to investigate whether estrogen substitutes inhibit neuronal cell death associated with Alzheimer's disease in postmenopausal women. Most teenage boys don't even know what postmenopausal means.

Though piano and research are two of Felix's primary passions, he is also involved with a myriad of other activities outside of his classes at Conestoga High School, which has been consistently recognized as one of the best public schools in the state. He is a volunteer EMT at the Berwyn Fire Department, captain of the quiz bowl, debate, and model UN teams, editor in chief/founder of *SciSpot Online Science Magazine* (his school's first science-focused newsletter), president/founder of Young Artists for People (a club that organizes talented high school musicians to perform in local retirement homes), and a three-year veteran of the Student Council.

On the surface, it might seem that Felix is a shoo-in for admission to Harvard. However, as an Asian American, Felix is also a member of a group that is overrepresented in the Harvard applicant pool, which could be a disadvantage in the admissions process. In the past two decades, selective colleges have been repeatedly accused of a bias against Asian Americans, and several students have gone so far as to file official complaints with the federal government at the Office for Civil Rights. No university has ever been convicted of discrimination, but an investigation into the admissions process at Harvard in the early 1990s uncovered a number of offensive remarks written by the staff in regard to Asian American candidates, including glib descriptions such as "he's quiet and, of course, wants to be a doctor."

A more recent study published in *Social Science Quarterly*, which analyzed data from 124,374 applicants to three highly selective colleges, found that qualified Asian American students had lower admission rates at these top schools than any other group of students. In addition to being overrepresented in the applicant pool, Asian Americans also tend to be excluded from many of the institutional priorities that guide the selective college admissions process. As immigrants or children of immigrants, they may be less likely to have a parent who attended a selective American college and may not benefit from the advantages of legacy in college admissions. They also do not qualify for most affirmative action programs and are a rarity on athletic teams. In fact, the only category in which Asian American students are likely to be given a boost in the admissions process is for high SAT scores, which is still a key variable in admissions decisions. Even so, the researchers projected that eliminating preferences based on legacy, race, and athletics would increase Asian American acceptances by approximately 30 percent at the three highly selective schools they studied.

Based on these statistical trends, Felix's background may hurt his chances of getting into Harvard. It also doesn't help that he's up against a number of his extremely competitive classmates. "Most of my friends are involved in lots of clubs," he explains. "There is even a story of a kid who tried to run for president of the Young Democrats even though he had never been to a meeting. Then he actually went to the Young Republicans and ran for a position, like secretary or something!" Felix laughs at the story without a hint of judgment or resentment.

"There can be a lot of competition, but mostly it's confined to a small group," he says of his high school culture. "You know, 'the smart ones.' They're good academically and do lots of stuff outside of school. There's definitely competition there, but it's friendly competition."

"Where do you think you fit in all of this?" I ask.

"I mean, I think I'm up there," he answers, referring to his academic performance, "but I know a lot of kids who are not on the AP track that are just as smart but don't bother with the AP tests. I don't know . . ." Felix looks down as he talks about this injustice, like he somehow feels guilty. "People have said that the school focuses only on nurturing the top kids and the others get gypped."

Selective colleges encourage students to take challenging high school classes to prepare them for the rigors of collegiate academics. As a result, high schools across the country have been adding more and more Advanced Placement, or AP, courses to their curricula. Felix's high school actually offers more AP classes than any other public or private school in the state. Last year, the 2,000 students at Conestoga collectively passed almost 1,400 AP tests, and the College Board officially recognized 219 students for their outstanding college-level performance. (These numbers are even more impressive considering that students in the earlier grades are ineligible for AP courses.)

Felix and his high-achieving peers are part of a nationwide trend of students taking more AP tests than ever before. About 1.5 million high schoolers nationwide now take at least one AP exam. And last year, 13,657 students took nine or more AP exams by the time they graduated from high school, more than seven times as many students who did this a decade ago.

The enormous growth of the high school AP program has not translated into significant academic gains for students in college, leading some to speculate that AP courses are less rigorous than actual college classes. According to two recent studies at Harvard and Texas Christian University, students who take multiple AP courses in high school have the same grades and persistence rates in college as those who took regular college-preparatory classes. This may explain why students at high schools like Conestoga are able to manage so many AP courses.

Like his classmates, Felix has loaded up on AP courses for his senior year. "I like to challenge myself," he explains, which is no surprise since he comes from a long line of overachievers. His parents are originally from Shanghai, where they both earned degrees in medicine and engineering before enrolling in Ph.D. programs at Massachusetts Institute of Technology (MIT). They now both work in pharmaceuticals.

I ask Felix if he hopes to go into the pharmaceutical industry as well.

"No way," he responds, shaking his head for emphasis. "After what I saw in China, I know I want to practice medicine on a personal level or somehow help people who really need it."

Two summers ago, when he was just fourteen years old, Felix embarked on a trip to a rural Chinese orphanage, where he lived in a hut with two doctors and their assistants. ("I didn't want to let him go," his mother later tells me, "but he insisted, so I trusted him. As a trained doctor, I wouldn't have been able to do that work. It's just too horrible.") Chinese children born with congenital diseases or deformities are often put up for adoption in the poor rural districts because their families do not have the means to properly provide for them. The state then places all the sick orphans together in special orphanages. However, because China has yet to develop the infrastructure to care for these children, these orphanages are often in a terrible condition with absolutely no medical facilities.

"Even though I always wanted to be a doctor, it was really a nightmare-type place. There were like fifty kids in a building about the size of this small area," Felix says, tracing his finger around the border of the café. "There was a three-year-old girl with severe mental retardation who had ripped out all her hair and another little boy with hydrocephalus—"

"Wait, what's that?" I ask, almost afraid to hear the answer.

"Oh, sorry," he apologizes. "It's when fluid builds up in the brain cells and the head swells. It kind of looks like an alien head. There was a three-year-old boy there whose head was sixty centimeters around!" The average head circumference for a three-year-old boy is about forty-eight centimeters.

"There were also many kids with spinal stenosis—you know, they were paralyzed—but the orphanage didn't have money for wheelchairs so they had to drag themselves around on the dirty floor by their arms." He raises his eyebrows as if to ask, *Can you believe that this actually happens in the world?*

I ask Felix if he was changed by his trip to China, and he takes a moment before answering. "It was amazing how everyone just accepted their fate. They sat there until they died. They had no other choice." The story seems too real and gruesome to be narrated in a suburban café.

"When I got back to the lab at Jeff Medical School, the doctors were all nice and clean," Felix continues. "I saw them worrying about things like the nameplates on their lab coats," he says, once again raising his eyebrows. "I really started thinking about the health care system in general, and started to appreciate Doctors Without Borders [a nonprofit organization that provides health care and medical training to needy populations] and those kinds of groups. I think I want to do something like that."

Felix's grandparents, who still live in Shanghai, also trained as doctors. They continue to practice medicine, and his grandfather is known as one of the best surgeons in the city. "My grandparents have very high expectations," Felix explains. "For me to build on the success of my family, it seems that Harvard is the only answer. It is one of the only schools outside of China that people know." Apparently, there is a hugely popular book in China called *Harvard*

Girl Yiting Liu, which was written by a mother and stepfather who tell the story of how their daughter got into Harvard. Since it was published in 2000, the book has sold millions of copies, inspired dozens of copycats, and made Yiting Liu, the "Harvard Girl" herself, a household name.

Even though they live so far away, the Zhangs still manage to arrange family reunions. In fact, they have a big vacation to Hawaii planned for mid-December—at exactly the same time that Felix will receive the verdict on his early action application to Harvard. "I don't really like it that everyone knows where I'm applying," he says. "I'm worried that I won't get in. It would be better if it was a secret so no one would be disappointed. I hate disappointing people."

I ask Felix if he feels pressure to live up to all that his family has accomplished. "It's sort of a blessing and a curse," he answers. "It's a blessing to look up to them. And my parents have an inside perspective on medical schools and all that. But sometimes they think that they know everything. My mom likes to teach me to play piano even though she doesn't even play." For the first time, Felix sounds like a normal, angst-filled teenager.

Felix has just returned from what he calls "the marathon college tour, otherwise known as I-95." The Zhangs drove up the northeast coast to visit Yale, MIT, and Harvard, where Felix had an on-campus interview. "Yale was unexpectedly breathtaking," he says, wide-eyed. "I loved the campus and environment and the residential colleges were just amazing. Of course, just when I thought Yale was the best thing ever, we drove to Harvard and I totally forgot about *that other Ivy*."

We all remember our first love. For Felix, that first love is Harvard University. He entered the Admissions Office, dressed down in slacks and an untucked button-down shirt, trying his best to mask his anxiety before his interview. "The guy who went before me was wearing a full suit and tie, kind of like the stereotypical Asian kid," Felix says. "When my mom saw him she started freaking out, saying, 'You're underdressed, you're underdressed.' But I had the exact opposite reaction. When I saw what he was wearing, I was happy because I figured that I would come off as the 'social guy' compared to him."

Felix was interviewed by a recent graduate, Erin Fehn, whom he describes as "really cool, definitely not the old bespectacled scholarly sage I was expecting." Ms. Fehn quickly demonstrated her affability. Only two years out of college, she is able to relate to the intimidated high school students who visit her office for interviews and ask questions at Harvard information sessions. Felix took to her immediately. The interview flew by.

"We were both laughing the whole time and relating to common interests," he says. "It didn't really feel like an interview at all but more of a conversation, mutually swapping stories. We talked about my Alzheimer's research for quite a while, piano, debate, my community service interests, parents, and before we knew it, the thirty minutes were up."

Before parting, Ms. Fehn dropped a verbal atomic bomb on the unguarded teenager. "Amazingly, she told me that she would tell the committee what a great person I was and how fabulous it was to talk to me. I'm hoping that's a positive," Felix says.

Interviews play many different roles in the admissions process, depending on the candidate, the interviewer, and the college in question. Some schools don't require interviews for undergraduate candidates at all, simply because they have a limited number of staff members and volunteers. For those that do, there are typically two types of interviews: on-campus and alumni, with some colleges offering both options.

On-campus interviews are generally the more important of the two. These interviews are usually handled by trained students or staff members who have a good perspective on the applicant pool with which to contextualize particular candidates. Admissions officers tend to put stock in their colleagues' evaluations, and, on rare occasions, students may even end up having their applications evaluated by the very same person with whom they interviewed. A positive assessment from Ms. Fehn could potentially help Felix's chances of getting into Harvard.

Alumni interviews generally do not carry the same weight in the admissions process because the interviewers are not trained professionals. They tend to have a limited perspective when it comes to the overall applicant pool. One alumna's "outstanding superstar" may seem like the girl next door when compared to twenty thousand other exceptional applications in the Admissions Office. Alumni interviews are used more to encourage graduates to stay connected with the institution as well as to give applicants an opportunity to ask questions about the school. These interviews are usually conducted somewhere close to the applicant's house, like a local Starbucks or a neighborhood diner, or sometimes over the phone.

As Felix excitedly tells me about his interview, I am pleased to hear how well he handled the situation. He managed to talk about his accomplishments without losing his sense of humor or being pretentious. Plus, he let the conversation drift to world events, books, movies, and the arts. Perfect, since for the most part, interviewers tend to give high marks to the kinds of people with whom they enjoy socializing. Achievement and intelligence count, but so does being kind, accessible, and humble.

A few weeks later, Felix hands me a stack of papers—things like his transcript, résumé, and a copy of his school newspaper—to give me some more information about him. Included in the pile is an essay that he published several years earlier in *Stone Soup*, a bimonthly magazine for young writers and artists that receives more than 250 submissions a week. I flip through the pages until I spot a photograph of a chubby, sweet-faced Asian American boy wearing glasses and a polo shirt. His identity is confirmed by the underlying caption: FELIX ZHANG, 13, BERWYN, PENNSYLVANIA.

The short story, entitled "Good Night Son," is a tragic tale about Ryan Carrol, a boy who spends his life trying to please his father. His father had worked hard to overcome the obstacles of his childhood and vowed to teach his son to achieve in the same way. Ryan grew up to be a remarkable man—intelligent, hardworking, kind, and talented. To escape the perfectionism forced upon him by his father, Ryan fell in love with music and evolved into a brilliant pianist. But his father failed to reward him with even modest praise for his accomplishments. He never even says "good night" to his son.

Ryan ultimately enrolls at Harvard and goes on to medical school. After his graduation (at which his father failed to congratulate him), he decides to practice medicine at an impoverished clinic in India—in defiance of his father's wish that he become a "big CEO of a large pharmaceutical company." Ryan ends up getting mortally wounded while overseas. He awakes in a hospital bed to find his father by his side. Just before his son's death, his dad says "good night" for the first time.

ANDREW

Founded in 1847, Jesuit High School is one of the most respected schools in the city of New Orleans. The all-boys school is known for scholastic excellence, athletic prowess, and a strict code of conduct, including a required military-type uniform and rules about haircuts and jewelry. In general, students enter Jesuit in the eighth grade and are selected based on their elementary school records; standardized test scores; and recommendations from teachers, principals, and/or a church pastor. Since Catholic schools are a popular and cost-effective alternative to New Orleans' struggling public school system, admission to Jesuit is competitive. The school enrolls a number of academically talented students from other religious backgrounds as well.

With sandy blond hair and an average build, Andrew Tessier makes his first impression as an inconspicuous clean-cut teenage boy. His school uniform, which he wears with pride, is a pressed monochrome khaki ensemble whose primary accessories include a shiny reflective belt buckle and a black plastic name tag pinned to his lapel. A gold class ring with a blue stone rests on his finger. It belonged to his grandfather, who, along with his father and uncle, also graduated from Jesuit.

Andrew, who was born and raised in New Orleans, is beginning his final year at Jesuit High School. He wants to go out with an academic bang and has loaded up on demanding classes, including AP Chemistry, AP Calculus, AP Government, AP English, Honors Physics, and a course in American military history (in addition to his required religion classes). Andrew is in the running for valedictorian. Keeping his perfect grade point average is a big priority.

"Down here, it's a big thing," he explains. "If you put on your résumé that you were valedictorian of your class at Jesuit, people will notice. It's just 'cause Jesuit has such a long history, and people who went to high school here know about it. If you meet a valedictorian, it's like, 'This kid's *gotta* be smart.'"

Though Andrew is a loyal Jesuit student, there was a time when his future at the school was in jeopardy. About a year ago, he was sitting in chemistry class when he heard a familiar announcement on the loudspeaker system informing students to tune their radios to 870 AM for school closure information over the weekend. A hurricane was heading toward the Gulf region.

"There are always big hurricanes," explains Andrew. His bold brows dominate his round beatific face, especially when arched in punctuation. "Ivan came by the year before that. It was coming, projected to hit us, made a last-minute turn, and we didn't even get any rain. That's happened several times before: 'The hurricane's coming, blah, blah, blah.'"

That Saturday morning, the Tessiers tuned in to media reports predicting that a major storm, Hurricane Katrina, was on course to hit the city. Katrina had intensified overnight and was now a Category-Three hurricane with winds of up to 130 miles per hour threatening to unleash serious damage. "We had a Category One, Cindy, that July," Andrew remembers. "I was working at the Red Cross at the time, and everyone was really surprised that it did as much damage as it did. We didn't have power for three or four days. It was a hassle, but that's just life."

After hearing reports of a looming Category Three, Andrew and his father went to Lowe's in search of wood and other storm supplies. They boarded the windows of their beautiful 150-year-old house in the Garden District, a neighborhood on relatively high ground compared to the rest of the city. The Tessiers knew this procedure well, having survived predictions of catastrophic hurricanes that failed to materialize into full-blown disasters before. However, the family discussed the possibility of evacuating later that day.

"I went to fill up all the bathtubs with water in case we stayed," Andrew recalls. "My dad remembered how the power was out for two weeks after Hurricane Betsy, which was just a mess. He suggested that we might as well leave. I was more of the opinion of waiting to see if it changed course."

By early Sunday morning, Hurricane Katrina was classified as a Category Five. And it was heading directly for New Orleans.

With his older sister off at medical school in Virginia, Andrew and his mother started packing, as his father, a real estate lawyer, headed to his downtown office to back up his files. By the time he returned to the house, Mayor Nagin had ordered a mandatory evacuation of all residents of New Orleans—the first mandatory evacuation in the city's history. Having survived more than three hundred years of close calls and false alerts, New Orleans residents started to wonder if their luck had run out. What would become of them if the "big one" actually hit the city?

Andrew remembers the events as if they happened yesterday.

"We had mixed emotions about leaving," he recounts in a careful, somber tone. "I think the mayor said that there would be six feet of water on St. Charles Avenue based on computer models. They've always had doomsday scenarios though. I think he used it as a scare tactic to get people to leave, which he should have. We really didn't know what was going to happen. I thought my mom was kind of overreacting when we were leaving. We're pretty high for New Orleans standards, plus we have steps to our house, but she made us move all the furniture to the second floor."

Andrew was more concerned with whether or not his family had enough gas to get out of the city. "Gas is a major issue. Right before any hurricane comes, gas prices spike. And the lines are just huge." Though they may have had more room for possessions and been more comfortable in Andrew's SUV, the family piled into his father's sedan because it was more fuel efficient—and more valuable.

"New Orleans has three or four major evacuation routes, so you basically have eight lanes to evacuate all the people. The plan actually worked reasonably well, but by the time we left, we couldn't go west to Texas because there was too much traffic. So we went east. It took us eleven hours to get to somewhere around Destin, Florida, which would normally take about five. We stopped at the first hotel that didn't have a mandatory evacuation."

To Andrew, the car ride felt exceedingly long. "I listened to music a lot, and complained about the traffic," he remembers. By Sunday night, the Tessiers had settled into a hotel. "The weather predictions were pretty ridiculous on the Web. The hurricane went from one hundred ten to one hundred twenty miles per hour . . . and then from one hundred fifty to one hundred seventy-five miles per hour. It was like, *Are you joking?* When it hit Florida, the storm was *six hundred miles across.* That's absolutely massive. It was pouring. There were massive waves. I've never seen weather that bad. My parents were worried, but what are you going to do? Eventually, we went to bed."

On Monday morning, in the calm after the storm, a collective sigh of relief flickered across the Southeast. By the time of Katrina's landfall near the Louisiana-Mississippi border, the storm had weakened considerably, back to a Category Three. Andrew says that it was like waking up from a heart-pounding nightmare. New Orleans had avoided a direct hit.

"It was like, 'Yay! New Orleans dodged the bullet,'" Andrew remembers. A glimpse of a smile spreads over his face before dolefully wilting in the blink of an eye. "Then Tuesday, it was like, 'Oh wait, there's flooding.' We didn't know how much our house was flooded, but we heard through the grapevine that uptown was okay."

The images on TV just made things worse. Andrew and his parents watched footage of looters on Canal Street and heard stories that his neighborhood was being raided as well. "The rumors were greatly exaggerated," Andrew says, defending his community. "We didn't have any looting. None of our friends had looting."

Unable to return to New Orleans, the Tessiers remained at their Florida hotel for days, cut off from most of their friends and family. Cellular phones in the 504 area code were useless because the city's cell phone towers were decimated by the flood. Using the hotel phone to call out, they contacted Andrew's uncle, who lives in Houston, and were able to secure a rental apartment for the family.

That Friday, the Tessiers set out for Texas, by which time the price of gas had doubled from only a week before. Because the interstate highway was unnavigable, they drove a meandering twenty hours over two days. "We were *really lucky*, because once we got to Houston there was physically *nowhere* to stay," Andrew recalls. His father now faced the daunting process of putting his law firm back together. He began contacting his partners and employees to reorganize and resume business operations.

Andrew was also faced with an enormous obstacle. His beloved Jesuit High School was basting in five feet of water. He had to find a new school to enroll in, at least temporarily. His mother, Carli, decided to contact Phillips Academy, one of the most prestigious and highly selective boarding schools in the country. She was familiar with the school because Andrew's older sister, Elizabeth, had briefly considered applying there several years earlier.

A polished, all-American beauty with long blond hair and willowy stature, Andrew's mom looks like she might be a local news correspondent or the host of a talk show. "I didn't know what to do or where to turn," she says in a soft and charming Southern accent, her hands clasped. "I called the Admissions Office at Phillips Academy to make them aware of the situation. They said they were sending someone to Houston to interview students from New Orleans. We were desperate." Phillips Academy had not only agreed to enroll students who needed to relocate after Hurricane Katrina, but also, because of the extraordinary circumstances, the school decided not to subject New Orleans residents to their standard admissions process. They typically have a lower acceptance rate than any college in the country.

Phillips Academy (also known as Andover after its quaint Massachusetts hometown) is an illustrious institution, whose history is intertwined with that of the nation. It was founded during the American Revolution as an all-boys boarding school. George Washington delivered the school's first graduation address, and John Hancock's famous signature adorns the school's articles of confederation. The lengthy list of notable Andover graduates includes John F. Kennedy Jr., Oliver Wendell Holmes Sr., and both Presidents Bush. Approximately half of Andover graduates go on to the Ivy League each year and a whopping 19 students matriculated at Harvard from the class of 2006 alone.

To say that Phillips Academy is one of the finest high schools in the country is somewhat misleading; the school is much more like a college than a high school. The 500-acre campus features two ice hockey rinks, eight squash courts, a crew boathouse, and eighteen sports playing fields. It also hosts several museums for art, architecture, and Native American artifacts. Andover students can participate in more than 350 extracurricular organizations and choose from more than 300 courses in a wide variety of disciplines, such as Art History, Classics, Philosophy, and Psychology. They also have the opportunity to study abroad in places such as France and China.

A few days after they arrived in Houston, Andrew had an interview with an Andover school official and was offered a coveted spot in their junior class. At the same time, he got word that Jesuit High School of New Orleans was preparing to reorganize in collaboration with an affiliated Jesuit school in Houston, where many of its students had been relocated. Though he knew it was an enviable opportunity, Andrew resisted enrolling at Phillips Academy. He insisted that he wanted to stay at Jesuit and eventually return to New Orleans. "Jesuit is just a different kind of school," Andrew says. "Both my father and my grandfather went there. We're really proud of loyalty and tradition. Plus, I didn't want to abandon my friends."

With their lives turned upside down by Katrina, Andrew's mother felt that her son would benefit from the stability that Phillips Academy would provide and tried to persuade him to enroll there. "I wanted him to go because I knew it was a great school, and I trusted them," she remembers. "I talked to the assistant principal, and she was exceptional. She said, 'Just let him come with us. We can get him new clothes, a place to stay, and everything he needs.'"

Phillips Academy is in a position to be generous, with more than $12 million in their scholarship budget and a $700 million endowment. But Andrew felt devoted to Jesuit High School and his hometown. He convinced his mother to let him enroll at the Texas location so that he could eventually return to New Orleans.

The semester kicked off with a rocky start. Because the Houston school could not simultaneously accommodate its local residents and the additional New Orleans evacuees, Andrew and his classmates attended impromptu evening classes from 3:30 to 9 PM, many of which were taught by the same teachers he had had a few weeks earlier.

"A lot of the teachers didn't even have their own stuff to give us," says Andrew. "They lost their books and lesson plans. There's this one English teacher who is famous for vocabulary words. He makes us learn two thousand nine hundred sixty-one words, but he lost all of his tests, every single one of them."

A few weeks later, in late September 2005, the Tessiers found themselves caught up in an unprecedented turn of events. The National Hurricane Center had detected a massive storm, Hurricane Rita, headed straight for Houston, Texas. They were in the path of another predicted Category-Five hurricane.

"We evacuated *again*," Andrew recounts, widening his brown eyes. "It was like, *Are you kidding me?* There were three Category-Five hurricanes that year. Only three had hit the United States in the last century."

This time, the Tessiers did not debate over whether or not to evacuate from their Houston apartment. They made sure to get on the road before the traffic got out of control and waited out Hurricane Rita at a friend's house, just outside of New Orleans. It was the first time Andrew had been back in the city since Katrina.

After Rita had passed, Andrew and his father went to check on the damage to their house in the Garden District. They were met by military guards—M16s in hand—upon entering Orleans Parish. "That was kind of freaky," Andrew recalls, his face tensing up. "The city was a mess. Dead leaves and branches everywhere. The only thing around were Humvees and Black Hawks."

Though their house was in one of the few neighborhoods that escaped flooding, the Tessiers were not as lucky when it came to wind damage. Most of the houses on their street needed completely new roofs. "My room was the only room that had significant visible damage," Andrew says, describing the scene in his second-floor bedroom toward the back of the house. "You could look up and see the sky. We went up to the attic to see how much roof damage there was. But when we climbed the stairs, we saw that there was *no roof.*"

Later that day, Andrew helped his father clean out their refrigerator, which they were able to save (New Orleans residents eventually discarded an estimated thirty thousand rotting refrigerators that year). Afterward, the family went back to their rented apartment in Houston.

It took months for officials to restore electrical power to New Orleans, during which most of the city remained empty. This made it impossible to get started on construction. The Tessiers' beautiful, old house lay empty and damaged, compounding its structural ailments. They now had to deal with major mold and water damage.

"My mom didn't see the house until December," Andrew says. "She just didn't want to see it."

On December 23, right after he had finished his final exams for the term, Andrew and his mother enjoyed a marvelous Christmas present. They left their Houston apartment for good and headed back to their house in New Orleans. Despite the fact that some of their streetlights still didn't work and much of the city was full of debris, Andrew felt great about being home. "Houston people are nice, but it's not New Orleans," he says.

Jesuit High School was the first school with major flood damage to reopen after Hurricane Katrina, a fact about which Andrew is noticeably proud. The cafeteria, which took more than a year and a half to remodel, now contains an oversize aerial photo of the school building and surrounding structures submerged in brown sludge. The big yellow school bus roofs peeping out from underneath the mess testify to the scale of destruction.

Unlike most schools in the area, the vast majority of Jesuit students returned that winter, and Andrew was able to finish his junior year in the same school where he started, almost as if nothing had ever happened. Now a senior, he is gearing up for the college application process.

Andrew has all the academic credentials to get into a top school. In addition to being a straight-A student, he is an excellent test taker. He scored 760 out of a possible 800 in both the Critical Reading and Math sections of the SAT and 770 or above on subject tests in writing, American history, math, and chemistry. He also received perfect scores on Advanced Placement tests in history, English language, and Latin poetry. Most of his extracurricular activities involve community service or church, but he plays tennis and competes in math competitions as well.

Andrew loves to learn and is the type of kid who takes extra classes for fun. The summer before his senior year, he enrolled in the Education Program for Gifted Youth (EPGY) Summer Institute, a competitive four-week engineering program at Stanford University. Admission to the program is selective. To be considered, students are required to submit transcripts, test scores, teacher recommendations, samples of their work, and an essay describing their reasons for wanting to attend. If accepted, students live in the campus dorms and attend daily two-and-a-half-hour classes with Stanford faculty in addition to completing three hours of homework each night.

"My dad kind of pushed for the summer program at Stanford. It helped me to focus on engineering as something I wanted to do," Andrew explains. Having spent a month at Stanford, he definitely wants to apply there, but he is also considering Harvard, Princeton, and the University of Pennsylvania, after visiting several elite campuses with his parents.

"I thought Harvard was really interesting," he says. "The tour guide definitely gave me a great impression. Harvard sort of has a stereotype—you know, kind of elite, whole lot of money, politically connected. But our tour guide was really open, just this nice, awesome guy. I thought much better of the school after visiting."

Andrew is also interested in applying for the George Washington Honor Scholarship at Washington and Lee University in Lexington, Virginia, which covers up to the full cost of tuition, plus room and board, for the few talented students to whom it is offered. His older sister, Elizabeth, turned down the Ivy League to accept this merit scholarship several years ago.

"My sister and I are very much alike," he says. "She really loved W and L and encouraged me to apply for the scholarship there. I mean, two hundred thousand dollars is a lot of money, and it's not like I'm exaggerating either," Andrew says, laughing at the outrageous figure. "If I get into W and L, I can double-major, versus Harvard or Stanford, where I will just get to do engineering. I don't know if I will have this decision, but it will be a blessing if I do." According to Andrew, Washington and Lee has fewer requirements for engineering majors and would accept more of his AP credits, which would give him flexibility in his course schedule.

Over the summer, Andrew polished off a draft of the Common Application, which he plans to submit to several colleges. The Common App began as a pilot program in 1975 when fifteen universities banded together to ease the burden on undergraduate applicants by replacing separate institutional applications with a single application. In 1994, Harvard became the first Ivy League university to accept the Common App, a decision that is credited for significantly increasing its popularity. This year, approximately 300,000 students are expected to use the Common App to apply to nearly three hundred colleges, including Harvard, Yale, Dartmouth, Cornell, Duke, Northwestern, and the University of Pennsylvania. Colleges that accept the Common App contend that it streamlines the application process for all students and encourages diversity by increasing the pool of minority applicants. Still, most of the more selective schools also require students to fill out lengthy supplements with extra essays.

To complete his Common Application, Andrew submitted his

transcript, two teacher recommendations, a guidance counselor recommendation, and a list of extracurricular activities. He requested and paid for the College Board to send official copies of his standardized tests—the SAT I and three SAT II subject tests, the standard for most Ivy League schools—directly to all of the colleges on his list. He also completed one 150-word short essay and a more substantial 250- to 500-word personal essay.

Not surprisingly, Andrew's personal essay talks about the impact that Hurricane Katrina has had on his life. In it, he writes:

If Hurricane Katrina has taught me anything, it is that humanity is both paradoxically fragile and invincible. This sentiment has personally and permanently changed my perspective.

I, along with many others, had always subconsciously felt that we humans controlled this world and should only be concerned with other humans. We thought that the greatest external threats to our country or our lives were Communism, totalitarianism, and terrorism. Weather was just an inconvenience, something to be irritated by, not something to be hated or feared. Everyone knew that nuclear weapons were the most destructive force known to man and that, even in this age of global terrorism, our cities and societies were beyond the reach of complete destruction. For what organization was strong enough to create weapons of mass destruction without a nation's support, and what country would be mad enough to use them against the United States? But after several levee failures, thousands of deaths, the blockade of our city by the National Guard, martial law, and inept politics and bureaucracy, my opinion has changed. The whole weight of the fragility of not only myself but also my entire society nearly crushed me. If my life could be ended by something as common as a falling tree and my society could collapse due to something as trivial as rising water, what other illusions do I still cling to? Is man really in control? Is my life my own, or is it entrusted to me?

How can the obvious be so wrong? With my own eyes I have seen trees five feet thick snapped in half, houses utterly annihilated, piles of debris half a mile long and one hundred feet high, water marks on roofs of raised houses, proof of a twenty-two foot tidal surge five miles from shore, an entire community abandoned, and a city deserted by the government. The combined efforts of the entire human race could hardly duplicate—or impede—such power. At first, the entire experience led me to doubt the existence of God because I could not understand how a loving God could permit this. However, my doubt changed into conviction, and although I do not believe that God sent the tempest, I now believe that God can bring good out of evil and make straight lines from crooked ones. I also believe that God calls each and every one of us to rise to the occasion and become the person that we can and should be. And if we do what is right, our fragility becomes irrelevant and our strength immeasurable. With my own eyes I have seen houses rebuilt, levees repaired, lives rekindled, communities reunite, and strangers volunteer. Seeing this determination in my neighbors has convinced me that I should not put my trust in human technology; but in the human spirit, that which makes us who we are and allows us to build not feeble houses or earthen levees but truth and kindness. And those cannot be touched by wind or rain.

TWO

"If colleges look at absences, I'm pretty much screwed"

MARLENE

Marlene Fernandez began high school in New Rochelle, a prosperous suburb just two miles north of New York City, as a very strong student. She finished her first year with straight As, including several A+'s, in predominately honors courses. However, by her sophomore year, she couldn't bring herself to care about how she did in school. Her grades quickly declined.

Marlene is intensely regretful about neglecting her studies. To punish herself, she constantly replays the events in her head and tells the story like she's confessing a "dark past" or "shocking secret" in the second act of a melodrama. "I would stay home from school because that would be the only time I had to myself, you know, some personal space," Marlene admits, shamefully lowering her big brown eyes behind her glasses. She is dressed casually in jeans and a T-shirt, her long, shiny mane secured in a ponytail.

At first glance, Marlene's ethnicity is somewhat ambiguous. With her fair complexion and straight, dark hair, it is hard to tell if she is from the Middle East or somewhere in Latin America. As usual, her pretty face is makeup free.

Though she was born in the Bronx, Marlene spent most of her childhood in the Dominican Republic, where her parents were both raised. "At the end of second grade, we took a trip to the DR. Our parents told us that we were just going on a vacation while they worked out the visa issues," she explains. "It didn't hit me that we were staying until I started going to school there."

Marlene and her family, which includes her mother, father, and two older sisters, ended up living in the Dominican Republic for more than four years before they were finally able to return to the States. When Marlene was in seventh grade, they moved into a modest apartment in New Rochelle so that the girls could enroll in a good school system. Despite having received most of her early education abroad, Marlene was able to place out of the district's ESL (English as a Second Language) track. She jumped into the standard curriculum at her middle school, where she excelled.

"I never knew we were poor till we moved here," she says with a subdued chuckle. "At first, I was embarrassed to tell people where I lived, but now it's okay." Marlene's mother works in a supermarket and takes part-time community college courses in nursing. Her father sells supermarket supplies. Together, they currently earn about $26,000 a year, which is well below the city's average family income of $73,000.

Unlike the vast majority of her classmates, who live in four- or five-bedroom houses, Marlene's family now lives in an overcrowded three-bedroom apartment. By the time she entered the tenth grade, Marlene found this living arrangement incredibly restrictive. "If you haven't noticed already, I'm a very reserved person," she says, half-joking. Desperate for some time alone, Marlene started ditching class so that she could have the apartment to herself during the day. She craved privacy the way many kids crave acceptance, which took a toll on her nearly perfect academic record.

"A similar story applies to my junior year," she says about her declining enthusiasm for schoolwork. "The fact that my sister had to get *so many* loans just to go to the college of her choice really scared me." Marlene's middle sister, Yvonne, is now a freshman at Elmira College in upstate New York. Because their parents could not afford to contribute much for college, Yvonne spent a good chunk of her senior year in high school agonizing over financing her education. She eventually decided to take out $72,000 in student loans, which was difficult for Marlene to watch.

"I said to myself, 'Why even bother trying to get good grades if I'm going to end up in a state school anyway, and I could get in with lower grades?' But"—she takes a deep breath and exhales loudly— "that was obviously before I knew about financial aid."

Toward the end of her junior year, Marlene came out from under her cloud of diminished expectations and decided to do some research on financial aid and scholarship opportunities. What she found was encouraging. If accepted, most Ivy League colleges would probably give her generous grants to cover tuition, and because her annual family income was well below the $60,000 cutoff, she could go to Harvard for free.

Over the past generation, rising college costs have outpaced inflation, needy students have been forced to take on large debt, and competition for a spot at our nation's best schools has intensified. These trends have had serious implications for students like Marlene. Hispanics are currently the most underrepresented group in the college-going population, and low-income students are much less likely to enroll in higher education than their wealthy peers. Money plays an even bigger role in admission to elite colleges. A study by the Century Foundation concluded that just 3 percent of students from the bottom income quartile were enrolled at the best 146 universities, compared with 74 percent of students from the

top. Kids who are the first in their families to go to college a̲̱
hard to find on the most prestigious campuses. William Bowen, the
former president of Princeton University, studied the populations
at nineteen elite colleges and found that these students made up
only 6 percent of undergraduates. The escalating competition has
hurt applicants who do not have access to tutors and supplementary educational resources that lend themselves to high SAT scores
and other desirable traits in the application process, like impressive
résumés or professionally edited college essays.

A few years ago, Harvard was the first prominent university
to openly recognize the lack of socioeconomic diversity on selective college campuses. The institution redefined admissions practices when President Lawrence Summers announced that Harvard
would expand its affirmative action program. Like the "plus factor"
granted to minority applicants, admissions officers would also give
special consideration to students from low-income backgrounds
and award these students generous grants instead of asking them to
take on overwhelming debt. Since Harvard's announcement, nearly
two dozen elite colleges have promised to increase their efforts to
recruit more low-income students, according to *The Chronicle of
Higher Education*. Some colleges, such as Princeton and the University of North Carolina at Chapel Hill, also revamped their financial aid programs and eliminated loans for the neediest students.

Even though more students are able to qualify for aid and the
financial awards are more robust, students whose families earn less
than $60,000 a year are still relatively rare in the Harvard applicant
pool because most eligible students are unaware of the university's
low-income affirmative action program. Marlene is on a path to
being one of the few students to defy this trend. After learning
about Harvard's financial aid program, she decided to apply and is
focused on submitting the best application that she possibly can.

"I know that some of the choices I made in the past were extremely stupid," Marlene says, drawing out her last two words. "If

colleges look at absences, I'm pretty much screwed. But unfortunately, there's nothing I can do about it now. I just thought you should know." Marlene then looks up as if she is waiting for my condemnation.

"I really don't think you're *screwed*," I reply. Marlene rolls her eyes, her usual response to my compliments. "Honestly, you have a lot going for you."

There's no denying that Marlene is smart. Even with her inconsistent effort, she is still in the running to rank in the top 10 percent of her class at a competitive college-prep high school. As a Dominican American from a low-income family, she is also an attractive candidate for selective colleges that want to recruit talented students like her who are currently underrepresented on their campuses. Though her academic record is not without its blemishes and she doesn't participate in many formal extracurricular activities, Marlene has a good shot at getting into a great school if things go her way.

Marlene is motivated to enhance her academic credentials in the time she has left before her college applications are due. In addition to working the snack bar at a local private beach club, she completed precalculus over the summer so that she could enroll in AP Calculus in her senior year. Marlene is also taking AP Physics, AP Spanish Literature, AP Macroeconomics, and, despite her introverted nature, she has "basically forced" herself to take Speech and Communications.

"New Rochelle has like four thousand students, so it's really big. It's diverse, but at the same time it's not," she continues without a hint of irony. "The kids are self-segregating. All the Hispanic and black students are in the regular classes together, and the white kids, who are mostly really rich and Jewish, are usually in honors." Marlene does not really socialize with the other students in her classes, where she is one of the very few students of color. "In AP Chem," she says, "it was me, one other Hispanic girl, and two black

kids in the entire class." In general, her friends are Mexican ⸺
can and on the nonhonors track, but she does have some friends
from other groups.

"A lot of the rich kids have tutors and stuff," Marlene observes. "I
remember when we got our PSAT scores back during AP Chem last
year. One kid was like, 'I only got a 720 on reading. My tutor will be
so mad.' I thought it was pathetic." Having fewer economic resources
than your peer group is a well-documented source of teenage angst
(just watch any John Hughes movie), and Marlene is no exception.

Unlike many of her classmates, whose parents ride them hard,
Marlene's parents are the opposite of college-obsessed. "My parents see absolutely no difference between Harvard and Westchester
Community College," she continues. "I obviously disagree. Sometimes it gets to me. If I took an AP class or a regular class it's still the
same thing to them. A few years ago, I was kind of kidding around
with my mom and said, 'I'm going to go to Harvard.' I had to tell her
that Harvard is basically *impossible* to get into, the hardest school
in the country. She was like, 'Why would you choose to go to such a
hard school when there are so many easier colleges?'"

Though Marlene sometimes wishes that her parents would push
her harder in school, she does not envy her classmates, whose parents are overly obsessed with where they go to college. She describes her sympathy for her friend Grace, who is "freaking out and
stuff because she's applying early to Penn, and her parents are the
crazy kind. Plus her brother goes to Cornell."

Marlene often compares herself to her classmates. Naviance, a
new online tool that reports the college acceptance rates for students at participating schools (including New Rochelle High School),
allows her to relentlessly assess her competition. She logs on frequently, measuring her GPA and SATs against the others', trying to
predict her chances of getting into a selective college. The routine
has become a wheel of self-doubt.

Because Marlene needs to compare financial aid awards, assemble her application materials, and bring up her grades, she has decided that she cannot apply anywhere early. "I mean, the thing with me is that sometimes I feel as if I have a slight chance at these schools that would be enhanced by applying early decision, but then I remind myself what I'm up against . . . and it's like *ugh*. I don't have the slightest chance, especially because everyone in the top of my class is applying somewhere early. So by the time I get to the regular decision round, it'll be over for me," she says.

Approximately 250 selective colleges offer some type of early admissions program, where students apply to one institution in advance, usually by early November of their senior year, and receive a response before the rest of their college applications are due. Early admissions programs generally fall into one of two categories: early decision and early action. Students who apply early decision agree to enroll if they are accepted; those who apply early action do not make a binding agreement. Marlene is correct when she says that she would have a better shot of getting into a selective college if she could apply early. Prominent researchers Christopher Avery, Andrew Fairbanks, and Richard Zeckhauser documented this phenomenon in their book, *The Early Admissions Game: Joining the Elite,* after examining 500,000 applications at fourteen elite institutions and conducting hundreds of interviews with students. They concluded that applicants can more than double their chances of being admitted to a selective college if they apply early decision and receive a boost that approximates the effect of adding one hundred points to their SAT scores.

The early decision advantage is generally bestowed on wealthier applicants. They are more likely to apply early because they do not have to compare financial aid packages among various institutions and have access to more sophisticated college counseling resources that prepare them to complete their applications ahead of schedule. Marlene typifies the sort of student who is generally left out of the early admissions game.

It's not that colleges make exceptions for early applicants or admit students who aren't qualified. With an abundance of outstanding candidates to choose from, most institutions prefer to accept early applicants because they drive up the admissions yield (the percentage of accepted students who eventually enroll), which is an indicator of the college's popularity. Other logistical considerations can also benefit early applicants. Because they are the first to apply, there is more room for them in the class, and admissions officers can give each candidate a little more attention as they have fewer to evaluate. By the time regular decision rolls around—when the vast majority of applications are submitted—the most selective colleges have already filled 30 to 40 percent of their classes. This exacerbates the competition for remaining spots.

"When I speak to other people about college stuff and how they have everything planned out, I get a little frustrated," Marlene exclaims, "because even if I had my essays ready and everything else, the one thing I would be missing would be the one thing out of my control—those darn recs. But, then again, it's my fault, so yeah . . ."

To submit her applications, Marlene must ask two teachers to complete recommendation forms. However, she is convinced that most of her former teachers, especially the ones she has had more recently, will not advocate on her behalf. Marlene has been agonizing over which teachers she should ask for weeks.

Most people tend to underestimate the role that recommendations play in the admissions process, perhaps because they never get to read them. It is also generally assumed that all teachers write nice things about their students. What makes one recommendation better than another? Aren't they all good?

While most teachers do submit flattering endorsements, not all recommendations are the same and admissions officers are well trained in deciphering between the exceptional and the mediocre. The best letters communicate a sense of how the student functions in the context of the classroom. Does he contribute to class discussion without dominating the room? Does she think critically? Can he write? Teacher recommendations are also used to corroborate the content of the rest of the application. If a candidate writes her essay about her passion for community service, colleges expect that her teachers will reference this passion as well. These individual pieces all contribute to the picture of the whole student that emerges in the admissions process.

In addition to a letter, most applications ask teachers to evaluate a student's performance in many different categories, according to a carefully crafted scale that ranges from "below average" to "one of the top few I've ever encountered in my career." The Common App, for example, asks teachers to rate students on the following criteria: academic achievement; intellectual promise; quality of writing; creative, original thought; productive class discussion; respect accorded by faculty; disciplined work habits; maturity; motivation; leadership; integrity; reaction to setbacks; concern for others; self-confidence; initiative; independence; and an overall assessment. The most selective colleges are looking for students who are consistently rated as "one of the top few I've ever encountered in my career."

Aside from stressing about her teacher recommendations, Marlene is also studying to take the SATs for the second time. "I really didn't study at all the first time, so I did really, *really* bad," she says.

I ask her to tell me her scores, assuming that they aren't as terrible as she thinks. After all, her performance on the PSAT was good enough to earn her a spot in the National Hispanic Recognition Program, which commends approximately 3,300 of the 124,000 Hispanic students who take the exam each year.

"I don't want to say." The look on her face says, *Please, please don't make me say it out loud.* "I promise I'll tell you both scores once I get the new ones back, okay?"

"All right," I agree. "Just remember, most kids do better the second time they take the test. I'm sure you'll do better if you study."

"Let's hope," she says, once again rolling her eyes at my optimism.

NABIL

"Not having friendships on a more academic level, or at least friends from other places who are interested in things similar to what I'm interested in, has been the most disappointing part of my high school life," Nabil Abdurehman says matter-of-factly. Though he tends to speak precociously, like the kind of kid who reads Beat poetry or wears black to school every day, Nabil is more nerdy than rebellious. We meet for the first time at one of the many Starbucks in Cordova, an enclave of retail chains and prefab housing communities outside downtown Memphis. The indistinguishable strip malls line the newly paved streets like customs officers protecting the border. They make the town seem like it is hard to escape.

Nabil is a handsome, lanky guy with a runner's physique and aristocratic bone structure. He wears spotty wire-framed oval glasses and doesn't sit very close to me. When I go to shake his hand, he backs away, lowers his voice, and explains, "We don't do that." Nabil's family is originally from Ethiopia and practices Islam. Like all observant Muslims, he prays five times a day, complies with halal dietary regulations, fasts on Ramadan, and does not make physical contact with the opposite sex—a custom about which I was ignorant.

Nabil diffuses the situation by immediately launching into a discussion about how much he loves math. He loves to do math problems, read math books, and go to math Web sites in his spare time. Having already exhausted his high school curriculum by completing AP Calculus his junior year, he even enrolled in Multivariable Calculus at the University of Memphis over the summer just for fun. Nabil also founded a math club at his high school. "Starting a club was a goal of mine to increase interest in the subject and to show some teachers that there are students interested in this type of thing," he says. "I'm the captain and teach the other students about concepts not usually covered in the high school curriculum. Right now, we're going over basics, like recursive and parametric equations, et cetera, which they should in theory learn in school, but don't."

Nabil doesn't really fit in at Cordova High, a no-frills public school in Memphis, Tennessee. "I don't know what the deal is with Cordova," he says, shrugging his shoulders. "It's like all the smart kids either go to one of the many private schools in the area or to White Station." Though Nabil was encouraged to enroll at White Station, the city's finest magnet high school, he opted for Cordova High because it was closer to his house. At the time, he had not anticipated that his social life would suffer over the next four years as a result. But, as he tells it, his good friends from middle school—the "smart kids"—sought out more rigorous high schools, and he was pretty much left alone.

Nabil is currently ranked first in his class and yearns to improve the intellectual atmosphere of his high school. He genuinely wants to inspire other students and teachers to challenge themselves, especially where math is concerned. "Last year, we had the AMC/ AIME at our school for the first time. Apparently no one asked before I did," he says in disbelief. The AMC (American Mathematics Competitions) are a series of difficult exams for high school math enthusiasts. Last year, more than 413,000 students took the AMC, and about 10,000 qualified for the AIME (American Invitational Mathematics Examination) nationwide.

"I love math, but I also want to study other things, like foreign language," Nabil says. "And I want to meet different types of people. Harvard seems like the most diverse of all the schools." Nabil is primed to apply early action, and believes that he has a good chance of getting in. Besides being the top student in his class, he is genuinely passionate about learning, which will surely come through in his essays and recommendations. For the most part, Nabil has also done well on his standardized tests, though, not surprisingly, his best scores are in math, where he got a 780 on the SAT I, 800 on the SAT II, and a perfect score on the AP Calculus test junior year. Except for the verbal portion of the SAT (he scored in the low 600s), Nabil got a 700 or above on subject tests in Writing, Physics, and American History. In addition to Calculus, he earned mostly 4s and 5s on a range of AP exams, including European History, American History, Chemistry, and Physics.

Nabil has more going for him than most students with solid academic credentials and significant extracurricular involvements. He is also a member of a group that benefits from affirmative action, which will be a plus factor in his application. The only thing that might hurt his Harvard application is the caliber of his high school. Nabil is a big fish in a small pond; admissions officers may question how he would fare in a more competitive academic environment.

Since Harvard's early action program does not force a student to enroll if accepted, Nabil also plans to apply to other universities with strong math programs. To narrow down his selection, he has already begun to read the published articles and books of various faculty members at the schools to which he is considering applying, including one of his "mathematical heroes," Paul Sally, a professor at the University of Chicago. He plans to make a trip to the University of Chicago in a few weeks, which is the only school on Nabil's list that participates in the National Merit Scholarship Program. "I think we had only one National Merit semifinalist in the past two years," Nabil says of Cordova High. "White Station has around twenty each year—yes, the highest in the state." He scowls a little when he talks about White Station, like he is tired of hearing about how great it is.

Each year, approximately 1.4 million juniors take the PSAT as a practice run for the notorious SAT, and fifty thousand high scorers on the PSAT are officially recognized by the National Merit

Scholarship Program. Of those, sixteen thousand are chosen as semifinalists (the selection process is conducted within each state to preserve geographic diversity), and approximately half of these students receive National Merit Scholarships—a one-time payment of $2,500—based on their academic records, schools' curricula, standardized test scores, recommendations, leadership experience, and a personal essay. "I know I'm a scholar and after comparing my score to the cutoffs from last year, I expect to be a National Merit semifinalist as well," declares Nabil.

In many ways, Nabil credits his father for his academic success. "Every time my dad reads something about education, he brings the article home for me to see."

Nabil often begins his sentences with the words "my dad":

"My dad gave me this article that said how the University of Memphis is looking for diversity, you know? So they're offering a five-thousand-dollar scholarship to any student with like a C average from a school in Memphis that's majority black."

"My dad was telling me the other day how I should double-major in math and a related field, something real or applicable like economics or electrical engineering."

"Initially my dad was strongly against me running varsity in college because the elite schools give too much work for you to do well if you also do a sport."

Nabil's father manages a couple of Memphis gas stations, and his mother helps out part-time as a cashier for checks and money orders. Though they are both originally from Ethiopia, his parents met and were married in Atlanta. The family moved to Tennessee when Nabil, the oldest of five, was six years old.

The growing African immigrant community is a new and distinct addition to a city with deep African American roots. Blues legend B.B. King is named after Beale Street, the center of downtown Memphis (his friends at WDIA, the first African American radio station, used to call him Beale Street Blues Boy). More significant,

Memphis is home to the National Civil Rights Museum, located at the site of the former Lorraine Motel, where Martin Luther King Jr. was tragically assassinated.

Though a majority of Memphis citizens—more than 61 percent, according to the most recent census—identify as African American, the census data does not distinguish between recent immigrants and those with long-standing familial roots in the United States. These communities differ in several ways, most notably in their religious practices. While the city's African American community is traditionally Christian with deep connections to local churches, many recent African immigrants are practicing Muslims, like Nabil and his family. There are also cultural differences, such as diet and music. "I don't like rap music because I can't understand it," Nabil says.

In general, Nabil dislikes racial categorizations and their associated stereotypes. "When was the last Nobel Prize awarded with separate consideration for different races?" he asks rhetorically when the conversation turns to issues of race.

A controversial debate has erupted on our nation's most prestigious campuses about the overrepresentation of black students from families who recently immigrated, as opposed to those whose ancestors were brought over as slaves and whose families have been here for hundreds of years. Last year researchers at Princeton and the University of Pennsylvania released findings from surveys given to 1,051 black freshmen at twenty-eight selective colleges. They found that 27 percent of African American students were first- or second-generation immigrants, which is more than double the national average for all blacks ages eighteen to nineteen. The percentage of immigrants was even more pronounced at the four Ivy League schools included in this study (Princeton, Yale, Columbia, and the University of Pennsylvania), where 41 percent of students were first- or second-generation immigrants. These numbers do not include international students who identify as black.

The authors of the study conclude that recent immigrants tend to be favored in the admissions process, especially at the most selective schools, because black immigrants are more likely to have higher grades and test scores. They also note that admissions officers may be subconsciously selecting applicants with more "sociable qualities" that they more readily perceive in immigrants over other African Americans. Previous research suggests that whites tend to find immigrant blacks more "likable" in general.

This tendency to admit black immigrants over other African Americans at highly selective universities is problematic. Though these students contribute to campus diversity, they face many of the same challenges of recent immigrants from other countries, especially Asian students, who do not benefit from affirmative action in the admissions process. In addition, they may be more likely to succeed in school because, as the study notes, "black immigrant fathers were far more likely to have graduated from college and to hold advanced degrees than native fathers."

Though Nabil's father did not graduate from college, he emphasizes the importance of education in his home and tells me how pleased he is with his eldest son. "Nabil is what every father wants his son to be," he says in a gentle Ethiopian accent. "When they were younger, I just tried to get all my kids to be interested in reading and studying. Nabil kept perfecting himself in his studies. He studies by himself—even when he is not in school."

Bucking the recent trend among high-achieving students applying to an increasing number of colleges, Nabil is determined to focus his energy on a few particular schools. "My dad gave me a pie graph from this *Newsweek* article that showed how a bigger percentage of students are applying to more schools, but I don't want to spend too much time applying to places that I'm not serious about going to." In addition to concentrating on schools with strong math departments, Nabil's college search is further restricted by the fact that he will only consider moving to a city in which there is a sizable Muslim community. "It's not something I want to neglect," he says of his religious practices.

A couple of summers ago, Nabil and three of his siblings spent two months in Ethiopia, which was their first visit to their parents' homeland. While there, Nabil found it difficult to communicate with his family, who speak both Amharic and their tribal language, of which he knows a little. "I couldn't do what I should have been able to do," he says of his inability to speak to his Ethiopian relatives. "Communication is really important. I couldn't say everything I wanted to say to my grandmother, which was disappointing." After the trip, Nabil was inspired to learn Arabic, which is similar to the tribal language his family speaks.

Nabil hates to disappoint others. He helps out around the house and regularly assumes the role of family chauffeur, shuttling his siblings and cousins to school, meetings, and sports practice. However, Nabil, like all of us, is not without his flaws. "I am the most forgetful person I know. Thursday, I locked myself out of my car again, the second time since school started. We—my dad and I—still haven't found the spare key yet and my car is still at school. The keys . . . well, they're sitting on the armrest between the two front seats."

LISA

We all communicate with our bodies, but Lisa Wang can shape hers into actual letters. First she's a "K," with her left foot and hand planted firmly on the ground, each muscle flexing in unison to support her right leg and arm, which reach out and up. Without skipping a beat, she then flies into the air to form an upside down "T," her toned legs extended in opposite directions, punctuated by her elegantly pointed toes. Next, she's a "J," stretching her arms out on the floor, effusively rounding her torso, and thrusting her legs up toward the sky.

When she is on that blue gymnastics mat, Lisa is in constant motion. She steadily molds and shapes her body, which looks like it's made of clay instead of flesh and bone, communicating with her audience like a swift sculptor. There is only one thing that is consistent about her mesmerizing metamorphoses. Whether she's leaping into the air Baryshnikov-style or rolling a ball across her neck like a Harlem Globe Trotter, Lisa does it with a smile.

Last August, Lisa placed first in the USA National Championships for rhythmic gymnastics. "I've been second and third consecutively the last few championships and I finally won the title this year! As a result, I've been assigned to compete in Japan for a World Cup competition in November!" she tells me over e-mail, having just gotten back from Minnesota, where the competition was held. Lisa is about to begin her senior year of high school, and she is officially ranked as the number-one rhythmic gymnast in the country.

It is mid-September at Adlai E. Stevenson High School in Lincolnshire, Illinois, where Lisa has been a star student for the past three years. Stevenson is one of only three public schools in the country to have received the Excellence in Education Award from the Department of Education four times. It has also been recognized on several occasions as one of the nation's top high schools by both *U.S. News & World Report* and *Newsweek.*

Almost all of Lincolnshire, Illinois, is under construction and the traffic is relentless. The two-lane road that funnels residents to and from the major highways is being expanded to accommodate the booming town, which is comprised of a combination of newly developed housing communities, golf courses, mini malls, and a few cornfields that have yet to be purchased by real estate developers.

Because of the traffic and construction, I am twenty minutes late to meet Lisa. After inching my way down Half Day Road, following the circuitous bright orange DETOUR signs, I finally arrive at her school. Panicked, I abandon my rental car, which is parked diagonally in a faculty spot, and run over the cut grass to the school's main entrance, hoping that Lisa hasn't given up on me.

More than 4,600 students are roaming around the enormous Stevenson High School campus. The mammoth beige building looks like it was originally constructed in the early 1960s and has idiosyncratic structural add-ons, like a man-made lake and a cavernous reception area with asymmetric glass walls. I manage to find Lisa through the maze of hallways. She is casually leaning against a partition that designates her school's counseling center, playing with the dyed streaks of reddish-purple in her naturally dark hair. Her guidance counselor, who I was scheduled to interview fifteen minutes ago, is waiting for us inside.

Lisa looks absolutely nothing like her pictures in newspaper articles and on her official profile on the USA Rhythmic Gymnastic National Team Web site. "It's fun 'cause I get to look really dramatic and just use a *ton* of makeup," she says of her stage persona. Her gymnastics regalia are elaborate second-skin leotards made of glitter and sequins, and she always has her hair pulled into a tight bun that sits atop her head when she performs.

Though she looks striking in her pictures, Lisa is noticeably more attractive in real life. Despite her tiny frame—she's barely five feet tall and weighs eighty-five pounds—you can tell that she is an athlete by the way she carries herself; her perfect posture comes from countless hours in the gym, refining her flexibility and developing her muscles. In person, she is much more "punk" than "beauty queen." Today, she's wearing a mesh black shirt with a tank top underneath and fashion-forward jeans. Bright purple eye shadow lines her almond-shaped eyelids, and she has painted her petite nails with flamboyant fuchsia polish.

Lisa leads the way to her guidance counselor's office. Mr. Roznowski greets me warmly, standing up from behind his monstrous desk to shake my hand. Lisa and I each take a seat in one of the two small chairs that are crammed into the available corners of the room, which is packed with catalogs and papers like an overstuffed suitcase.

Mr. Roznowski is one of the two full-time college consultants at Stevenson who work alongside a staff of sixteen guidance counselors. "This high school is unique in that it's really a college-prep school," he says. "Ninety-seven percent of the kids go to college, eighty-four percent go to four-year schools, but two thirds of the students stay within three hundred miles of home. Lots of them go to the University of Illinois, of course."

I ask Mr. Roznowski how the college admissions process at Stevenson has changed in the twelve years that he has been working at the school. "Well, I'm really excited about how some of the colleges are leaning toward deemphasizing testing—especially the fact that there are even a couple of public schools doing it," he answers, trying to lean back in a chair that doesn't give him the space to do so.

Top colleges have required standardized testing as part of their admissions processes for more than a century. In 1900, a small but prominent group of Northeastern colleges formed the College Entrance Examination Board (CEEB) to administer a common blue-book essay exam, which they named the College Boards. A newfound emphasis on academic scholarship coupled with improvements in the nation's railroad transportation inspired colleges to look beyond the "feeder" prep schools from which they traditionally drew students.

To make entrance exams more accessible, CEEB recruited psychologist Carl Brigham, a professor at Princeton, to expand on a multiple choice test used to sort army recruits for military assignment during World War I. The Army Alpha Test was an attractive blueprint for a college admissions exam because it tested general reasoning ability, not what you learned in high school. Multiple choice exams were also appealing because they ask many questions in a short amount of time to get a broad sense of what students know. Unlike essay exams, they can be quickly and mechanically scored. Brigham's work with CEEB produced the Scholastic Aptitude Test, or the SAT. The first SAT was administered in June 1926.

In the 1930s, administrators at Harvard instituted a National Scholarship Program to attract talented students from all parts of the country who could not otherwise afford to attend. However, they needed a way to compare students from different high schools. Unfortunately, the College Boards were too narrow to accurately assess the academic preparation of most students, except for those enrolled in private New England boarding schools. Admissions officers found that the SAT coupled with high grades was more effective in identifying gifted students across the country.

The SAT did not replace the College Boards as a requirement for admission to a top school for some time, mostly due to faculty skepticism of this new assessment. However, by 1941, wartime travel was difficult and resources were scarce. It made sense to replace graded essay exams with multiple choice tests. In addition to the SAT, multiple choice tests in particular subjects (called Achievement Tests or the SAT II Subject Tests) were also developed for use at the most selective colleges. These tests came in handy in evaluating the scholastic preparedness of World War II veterans, who applied to college in unprecedented numbers as a result of the G.I. Bill. Since then, the SAT has become a college admission staple that has fostered a billion-dollar test-prep industry. Even as many colleges are trying to put less emphasis on standardized tests, like Mr. Roznowski noted, the average SAT scores at the nation's most selective colleges continue to increase each year.

"Also, demographically, there has just been a much larger number of applicants in the last couple of years," Lisa's counselor continues. "The students are each doing more applications, more of them are applying to competitive schools, like Lisa."

Lisa epitomizes her generation of overachievers. In addition to her nationally recognized athletic ability, she is a straight-A student on the honors and AP track (the only B+ on her record was in Driver's Ed). Yet, as Mr. Roznowski brags about her achievements, she raises the corners of her mouth into a placid smile. She seems to be tuning out the conversation as she sits quietly in the corner, swinging her little feet back and forth.

"Another big change is that activities have really taken over," Mr. Roznowski continues. "Not necessarily just athletics. Extracurriculars are a big part of the lifestyle here. We encourage the students to *really* get involved. Even if someone became president of the knitting club, it would be impressive. I think that's why—in addition to the students getting a great education—our kids really go on to the top schools."

Though academic credentials are the most important variable in admissions decisions, colleges are also looking for students who are involved in extracurricular activities. In general, students who demonstrate genuine passion in one or two areas, like athletics or politics, give admissions officers a better sense of how they could potentially contribute to campus life. Because of this, they can be more appealing than those who submit a lengthy roster of superficial involvements. Lisa's impressive accomplishments in gymnastics will undoubtedly make a positive impression on colleges. She is clearly a dedicated athlete who has excelled on a national level.

Mr. Roznowski hands me a copy of the 2005–2006 PROFILE OF ADLAI E. STEVENSON HIGH SCHOOL, a document that includes information about the community, courses, college enrollment rates, and standardized testing. High schools send these types of profiles to colleges so that admissions officers can compare students from the same school by referring to the average GPAs and standardized testing scores within each class. They are also used to evaluate the overall rigor of their academic course offerings—like the fact that Stevenson offers 32 AP classes and more than 66 percent of students are enrolled in at least one of them. Colleges prefer students, like Lisa, who excel in academically rigorous high schools because these students tend to be better prepared for challenging postsec-ondary course work.

After leaving the guidance office, Lisa offers me a tour of the campus. Walking down the fluorescently lit hallways, she casually glances into the classrooms, which each contain about thirty stu-dents taking notes on various subjects. A chorus of Spanish words echoes throughout the corridor, which morphs into a runway as a group of girls squeezed into low-rise jeans strut their stuff.

Lisa leads the way out of the building to Stevenson's two-week-old "Garden of Peace, Hope and Remembrance for the Victims of September 11th" with a newly erected $110,000 abstract metal sculpture at its center. "It's pretty useless—especially for all that money. There's a whole uproar about it in the student newspaper," she says. There are no benches or swaths of grass inviting students to spend time visiting the site. Standing apart from the building, almost destined to be ignored, something about the overpriced and underused memorial seems to make an impression on Lisa. It is the first place she stops on the tour.

The excursion continues on to the athletic facilities. Lisa starts to talk about her family as she strolls past a huge football field with freshly cut grass. Her younger brother is in the sixth grade. "He's the polar opposite of me," she says. "He's so laid-back and outgoing, while I'm pretty quiet and more of a perfectionist. If I'm not giving my best I feel like I'm not meeting my own standards.

"I've always been like this. I'm just a hard worker," she reflects. "My dad's also kind of a perfectionist—he's always working, trying to do more. My mom more accepts things for what they are." As we circle back to the main building, Lisa tells me that her parents are both originally from China; her father works as an analyst for an insurance company and her mother dabbles part-time in real estate.

Once inside, we settle in a lounge area and sit cross-legged on the big carpeted blocks that substitute for benches or couches. I ask Lisa how she finds the time to train for gymnastics and keep up with the five AP classes that she's taking this semester.

"Sadly, I have no social life," she says without pause. "I take five classes in the morning and my mom picks me up at five after one. I eat lunch in the car on the way to gymnastics practice, then eat dinner and do my homework. I was up until like two thirty last night finishing all my work." Lisa is at the gym five hours a day, six days a week, twelve months a year. "It's really hard to train on so little sleep but I have to keep up my schedule," she explains. "Otherwise, I'd feel it right away. You need to keep your body really flexible."

According to Lisa, her teammates often talk about food and weight. Because judges evaluate a competitor's appearance in addition to her performance, coaches are known to put these athletes under pressure to lose weight. "I'm really lucky because I have a fast metabolism," Lisa responds when I ask if she worries about what she eats. "But I am still cautious. If I didn't eat healthily, it would affect my performance."

Most Americans are familiar with what is known as artistic gymnastics, having watched triumphant gymnasts like Mary Lou Retton and Kerri Strug win gold medals for elaborate dismounts off balance beams and uneven bars. Rhythmic gymnastics, however, takes place entirely on the mat, with props like billowing rainbow-colored ribbons or leather spheres that look like small basketballs. "Rhythmic gymnastics isn't really big in the United States," Lisa explains, "but I think it's the best sport. Anyone can attempt to run back and forth, throw a baseball, whatever. With gymnastics, people look at it and can't even *attempt* to do it."

Rhythmic gymnastics performances are meticulously choreographed. Like ballerinas, these gymnasts stretch the limits of the human form in harmony with music, twirling, jumping, tumbling. Tossing props into the air, they glide through the atmosphere and sashay across a mat, emerging from the dance at precisely the moment that gravity takes over and the object falls back into their commanding grasp.

In general, the best rhythmic gymnasts in the world are from Eastern Europe. "In places like Russia and Ukraine, they handpick the most flexible baby girls and put them in special schools for gymnastics when they are very young," Lisa explains. From that point on, these girls devote themselves entirely to the sport. By contrast, Lisa didn't start taking gymnastics lessons until she was in the third grade, which gives her a relative disadvantage in competitions. "In America, there are competing interests, like education and college," she continues. "Over there, kids get paid to compete. Here we have to pay." Because she is so accomplished, Lisa is one of the few American gymnasts whose training and travel is subsidized by the USA Gymnastics Federation.

Gymnastics takes Lisa all over the world. "The judging is still subjective, so it's good to make political alliances," she reports. Last summer, the U.S. team sent several of the top American gymnasts to Montenegro to train and network with judges from Eastern European countries. While there, Lisa got to work with Irina Viner, the most highly regarded rhythmic gymnastics coach in the world today.

"She practically *controls* the sport. All her gymnasts are at the top. She commands such enormous respect that you don't even question her."

I ask Lisa how she measured up to the other girls at the training camp. A self-assured smile appears on her face. "I held my own."

Most gymnasts who have reached Lisa's level would have already dropped out of school to train full-time, but she has strongly resisted leaving high school. Lisa prides herself on being able to do it all. "Gymnastics is like my anti-drug—not that I'd be doing drugs—but it gives me something to strive for. I wonder if I'd be doing as well in school if I wasn't doing gymnastics. I've developed such a ridiculous work ethic. I can *take* pain and criticism," she says with a bring-it-on swagger.

Lisa recently applied for funding from the USA Gymnastics Federation to train full-time with Irina Viner in Russia next semester. By then, she will have all the credits she needs to graduate with an Illinois high school diploma a semester early. "I won't hear until January though," she explains, "so I'm not really thinking about it. If I don't get to go to Russia, I might stay another semester at Stevenson and keep my training schedule."

Considering that she is a tremendously goal-oriented person, Lisa possesses an almost incomparable ability to focus on the moment. She tends not to fantasize about things she can't control, or lose herself in what-ifs. "I don't want my whole career to be based on whether or not I get to the Olympics," she says. "Everything I've done so far has been for the experiences . . . the *experience* of being a gymnast, the *experience* of competing and traveling, even just for little state meets."

If Lisa continues on the path to the 2008 Olympics, she will have to defer her college enrollment for one year. After that, she plans to retire from the sport and concentrate on being a regular student. "I have gymnastics but I also have school. I want to have an actual college experience. If I keep going after 2008, I will have spent my whole childhood only doing one thing. I love the sport. I love doing what I do—it's something that sets me apart and something I can keep forever. But the lifespan of a gymnast is only so long. If I could go to college and be normal . . ." Her voice trails off wistfully.

"Do you ever get to hang out with your friends?" I ask.

"Not too much. My closest friends are my teammates. I mean, I know people who are on the AP track in my school because they're in my classes. But there are so many kids that I have never even met at Stevenson," she says, looking around at the passersby. When she does socialize, Lisa and her friends do conventional things like hang out at the mall, watch movies, and play mini golf. "I'm kind of into laser tag too," she brags with a devilish grin.

"Do you guys get competitive about college stuff?"

"I don't feel like anyone I know is competing all the time. They're mostly focused on making themselves do better," she answers, shifting her tiny body by uncrossing her legs.

A few weeks ago, Lisa took a trip to the East Coast to check out some schools with her parents. "I visited Yale and Harvard a few weeks ago, and I think I'm going to apply to Yale early action and then Harvard and Stanford for regular decision." Since early action policies are nonbinding, Lisa can still apply to other schools even if she is accepted to Yale.

"I guess it was just that the student feedback at Yale was so positive," she answers when I ask what made her choose Yale over Harvard, where she was originally considering applying early. "You know . . . Harvard is *Harvard*," she says, spreading her hands wide to illustrate the scope of her intimidation. "As much as that can be a big plus, it also makes me hesitant. I don't want to stereotype, but I feel like Harvard is a lot more competitive from what other people say. Yale just seems more open and happy."

Unsatisfied with the results of her first SAT—720 Math, 700 Critical Reading, and 680 Writing—Lisa is planning to retake the test in a few weeks. "I think if you looked at my standardized testing so far, I'd be pretty mediocre," she says. "I'm hoping that my personal statement and academic record will help." She's right—her grades and athletic accomplishments will likely impress any admissions committee. However, like Felix, the fact that she is an Asian American could be a disadvantage, and the results of her standardized tests are weak in comparison with other applicants at places like Yale and Harvard. She needs to do better on the October exams.

Lisa has already started working on her college essays and, naturally, she plans to write about her involvement in gymnastics.

"There can be a lot of emotional stress in the sport, like with the weight thing or just the pressure to be perfect. There are no guarantees. If you can do it today, you might not be able to do it tomorrow. I probably put the most pressure on myself though. Half the reason I keep doing it is because I'm on top."

· THREE ·

"Success breeds success"

FELIX

The two thousand students at Conestoga High School are literally in the dark. Rumor has it that the blackout was caused by a small explosion in the power generator in the building, which was originally constructed in the mid-1950s. Unlike most high schools, where operational malfunctions warrant early dismissals, Conestoga classes continue uninterrupted on this mid-October afternoon. The dimly lit halls, scarcely illuminated by the emergency power supply, are quiet. There are no signs of frantic teachers or rowdy teenagers looking to take advantage of the possibilities that lie in the shadows. The imposing sense of orderliness may explain why *Philadelphia* magazine just named Conestoga the best public school in the metropolitan area.

At the center of the large atrium in the school's main entrance is Conestoga's prominent "College Board," an oversized map of the United States adorned with little red flags. At the end of the year, the school sponsors an annual ceremony during which each graduate places a sticker with his or her name under the flagged location of the college that he or she plans to attend. Felix immediately points out that three students from last year's class are now at Harvard.

The "College Board" is one of Conestoga's many trophies, simultaneously inspiring and intimidating students. Even after they have graduated and moved on, the "winners" and "losers" of the class of 2006 still linger in the school hallway, readily identified by their postsecondary plans.

OH, THE PLACES YOU'LL GO. At the end of eighth period, Felix finds me standing under a banner prominently displaying the famous words of Dr. Seuss. Today is the first day that guidance counselors will review college applications for the students in this year's senior class. Felix can't wait to turn in all his paperwork for his early action application to Harvard. We stumble down the dark corridors of the recently renovated redbrick building to the college office, a separate wing of the school devoted entirely to college placement. The reception area, wallpapered in school flags and accessories with huge bookshelves full of catalogs, is a monument to all things "college." Felix feels his way to his counselor's office, though she is nowhere to be found. An older woman informs him that the school will be closing immediately because of the blackout. "God!" he exclaims, clutching his Harvard application, "I just want to get it out of my hands, you know?"

This is the last year that Harvard will be accepting early action applications. A few weeks earlier, in late September, interim president Derek Bok stunned the admissions world by announcing that the university would do away with the policy. It has been the consensus among academics and administrators in the world of higher education for some time that early action and early decision policies give an unfair advantage to wealthier students, who tend to be better prepared to submit application materials early and do not have to compare financial aid awards among colleges. Still, Harvard's decision to end the thirty-year-old policy was a bombshell. When Felix first heard the announcement, he literally fell out of his chair in the school library.

"All I saw was the headline and not the detail that it would not be in effect until next year," he explains, thankful that the new policy will not directly impact his own early action application. "For this year though, I'm worried that they will take fewer students early action, and wait until the regular decision round to decide, maybe even waitlist people to prepare for next year. This isn't exactly the best thing for kids like me, who would be competitive in early action." Felix is just speculating. There's no reason to assume that Harvard will change its early action policies this year just because they plan to eliminate the program in the future.

In preparation for a busy senior year, Felix finished his Harvard essays over the summer. He spent evenings, weekends, and his downtime at the lab writing. They are both beautifully written. The first essay, "The 88 Keys of Learning," explores his love affair with the piano. "Her Field of Flowers," Felix's second essay, is about the time he spent in the Chinese orphanage. In it, he describes the feelings of helplessness he experienced after realizing that these hopeful children would never receive basic medical care:

Crawling along in rags that once were white, Kai Feng reached out, grasping at objects she could only see faintly. She was eight years old, paralyzed from the waist down, and losing her eyesight. Unable to afford a wheelchair, she was forced to drag herself along the filthy floors. Her case was no worse than any of the other 50 children in the special orphanage where I had volunteered last summer, all of them were suffering from rare congenital diseases or some sort of defect.

The orphanage was located in a rural area in northern China, an hour drive from nearest town. The building itself was night-marish, with walls painted an off-color white, smeared with the dirty handprints of passing children, and corridors filled with sights I still sometimes see when I close my eyes: a seven-year-old pulling out and eating the wispy strands of hair from her nearly-bald crown; a three-year-old with a case of hydrocephalus so dire the circumference of his head measured 57 centimeters; huddled in the corner, a five-year-old who had lost her eyes at birth, sitting immobile, her empty sockets wrapped in a dirty cloth. These were some of the most unfortunate human beings I have ever met; and I often wondered how many more of these utterly forgotten children were in this world.

Often Kai Feng would ask me to take her into the small gar-den in the orphanage's backyard. I would carry her on my back and reach down to pluck flowers as she called out the colors. She would seem so happy and kiss the petals. One day, when she had armful of lovely flowers, she turned to me and whispered, "Can you fix me?" How I wished I could pull out a magic wand and just tap her legs back to life and clear the blurry world around her, but I couldn't. "It's okay," she giggled, "One day, I'll get all better, and then we can go to a field full of these flowers and see all the colors in the world!"

Whenever I think now of my future career in medicine, I cannot help but recall that moment. Here was a girl so ready to believe that help was on the way when, in fact, there was none. There should have been. There should have been a doc-tor present to help all of those children, tending to their daily urgencies, and working to improve their lives. Too often today, people think that, a stethoscope and "M.D." following their names equates to high salary and bragging rights at the dinner table. But this can't be true, can it? If this is true, then what of those unsung heroes with organizations such as "Doctors with-out Borders" or the Red Cross? If this is true then what does the future holds for those children in that orphanage who so desperately need help?

But before change can occur, my generation, the future world leaders, captains of industry and citizens of the world must first know a change is needed. I have since worked with children's hospitals in Shanghai to accomplish just that, establishing an International Clinical Internship program which brings students interested in health care from around the world to China to work with doctors treating these poor children.

Perhaps my view of medicine and the health care system is idealistic. But then my goal, my mission in life is to change the health care system to that very ideal. May we never forget that doctors should be where patients are. Location, environment, or society should not be limiting factors but catalysts for medical care. How else will we ever be able to take a little girl to her field of flowers?

"Did anyone help you with your essays?" I ask, noting how well-written they are.

"Just my mom," he replies. "Oh yeah, I'm also going to ask my English teacher to look at them before I send out my application. If it was up to my dad, they'd already be in the mail, but I wanted to get some more feedback."

Before exiting the College Office, we run into Felix's friend Andrew, who is also eager to officially hand in his early action application forms for Harvard. Dressed casually in a maroon hooded sweatshirt and jeans, Andrew first appears like a typical upper-middle-class white suburban teenager of average height and build. However, his ability to articulate complex ideas in rapid succession, coupled with the anxiety that permeates his voice and fidgety mannerisms, make him seem far older.

"You should talk to Andrew," Felix says, giving his friend an affable pat on the back. "He's also applying early to Harvard." Without prompt, Felix steps aside and Andrew starts to describe his college admissions experience. Having worked on his application, especially his essays, for three to four months, Andrew is banking on the power of his writing to persuade the Harvard Admissions Office to offer him a place in the class of 2011.

Andrew's Harvard essay is about his formative experiences in fighting against a bureaucracy that condemned originality and progress. Back in the Cub Scouts, he spent hours working on building a groundbreaking model car to enter into the Scouts' design competition. Though he had broken no rule, his submission was rejected by the judges for being "too creative." When his father, who is an attorney and professor, was made aware of the incident, he invited his son to speak to his law school classes about the barriers to innovative enterprise that plague our society. It is almost unheard of to have a high school student lecture in a graduate-level course.

Though Andrew is applying to Harvard early, he realizes that the odds are against him. So he decided to cast a wide net in the college application process. His "safety schools" include Muhlenberg College, where his parents both went; Dickinson College; and American University. "A lot of people I know went to smaller colleges and they're doing great," he exclaims firmly, "maybe even better than if they went to the Ivy League. There is an inherent privilege in going to the Ivy League that makes those who don't get in work even harder." Andrew has already finished the majority of his nine applications several months before the deadline "so that my parents won't nag me when December rolls around," he says.

Aside from being required to wake up early, Andrew really likes his high school. Of course, Conestoga is competitive, especially senior year when everyone seems obsessed with getting into colleges. "If you sit down at any table of seniors the only topic you'll hear about is colleges," he observes. "I expect that this will probably only amplify as the year goes on."

. . .

FELIX'S FRIENDS SEEM to cluster around the College Office. He introduces two girls and two guys, each of whom is either of East or South Asian descent. Like Andrew, they report being quite happy at Conestoga, though they complain about the stress of their senior years. College applications, homework, and SATs ("For those of us who have to take them again," one of Felix's friends jabs at him) all contribute to the pressure they are experiencing.

"It's not necessarily just the school," says a waifish girl, folding her arms across her chest and leaning forward to balance the weight of the enormous book-filled bag strapped to her back. "It's the students and everyone around you. There are so many people taking seven or eight APs that the balance is completely off. Taking only one or two is considered below par." Each of the students in this group is taking between six and eight AP classes this year. They all have their hearts set on getting into highly selective colleges, like the University of Pennsylvania, Johns Hopkins, and the incredibly competitive six-year medical program at the University of Pittsburgh.

"My dad wanted me to take two full practice SAT tests every day for four months," says one of the boys, who is sporting a full mustache. Considering that the new SAT exam is three hours and forty-five minutes long, this schedule requires that he spend seven hours a day on SAT prep. "Of course, I didn't do it. My dad is kind of psychotic."

"Yeah," the other boy in the group agrees, "*both* my parents are kind of psychotic." The kids all laugh. I ask them why their parents are so invested in where they go to college.

"You know, it's important to go to a good college to do better than our parents did. It's the only way to succeed," one of them responds in a singsongy voice that borders on mocking, perhaps because he's heard the sentiment repeated so many times before.

The girl who wants to enroll in an accelerated medical program proudly interrupts. "I took one SAT every day for the past two weeks!" The rest of the kids all but ignore her. For the first time that afternoon, no one wants to talk about college stuff.

"YOU CAN DIFFERENTIATE between students who are in it for grade grubbing and those that really want to learn," Felix's AP Government teacher, Mrs. Ciamacca, tells me later that afternoon in her dark, empty classroom. "Felix sees connections between things that others wouldn't see," she says matter-of-factly. "In ninth grade, we did these simulations where students had to use the Nuclear Non-Proliferation Treaty to prevent a crisis in Asia. All the students had to take on the perspective of different countries and many of them just sort of went through the routine. Felix really went above and beyond. He got everyone to agree to a consensus and wrote up a really excellent resolution paper. Even in ninth grade, he had a love of learning for the sake of learning." Felix is not in the room to hear the compliment. After introducing Mrs. Ciamacca, he headed gone down the hall to pack up the schoolbooks in his locker.

Mrs. Ciamacca has been teaching at Conestoga for seven years, having had Felix as a student in both her ninth-grade World Cultures and her twelfth-grade AP Government courses. Her students love to talk about her fascinating past, which includes a stint as a military policewoman in the Marine Corps. After what she calls her "second career" in business, Mrs. Ciamacca went back to school to get her teaching credentials before embarking on her current "third career" as a high school instructor and head of the teachers' union. "I'm trying to get kids to get involved in government," she exclaims. Her political passions are shared by her husband, whose campaign signs for the Pennsylvania State Senate line the streets of Berwyn.

With the high school rankings issue of *Philadelphia* magazine tacked onto one of her classroom corkboards, it doesn't take long before the conversation turns to the topic of college admissions. Mrs. Ciamacca depicts the school as having a climate of high expectations and describes the pressure that students are under early in the year. "A couple of years ago," she says, "I actually took the kids aside to talk about how this 'AP culture' is not conducive to fostering the whole student. They're so driven to succeed, but what does 'success' mean anyway? It's so competitive that I make a point never to congratulate the students who get into Brown or Harvard in front of other students because they see themselves as 'less than' for not getting into the top schools."

Of course, there are some benefits to having so many students who are intensely driven to succeed in school. "The people are great here, the students are great here," she declares. Everyone at Conestoga seems eager to praise the school, challenging the widely held perception of high school as a place for discontent and alienation.

"There are no disciplinary problems," the teacher continues, "but this is a high-pressure place because the expectations are so high. The students are so overwhelmingly bright. Parents seek out this district when they are looking for places to move. They call it the 'gem of the Main Line.'"

Parents have high standards for the Conestoga faculty. "The teachers here really strive to develop critical thinking," Mrs. Ciamacca reports. "You just can't stand up there and read notes. You really have to engage students, to guide them rather than tell them what to think. Some kids, like Felix, could always make those kinds of critical connections. Others have to work at it.

"When I think about what I was doing in high school . . ." Her voice trails off and she smiles. "The load of work that these students have is astronomically more. These guys are *years* ahead of what I was doing in high school." The teacher lights up when she talks about her students.

"I guess it really is the parents. They really seek out this school," she says after a moment, trying to present a more balanced perspective. "Many of them are attorneys or executives at big pharmaceutical companies in Philadelphia. There are also some Asian parents who rent small apartments in the neighborhood just so their kids can get into this school."

"I'm sure that contributes to the pressure," I reply. "I know if my parents actually moved their whole lives somewhere just so I could go to school there, I'd probably feel pressure to work harder."

"Exactly," Mrs. Ciamacca agrees. "Also, there's the fact that success breeds success."

FELIX'S PARENTS MOVED to Berwyn about fifteen years ago when his father was offered a position on the Jefferson Medical School faculty and his mother accepted a job at a biotech company nearby. They had both just graduated from MIT, where they were the first graduate students from Chinese universities who were admitted without sponsorship from the Chinese government. Prior to 1983, Chinese students who studied abroad had to be sponsored by the state, which meant that they were subject to restrictions on their course of study, as well as required to return to China upon graduation. In many ways, Felix's parents were pioneers.

"We always had a sense of adventure," his mom says later that evening over dinner in a local Asian-fusion restaurant. The whole family is together, including Felix's father, James, and his adorably precocious ten-year-old sister, Alexandra. She arrives at the restaurant with a thick book in hand and orders sophisticated dishes like sashimi. Felix's attention is focused on Alexandra throughout the evening; he loves to make her laugh and teach her things, like useful chopstick techniques to avoid dropping the fish in her lap.

"I never planned to have another child, but Felix kept begging me," his mother says, looking over at her son and daughter. "So I told him that the new baby would have to be partially his responsibility. He takes that seriously. Ever since his sister was born, Felix has always looked after her."

Felix's mother, Danyi, is slender and well dressed in a champagne sweater with large monochrome sequins sewn around the collar. She speaks English with a hint of an accent, more British than Chinese. "The thing about Felix is, even though he is sixteen years old, he still brings home stories and shares his life—still hugs his mom and wants to connect," she explains. "A couple of times, Felix would have other plans but if his dad didn't know and offered to watch a movie with his son, Felix would quietly cancel his plans to spend time with his parents." After dinner, Felix drives Alexandra home, and his parents immediately launch into the story of how they first arrived in America from Shanghai.

Danyi was determined to earn a Ph.D. in biomedical engineering. She had just completed a five-year interdisciplinary program in medicine and engineering at a competitive Chinese university, where she and Felix's father were classmates. With limited graduate programs in China, Danyi decided to pursue her studies abroad. However, before she set out for the West, she faced an exigent dilemma: accept a full scholarship at the University of Southern California or enroll as an unfunded student at MIT, hoping she would somehow find a way to finance her education. She took a formidable risk and chose the latter.

In December 1983, Felix's mother flew from Shanghai to San Angelo, Texas, a quaint, isolated city in the middle of the state. A first-time flyer, she was the only passenger on the small plane that night. By the time she touched down on Texas soil, Danyi was completely disoriented from the distance and duration of her trip.

"I got very upset because I thought that I had accidentally gone to Germany!" she exclaims, laughing. When a local woman came out to greet the arriving planes, Felix's mother recognized the woman's "German" accent from old World War II movies. At the time, she had no idea that the Nazi characters in these movies were usually played by American actors speaking in fake German accents. Luckily, the German-Texan woman led her to a phone and she was able to reach her aunt, with whom she had arranged to stay for six months before going to graduate school.

"Oh, we were so poor," Felix's mother laughs again. "The Chinese government would not allow us to leave the country with more than a hundred dollars. Right away I had to work. The first thing my aunt told me was that you need a car in Texas. I had never even touched a car before. What could I do? I learned how to drive and bought a seven-hundred-fifty-dollar Lincoln Town Car."

While his mother was working and saving in small-town Texas, Felix's father was getting settled with relatives in Seattle. He had also come to the States to study engineering on scholarship at the University of Michigan. "He basically followed me around," Danyi chuckles, resting her hand on the arm of the good-looking man sitting next to her. Felix's father, who is broad-boned like his son, wears designer glasses with a sharp black blazer.

"I was *terrified* because I had never driven on a highway before," Danyi continues. "So he came from Seattle to Texas to help me drive the Town Car to Boston before school started. He also had never touched a car, and I had just got my license. The first day was *awful*. We drove in the pouring rain and had no idea how to get on and off the highway ramp. I started crying so much that I got really tired and we slept in the car at a gas station. When I woke up the next day, the sun was shining. Then," she makes direct eye contact and finishes her sentence slowly, "the hope came back."

After two nights and three days of inexperienced—and unlicensed, in Felix's father's case—driving and sleeping in the car, the couple arrived in Boston excited by the prospect of what lay ahead. They were up for adventure, having fallen in love on the trip to their new home, the best technological university in the world. Felix's mother quickly found a funded position in an aeronautics lab, and his father joined her less than two years later when the nuclear engineering department agreed to take him in. They were married in an MIT chapel shortly thereafter. Upon graduation, the couple bought a house in Berwyn. "You can't beat the schools," Danyi reaffirms. They have been living in the area ever since.

"We always encourage our kids not to fear," James says, shifting his weight from left to right. "We are more dominant, like most Chinese parents. We decided on medicine when Felix was young."

"He decided too," his mother interrupts.

"Yeah, but we tried to lead him. He was so good at music, but I told him that music does not equal a profession. The pressure that we give him to be an overachiever is the thing that he should be proud of."

"That's why I say to Felix that he's so much better prepared than we were," Danyi continues. "We were so sheltered."

ANDREW

The main entrance is the most striking feature of the otherwise conventional brick building that houses Jesuit High School in Mid-City New Orleans. A concrete statue of the Virgin Mary hovers above the large metal double doors, etched into the structure's facade. She looks down from atop her perch at all those who enter like the Statue of Liberty welcoming huddled masses.

Inside, the first floor, which was submerged in five feet of water for three weeks following Hurricane Katrina, has been completely gutted and rebuilt as part of a colossal $12 million reconstruction project. "It's kind of funny, because they spent all this money to make the building exactly the same as it was. Same carpet, paint, everything," Andrew jokes. The only thing missing from the original floor plan are the classroom doors, which have yet to be replaced. Bystanders can easily peer into the various rooms, filled with studious boys in uniform sitting upright in their desk chairs.

Each room also has a large wall-mounted cross and a statue of the Virgin Mary similar to the one above the entryway.

The four color-coded stairwells function as the building's main arteries, channeling Jesuit's 1,350 students to their assorted destinations. There is nothing flashy about the hallways and classrooms except for the assembly of trophy cases that line the corridors like soldiers standing guard. Each shelf is packed with prizes displaying decades of victory while other historic achievements are marked by plaques and photos suspended from the walls. "These are some of the most impressive things I have ever seen in my life," Andrew says, tilting his head back to admire a worn wooden scorecard. "In '46, they won every single game, including the state championships, in every single sport. Incredible."

As a newly anointed member of the Jesuit senior class, Andrew is looking forward to cashing in on his "head of the line" privileges. Unfortunately, he and his classmates have to wait a few weeks for construction to be completed on the first-floor lockers. Not having to carry your books up and down the stairs is one of the more significant benefits of upperclassman status. But until their lockers are repaired, the seniors must lug their textbooks in huge backpacks like nomads.

Because the cafeteria is subsidized by the archdiocese, it will also take time to reopen. "For two dollars, you get a good full meal," Andrew says, proud of the Church's contribution. "I have never eaten in the cafeteria in my life, though. I've eaten the same lunch every day since eighth grade—ham and cheese on wheat with an orange and kiwi." He chuckles, acknowledging the absurdity of his dietary monotony.

Andrew is not big on change in general. "See this picture of Jesuit in 1985," he says, happily pointing to an old blown-up photo of the school grounds. "We look exactly alike now. See."

• • •

MR. WRIGHT, ONE of Andrew's favorite teachers, has been teaching AP Calculus at Jesuit High School since 1976. He originally migrated to Louisiana from the Midwest for a teaching position in the math department at the University of New Orleans in the early 1970s. While there, he realized that he "liked teaching and hanging out with the students," so he asked his pupils for the low-down on the city's best high schools. They led him to Jesuit, where he's been teaching ever since.

Mr. Wright, a tall man with receding gray hair, gets up from behind a school-issued faux-wood desk in the math department faculty office to shake my hand. He has that "teacher look," somewhere between groomed and disheveled. A green tie with a subtle print hangs down the soft creases of his white dress shirt.

We sit down across from a distraught junior buried in a mammoth math textbook while another teacher splits her attention between looking over his shoulder and tending to the mound of ungraded papers on her desk. The boy cringes and recoils while working through the problem, a gnawed-on yellow pencil dangling from the corner of his mouth. "You'll get it, just relax," the teacher reassures him.

I ask Mr. Wright about his thirty-plus years of experience at Jesuit High School. "Students from all over are looking to excel, and Jesuit is a prime candidate for that because we have a reputation of motivating them to do more," he responds. "I guess Jesuit is perceived as elitist by some people, but I don't perceive it that way. It's not a 'rich' school. About 44 percent of students have some type of financial assistance. Finances don't get considered until after a student is accepted."

Mr. Wright is a keen observer of changes in youth culture over the years. "New Orleans can be provincial, especially back in the mid-seventies," he says, reclining in his pleather swivel chair. "The students now have a much broader worldview. They also catch on more quickly. I think it's the whole acceleration thing. The kids are hungrier, more stimulated. Also, the students who are doing well now are not the geeky ones. I have many football players taking AP Calculus." Mr. Wright pauses and focuses on the frazzled student still grappling with the math problem. "School equals cool now, right?" he jokes with the boy, who cracks a weak smile and barely looks up except to roll his eyes.

Over the years, Mr. Wright has seen the enrollment in his AP Calculus course more than double. "I do think they miss some things," he says of his ambitious students. "They get so caught up and always have to be responsible. It's not *bad*, but sometimes they might regress to sort of childlike behavior. That senioritis thing shows up first in the most motivated students. Some of them never got to be just kids."

Though he doesn't seem like the type to put any student up on a pedestal, Mr. Wright clearly has a good deal of affection for Andrew. "Andrew was more intense at first, but the more he matures, the more open he is to being challenged without worrying about grades," he observes. "He quickly learned that it was safe to put himself in a position where the grade doesn't come first and trust the process. When he's quote-and-quote 'struggling,' I see it as a learning thing. I get to go with him on this journey. The best way to get the students' attention is to take away their security blanket. I try to get the students to let go and *experience* success.

"Of course, Andrew still sits in the front row," continues Mr. Wright, not quite letting his pupil off the hook. "He always sits in the front row. I can't see him in the back row. But he still has some humility about it. It can be a fine line when you're as talented as he is. He knows that he knows enough to be confident, but he also makes mistakes. My class is all about that—making mistakes."

Unlike most high schools, which have done away with the dreaded parent-teacher conference, Jesuit organizes these meetings each quarter. This means that parents are updated on their sons' progress every nine weeks. "That's the double-edged sword. It's easy to get kids to perform because you make one phone call and the parents snap to attention. The negative side is that they can be so involved that they lose track of the larger picture. It's not all about grades."

LISA

Lisa's parents live a world away from the central Chinese province of Guangxi, where they were both born. On this unusually sunny fall afternoon, we are having breakfast at Einstein Bros. Bagels, located in one of the many shopping centers near their home. Her father, Ping, describes his family's epic journey from rural China to suburban Chicago.

"In those days in China you don't have too much choice," her father says. He is a tall man with a kind face, who smiles frequently and speaks English with a distinct Chinese accent. "Smart kids go to physics because it is the hardest thing to do. The whole society pushed you. If you are a good student, you're supposed to do physics or math," he says, explaining the choices he made that eventually led him to the United States.

In 1987, Lisa's parents moved to Madison, Wisconsin, so that her father could study physics with a well-known professor at the University of Wisconsin. However, after completing his Ph.D., Ping realized that atomic physics was not his calling and decided to make a major career change, which led him to enroll in a master's program in quantitative mathematical finance. He later accepted a lucrative position at Allstate Investments, moving his family from Wisconsin to Illinois. "We use sophisticated software to forecast interest rates and other things—and try to figure out the economy, basically. I enjoy doing it because it has a much more direct impact in daily life than atomic physics." He grins.

Lisa's mother, Cindy, speaks with the same accent as her husband—and smiles even more often than he does. She is a petite woman (though not as small as her tiny daughter), dressed in a bright pink sweater. "I never predict I would stay here. I didn't think it was really realistic," she says, recalling her state of mind twenty years ago. "But my family always say if you can stay, just stay there. Don't come back." Her last sentence is startling. However, the situation in China at the time was dangerous for Lisa's mother and her family.

In 1966, the Chinese Communist Party, led by Chairman Mao Zedong, created the Red Guards, a mass youth militia, to take down the establishment and embolden the proletariat. This uprising, known as the Cultural Revolution, is estimated to have killed millions of people. Because they had been members of the local elite, most of Lisa's mother's family was persecuted during this time. "We were in three different places until 1972," Cindy explains in a shaky voice. "My father was in a labor camp. My older sister went to live with an aunt in the countryside. The three youngest stayed with my mom in our town." She pauses for a moment before continuing, "But my family was actually on the lucky side. No one got killed."

"Have you ever been to Madison?" Lisa's dad asks, changing the subject.

"No, but I hear that it's very nice."

"Well, they say that there are two college towns that you never leave. One is Boston, the other is Madison. We lived in Madison for a long time. Lisa was born there." He puts his arm around the back of his wife's chair and continues with his trademark smile, "I'll never forget it. It was the night that Carl Lewis won the hundred-meter final in the 1988 Olympics."

Lisa's mother interrupts excitedly, "Oh yes. I kept saying, 'I need to go to the hospital! I need to go to the hospital!' but he didn't want to leave. He said, 'Wait! Wait! I want to finish the game!'" She and her husband both laugh at the implication that Lisa has some sort of cosmic connection to the Olympics.

After the race was over, the Wangs finally set out for the delivery room. Lisa arrived a few weeks early, right before her father was scheduled to defend his dissertation. When she entered the world, she weighed only five pounds. She has been small ever since.

About a year after Lisa was born, her mother enrolled in a master's program in engineering physics at the University of Wisconsin. At this point, the Wangs were both full-time students (her father was in a postdoc program), and short on money and time. "It was very hard to have a little baby," her mother says. "Lisa was really tough. She was not a good baby. Really tough." For the first time that afternoon, neither of Lisa's parents is smiling.

"She was born three weeks early so she couldn't eat well," her mother continues. "She was always vomiting. Always vomiting. And she was so small. I always needed to hold her. I could not put her down in the crib. I could not put her down on the bed. *No way.*"

Cindy is now visibly upset. As she speaks, she seems to be transported back to that time in her life. Somewhere deep inside this cheery middle-aged woman is the voice of a desperate new mother living thousands of miles from home—culturally and geographically—frantically trying to meet the demands of a full-time graduate program and a fussy newborn baby.

"The doctor told us to put her in the crib, close the door, and let her cry. He says when she cries she will sleep. We put her in. She stood up in her crib and cry. She never gave up. She kept crying. Finally we gave up. *We gave up.*"

Lisa's father does not speak about the struggle with as much emotion as his wife, though it is clear that he remembers what they went through. "We tried twice to put her down and let her cry," Ping says. "But it carried over until now. She never gives up." Cindy chuckles at the happy ending.

Earlier that morning, Lisa told me how pleased she was with the results of her latest SAT. She managed to improve her scores by 100 points overall, raising them to a 2200. These new scores, coupled with her near-perfect GPA and impressive extracurricular résumé, speak well of her chances for admission to a top college. I ask Cindy and Ping if Lisa was always such a talented student.

"Yes, always, always a very good student," her mother responds. "In kindergarten they picked two kids for a reading program, like an enrichment program. The teacher told me that she was doing second-, even third-grade reading."

"I think Lisa is a bright student, but I never think she is gifted," Ping says. His candid comment is startlingly unusual. Most parents go to great lengths to brag about their children's intellectual prowess, especially when they have children like Lisa.

"A lot of Lisa's accomplishments come from working hard," her father adds. "She works really hard, and she can *really* concentrate. That's ninety-five percent of her success. She's bright but not the most smart. We also have friends' kids who are very smart, but lazy."

"Very lazy," agrees his wife. They laugh at the inside joke.

I ask the Wangs to describe their impressions of the college admissions process, expecting them to complain about the stress.

"Lisa actually takes care of everything in terms of college," her mother answers.

"We trust her one hundred percent," her father agrees. "But we do have some input on what college she applies to." Cindy rolls her eyes slightly.

"I don't care. They're all good schools," she says. As of now, Lisa is applying to Yale, Harvard, Stanford, Columbia, Northwestern, and the University of Michigan.

"Very few Chinese parents don't impose. We're one of the few," Ping says. "We went through the process so we know how hard it is to do something demanding if it's something you really don't want to do."

"She can study anything she wants as long as she's happy," adds Lisa's mother.

MARLENE

L ater that week, Marlene introduces me to her guidance counselor. Mrs. de Miranda, a small Cuban American woman, works almost exclusively with the Hispanic students at New Rochelle High School. It is not uncommon for schools to assign counselors to specific subsets of students, especially when there are language or immigration issues to consider. Mrs. de Miranda's fluent Spanish helps her communicate with the families she advises. We stop by her office one afternoon to discuss her philosophy on the college admissions process. She greets Marlene with a big hug and welcomes us in.

"So many recent Mexican girls—the new arrivals—tend to not take care of their education because they want to get married. Marlene is really a star for us, even among her sisters," she says. Mrs. de Miranda seems simultaneously involved in and unaware of the details of Marlene's life, like she remembers her sisters well, but forgets that they are Dominican instead of from Mexico.

"Marlene's family values are so strong, and they have kept them," continues the counselor. "But some of the other more recent immigrants haven't had exposure to good education. They don't have the same stability. Many of them live with cousins or siblings who are only a few years older."

The petite woman is enthusiastic about the ways in which the New Rochelle public schools try to provide additional support for students of color. She explains that every ninth and tenth grader is assigned to a "team"—a subgroup of students with the same advisors and teachers. These smaller learning communities help students adjust to their high school routine and enable teachers, counselors, and parents to monitor them. They also encourage diversity in the classroom until students move up to AP and honors courses later on. At this point, the classes tend to resegregate along racial lines, with the majority of white students in more advanced classes.

"I think they should eliminate the qualifying exam in this school," says Mrs. de Miranda. "Kids need to score a ninety on the exam to get into AP courses, which excludes many students. But Marlene is in—she's going for it!" She smiles warmly at Marlene, who sits quietly in a plastic chair in the corner of the cramped room.

"Well, I know she's concerned about loans, so I've encouraged her to apply to state schools," the counselor answers when I ask which colleges she thinks will be best for Marlene. "I want her to go away. I want her to get scholarships, to get away from home. The oldest sister is really tight with the mother, and the middle one is the social butterfly. I'm excited for Marlene to socially experience herself away from her family. They are so close and have solid values. But she needs to take those with her and make them her own."

"My mom wanted me to go to City College or Lehman or Columbia," Marlene explains, listing colleges that are close to home.

"I know when I went to college I was out of Cuba for only four years. It was so enriching. I have three siblings who didn't go, and it makes such a big difference. Go away, honey. You will really blossom." Mrs. de Miranda reaches over and puts her hand gently on Marlene's knee. "And don't miss those scholarship deadlines, okay? They go by really fast." She then turns to the pile of papers on her desk and holds up the letter of recommendation that she has already written for Marlene's applications. "I tried to encourage her to participate in more activities for college, but she didn't," she says, as she gives Marlene a look of disappointment.

"I couldn't because my sister wanted to, and we always argued about getting a ride home from school," Marlene protests.

Mrs. de Miranda promptly resumes her upbeat attitude. "Some parents are just living through their kids. That's their whole identity—where their kids get into college. Your parents aren't like that at all. You don't have that problem. They love you no matter what." She then jumps up from her chair to give Marlene another big hug, rocks her back and forth in an embrace, and exclaims, "You're gonna fly, butterfly!"

· FOUR ·

"I'm scared I'll like the school too much"

NABIL

P layers for Bolton and Cordova, please line up over here," instructs a female voice in a heavy Southern accent. It is the night before Halloween, when most high school students are putting the finishing touches on their costumes or scanning the grocery store dairy section for rotten eggs. Instead, Nabil can be found among a small group of racially mixed and consistently nerdy Memphis teenagers in the reception area of the local CBS affiliate. About twenty people, students and their parents, quickly form a line in the left-hand corner of the room, then disappear down a tiled hallway with strong fluorescent lights.

After navigating the winding corridors outside and back inside the building, the group arrives at the *Knowledge Bowl* set. Two teams of high school students take their places behind the old-school podiums, configured in two rows of four; each row faces out to the audience, and there is a spot for the host where they meet.

The podiums have silver plastic triangles adorning their trunks and long microphones snaking upward like branches. The players' names are etched onto the Plexiglas signs under their microphones, which will later be illuminated when they buzz in to answer questions. The kids, smiling and joking around with one another, pretend that they are gearing up to win big on *Jeopardy!*

The barebones *Knowledge Bowl* set looks like something out of *Saturday Night Live*, and the goofy host would fit right into a comedy sketch. With his cheap navy suit and classic 1970s coifed hair, he is almost a caricature of the game show host. He approaches each team member to review his notes, carefully nodding down at the paper in front of him and repeating terms like "National Merit semifinalist" and "cross-country team" in a robust, deep voice.

Nabil appears handsome and assured as he waits his turn. Standing tall, he is dressed in a black suit with a white button-down shirt. His look-alike younger brother, wearing a white track suit and Nikes, sits next to me in the audience. He taps his feet with anticipation, rests his elbows on his knees, and cradles his chin in his hands.

"Na-bill Ab-du-ra-man?" asks the host, sounding downright hostile.

For the first time that evening, Nabil seems shy. "It's Ab-dur-reh-man."

"Ab-du-ramanan?" The host tries to pronounce Nabil's last name again.

"Ab-dur-reh-man."

"That's okay, I'll just do the best I can," the host resolves. He continues down the line reading off the students' list of credentials. The kids respond appropriately by laughing politely at the corny jokes he makes.

"Y'all, please give us good claps so that we don't have to use the fake ones in the machines," the director pleads with the audience from the shadows.

"Ab-dur-reh-man?" The host checks in with Nabil before taking his place under the *Knowledge Bowl* logo center stage.

"Yep," Nabil beams back, standing taller than before.

"That was a lucky shot."

Nabil looks uncomfortable. "A lot of people have trouble with it," he responds.

"Stand by," says the director's voice, "and . . ." One, two, three, *"NOW!"* The mood instantly changes from mild to full-blown tension as the muted *Knowledge Bowl* intro appears on the monitors that are scattered around the set. The students stand stiffly with their arms by their sides behind the podiums.

"These are the Wolverines from Cordova High School led by Nabil Ab-dur-rach-man, who is a senior," says the host, almost getting the name right. He then introduces Nabil's teammates, as well as the four boys who make up the Bolton High Wildcats, and immediately launches into the questions.

"Among the world's greatest museums, there is the Louvre in Paris, the Metropolitan Museum in New York, and the British Museum in London. What is the name of the great museum in St. Petersburg, Russia?"

Silence.

"That would be the Hermitage. Next question. What famous criminal couple in the 1930s died—"

Bzzz. "Bonnie and Clyde." Brian, the Bolton team captain, gets it right. The questions and answers continue.

"Which historian is remembered for his accounts of Greek heritage?"

"Which Shakespeare character said, 'A rose by any other name would smell as sweet'?"

"Leopold and Loeb."

"The Lindbergh baby."

"Tasmania."

A few minutes and several questions later, the host abruptly ends round one with Bolton in the lead, 75 to 40. Nabil starts to look a little nervous, until he makes eye contact with his brother. The two boys exchange smiles, and he stops shifting his weight from side to side.

"We'll be right back to meet our students," says the announcer, transitioning to commercial break with a big game-show-host grin.

The short break flies by, and the audience applauds when the host welcomes us back to the show. Nabil is wide-eyed and glowing as he prepares for the spotlight, like a child waiting to be served an ice cream sundae in a restaurant. As team captain, he will be the first student introduced.

"So, Nabil with-the-very-complicated-last-name, it says here"— the host lowers his head and robotically reads from his prepared notes—"you're a National Merit semifinalist who runs cross-country and is learning Arabic. You'd like to major in math or a foreign language in college. Tell me, what sort of foreign language are you thinking of majoring in?" Anyone who knows Nabil knows that this is a silly question. He is much more interested in math than in foreign languages.

"Um," Nabil answers in his best mock-adult voice, "I'm thinking Chinese because I'm interested in how the language structure works. Or maybe French, 'cause lots of good work in math has been done in French." Nabil looks flustered, unprepared to answer questions about foreign languages.

"Uh-huh," the host responds dismissively and moves on to the other kids, asking questions like, "What kinds of things do you like to photograph?" and "Do you write music or just listen to it?"

The director holds up his fingers. One. Two. Three. It's time for round two.

"Identify the movies based on the literary works with the following quotations," instructs the host. "Frankly, my dear, I don't give a daaamn," he continues in his best Scarlett O'Hara.

Nabil buzzes in for the first time that night. "*Casablanca*?" His brother slaps his palm to his forehead, knowing this is the wrong answer.

"Nope. Bolton?"

"*Gone with the Wind*?"

"You got it. It's a far, far better thing that I do, than I have ever done befo—"

"*A Tale of Two Cities.*"

"Nice work, Brian." Brian, the Bolton team captain, is responsible for at least four out of five of the team's correct answers. Though he is trying his best to remain calm, Nabil lowers and shakes his head from side to side each time Brian gets one right. The host fires off questions for the next five minutes before transitioning to a commercial break.

"That brings the score to one hundred seventy for Bolton and sixty for Cordova. But don't worry," the host turns to Nabil, "we'll be right back for the lightning round and there will be plenty of time for you to catch up!"

The lightning round is aptly named. The questions, which come much faster now, are all plucked from news headlines. Buzzers go off one after the other.

"Element 118." Brian from Bolton again.

"Human remains." Yeah, Nabil!

"Stevie Wonder." David from Bolton.

Bzzz. Cordova.

Bzzz. Bolton.

Bzzz. Bolton.

Bzzz. Damn it, Bolton.

"We're all out of time, guys," the host announces and turns to face the cameras. "We'll be right back with our winners and our"—dramatic pause, fake frown—"not-so-winners."

Cordova not-so-wins, 70 to 200.

"I'm freeeee!" exclaims David from Bolton as he forcefully pulls his tie from his neck, like a prisoner loosening a noose. Nabil stands there for a moment, looking disappointed. He then leads his teams in congratulating Bolton for a game well played. The kids exchange high fives and hugs, and everybody seems to come back to life—even not-so-winner Nabil.

"I GOT A LETTER from the University of Chicago congratulating me on being a National Merit Semifinalist. It said that semifinalists are often qualified for one of their scholarships—they give like thirty—so I'm definitely going to apply," Nabil reports the following afternoon at Cordova High School. He just got out of quiz team practice, and doesn't have much time to talk because his brother is waiting for a ride home from school. We end up sitting on the hallway floor in front of his locker while the step team stomps and claps through their routine in the background.

A few weeks ago, Nabil, his father, and his two younger brothers set out for the nine-hour drive from Memphis to the University of Chicago, while his mother and two younger sisters stayed at home. It was their first trip to Chicago, and the Abdurehman men were impressed with the city's beautiful skyline and urban pulse. They made their hotel reservations on the road, and ended up at a Best Western late Sunday evening. "I guess they were just about full because the room we did get was on the *seventeenth floor!*" Nabil exclaims, making it obvious that he's never stayed in such a tall building.

The family woke up early Monday morning and headed directly to the University of Chicago campus to catch the first tour of the day. The tour guide reminded Nabil of Napoleon Dynamite "because she was really nerdy and into theater," he jokes. She told the group how much she loved answering questions, and when no one asked her any, she asked and answered her own.

Like many students who visit college campuses, Nabil decided to sit in on a class later that day. Unlike most students, however, he picked one of the most difficult classes, one taught by Paul Sally, a professor he really admires who has a reputation for being tough. Nabil proudly tells the story of how he actually shocked an undergraduate at the reception desk when he told her that he planned to sit in on Paul Sally's Honors Analysis class, so much so that she stopped one of her friends to pass on the news that a high school student wanted to take Professor Sally's class. True to form, Nabil was looking forward to the challenge of engaging with the toughest instructor.

There were six other students in Honors Analysis that afternoon, all seniors. Paul Sally was more than a little eccentric—he bit little pieces of chalk and wore an eye patch under his glasses. Even so, Nabil loved being in a serious academic environment. "I'd never done what they were learning, but I picked up some stuff," he says.

After lunch, the Abdurehmans began their trip back to Memphis. By this time, Nabil had really fallen in love with the college. He reread the University of Chicago brochures and catalogs during the nine-hour drive.

Aggressive college marketing is not a new phenomenon. By the early twentieth century, American universities had evolved into large and powerful institutions that actively recruited students and seemed to thirst for competition. Colleges organized football teams and adopted mascots, school colors, and school songs. They also raced to develop their impressive campuses by building luxurious dorms, laboratories, libraries, and theaters by following similar models of expansion. Despite this, the best universities tried to distinguish themselves from the pack, and the first public relations offices were soon established at colleges across the country.

This period marked the beginning of a new era of college advertising in which the first college admissions brochures and catalogs were published. Most brochures described the benefits of enrolling in a particular college, such as successful alumni, quality teaching, and beautiful dormitories. Technical colleges could boast about their ability to provide students with essential skills for economic prosperity. However, liberal arts colleges, including those in the Ivy League, had to convince students of their relevancy by playing up the intangible benefits of a liberal arts education. They claimed to promote strong moral convictions and tight-knit residential communities. Some schools also addressed parental concerns, assuring parents that their children would be safe and cared for. The image of the "college on a hill" was popular at this time—and remains so today—because it gave parents a sense that colleges were above the harsh realities of the outside world, and that their sons and daughters would be protected.

Aside from keeping their children safe, parents nowadays are also concerned with college costs. "My dad still wants me to look at financial aid packages before deciding on a college," Nabil says. Taking his father's advice, Nabil is applying to five colleges—Harvard, Princeton, MIT, the University of Chicago, and probably Boston University. "Harvard sounds like they're the most generous, but if I get a scholarship to the University of Chicago I might go. My dad also wants me to apply to Boston University because they have been sending us so much mail, and I could probably get a scholarship there," he explains.

Though he originally planned to apply early action to Harvard, Nabil changed his mind and decided to wait until the regular decision deadline in early January so that he could compose a more cohesive application. "With cross-country coming to a close, and me trying to start the Math Club off with regular meetings, the early Harvard app I was trying to send off seemed like it was being rushed," he explains. Nabil is either unaware or unconcerned about the statistical advantage to submitting an early action application. "If I could get in with an application I'd fill out and send now, I don't see why I wouldn't get in if I make progress on everything that I want to work on this year first," he says.

MARLENE

"O h. My. God. I LOOOOOOOOOOOOOOOOOOOVED it," Marlene tells me over e-mail, after her visit to the University of
Pennsylvania. She and her parents woke up early and drove down
to Philadelphia on a Saturday morning to attend the college's Multicultural and Diversity Open House, to which she was invited
based on the results of her PSAT. "This was the first school I visited
that I actually like, like *really like*," she says. "But this is really unfortunate because . . . aah! It's exactly what I didn't want to happen
since almost all of the highly competitive people from my school
really like it too, and so far, five people are applying there early
decision."

The Fernandez clan began their day by attending a student presentation for La Casa Latina, the university's Hispanic student association. The director of the organization also addressed the group
of prospective students and offered her contact information to any
applicant who had questions. Afterward, two admissions officers
gave a presentation about the university's application process and
admissions requirements.

"Someone from financial aid came and said the usual, 'We'll
make it affordable for you to come to Penn.' Then I went to their
engineering info session and it was a Hispanic female student who
was doing the talking. She said the expected 'Penn is so great,'"
Marlene recounts, with her trademark skepticism. The student told
the group about her freshman and sophomore internship experiences at General Motors and talked about participating in study
abroad and community service programs. By the time she left the
meeting, Marlene was highly impressed with the myriad of opportunities being presented to her.

After lunch, she and her family proceeded on a tour of the campus. Their first stop was Locust Walk, the heart of the University of

Pennsylvania. The stunning tree-lined lane was jam-packed with student organizations trying to recruit newly arrived freshmen. The tour group then explored the rest of the spectacular university grounds, including the cultural center, museum, gymnasium, and academic facilities. Marlene couldn't help but become enamored.

"At the end there was a Q and A section," she says. "And I liked that because for the most part parents didn't ask ridiculous kinds of questions. For instance, toward the end of my junior year, I went to this info session for Harvard, Penn, Duke, and Georgetown, and when it got to the Q and A section, most of the parents were asking the most pointless questions ever. And also most of the people there were the white-Jewish-overachiever kind—no offense—and I hated that because I felt so intimidated. Usually schools like Penn do not have to try to sell their school to anyone, but since this event was specifically for 'minorities,' they care more about selling the school to the kids and parents."

Selective colleges recruit high-achieving minority students in several ways. Admissions officers often collaborate with independent educational organizations that work with gifted students of color, arranging special tours or accommodations for students in these programs. Colleges also purchase information from the College Board to identify minority students with impressive academic credentials. Using the results of their PSATs, they target kids like Marlene with brochures, phone calls, and invitations to exclusive campus tours or events. In addition to visiting the University of Pennsylvania, Marlene had planned to attend the Multicultural Open House at Yale the following weekend. However, at the last minute, she decided against going so that she could devote the weekend to studying for the SAT. Her trip to Penn has motivated her to work even harder to prepare for her standardized tests. "That's exactly what I didn't want to happen—me fall in love with a school," she says, frustrated, "especially an Ivy school. *And especially the Ivy school that everyone wants to go to.* I know this might sound stupid, but that's why I'm not too fond of visits. I'm scared I'll like the school too much."

ANDREW

Of all the activities, interests and experiences listed on the previous page, which is the most meaningful to you, and why?

Sharing intellectual interests is an important aspect of university life. Describe an idea or experience that you find intellectually exciting, and explain why.

Write a note to your future roommate relating a personal experience that reveals something about you.

After much deliberation, Andrew has decided to apply early action to Stanford and these are just a few of the questions that he must answer in essay form to complete his application. "They had like three times more acceptances for early than for regular decision," Andrew says, aware that applying early could be a plus in the admissions process. "It's not binding so I can still apply to other schools for regular." He also really likes Harvard and is considering other Ivies like Princeton and the University of Pennsylvania.

Andrew's decision to apply early to Stanford was somewhat influenced by the fact that he had attended the Stanford EPGY Summer Institute. When a Stanford admissions officer visited New Orleans in the fall, Andrew asked her if his participation in the Stanford summer program would give him an advantage in the application process. "She said that the program would help me get in, but not because it was Stanford's," he explains. "I wasn't expecting her to say, 'Clearly, the fact that you went to Stanford's program is superior to a program at Duke or another school.' But I definitely put the summer program on Stanford's application when they asked me to list a couple of things I'd done over the summer. I think that the summer program, plus the fact that I'm applying early action, will help me at Stanford."

These days, virtually every prestigious college is cashing in on their elite reputation by sponsoring summer programs, which are often marketed as a way for students to prepare for college in high school. Though universities make no guarantee that students who attend these summer programs will eventually be granted admission, parents routinely shell out thousands of dollars for these academic camps. Eight weeks at the Harvard Summer School, one of the most popular programs, costs $4,550 for courses and $3,975 for room and board. The program posts the following message on their Web site:

> Though attending the Secondary School Program is not a guarantee of admission to Harvard College, students can take advantage of being on campus by visiting the Harvard College Admissions Office and attending a talk given by a Harvard admissions officer. In addition, interviews are granted to qualified SSP students who live far from Cambridge.

It is easy to see how an anxious applicant or desperate parent could perceive that students who attend a costly summer program on a university campus might benefit in the college admissions process. Many of these programs take students on campus tours and encourage them to attend information sessions by admissions officers. Some programs also offer SAT prep classes, and students can benefit from pursuing their academic interests in their free time. However, enrollment in these types of programs generally offers students few, if any, tangible advantages in the admissions process. An applicant may do just as well taking classes at a community college or visiting campuses with his or her parents, both of which are less expensive alternatives.

"The summer program application was like a college application," Andrew says, describing his Stanford experience. "It wasn't quite as long but it wasn't just 'fill in your name.' When I got into the summer program, I definitely saw it as positive feedback from the school." Though Andrew's logic is understandable, he may be setting himself up for disappointment by making assumptions about the connection between getting into the Stanford summer program and getting into the college.

ANDREW'S MOTHER IS his primary source of college planning information. "My mom has a billion books about every college that was ever created," he says. "She already went through the whole college thing with my sister."

Andrew is one of the few students in his class who aspires to enroll in a highly selective college. "Nobody freaks out about college at our school," Andrew explains. "I mean, we talk about it, but nobody is really whiny. People don't really apply to the Ivies. There aren't that many people that would want to or could pay for it. That's one thing that is different about the kids at Jesuit compared to a lot of other good private schools. Most of the kids are solid middle class. Almost everyone goes to LSU. And lots of the upper track kids get full scholarships."

"Why do you think you want to go to such a competitive college?" I ask Andrew one afternoon at a local coffee shop.

"I guess I'm just very competitive. I like winning. I am very gung ho about the things I do," he answers with a clever grin.

Andrew's remark reminds me of one of his Stanford essays. When asked to address something that someone has said, written, or expressed in some fashion that is especially meaningful to him, Andrew selected the following quote: "Of all the men who have ever said that they were burnt out, none of them was on fire." He writes:

If by "burning out" one means that he has worked so hard, he no longer cares, then clearly "burning out" is dangerous and ought to be avoided. But I could never become "burnt out" while I am passionate. I find myself always ready to learn more strategy (whether it is how to beat a chess opponent or how to solve a math equation), mathematics, physics, or military technology (where the most exciting, most expensive, and highest technologies always mesh). My passions are what drives me, what make me who I am and what I enjoy. . . .

I am what people call an overachiever, though I believe that overachieving is impossible—achieving one's goal is difficult enough. To put in the necessary interest and time worthy of any activity, I must be passionate about that activity; or else it becomes merely a hobby, or worse, a chore. . . . Just as in the parable of the talents in the Bible, I ought not to bury the gifts given to me by my master but rather to share them with the world and to develop them to multiply their value.

Most of Andrew's essays make reference to God or the Bible. "As a person, my religion is pretty important," he says. "If someone asks me to write something that describes myself, well, I couldn't not put God in there. Religion is a pretty big part of my life."

Ever since William F. Buckley Jr. published *God & Man at Yale* in 1951, the Ivy League has been accused of a liberal atheistic bias. Drawing from his own undergraduate experiences, Buckley's book went into great detail about how individual professors at Yale discouraged students' religious beliefs. Current research confirms that most college professors tend to lean to the left of the political spectrum and are not actively affiliated with an organized religion like Andrew. This potential conflict has been gaining attention in the media as religion has become more popular with students in recent years, especially on elite campuses. Over the past two decades, participation in Campus Crusade for Christ has increased by 163 percent at Brown, more than 500 percent at Harvard, and 700 percent at Yale, according to the Christian Broadcasting Network. A representative from the antiabortion group American Collegians for Life told the *Christian Science Monitor* in 2005 that attendance at their annual conference grew from 70 to 350 students over three years, and included many participants from Ivy League campuses.

In 2004, a right-leaning organization, Students for Academic Freedom, introduced the Academic Bill of Rights. The bill, which consists of eight amendments designed to protect religious and ideological freedom on college campuses, was crafted as a response to the perceived bias against conservative students and their beliefs in the classroom. Although the American Association of University Professors and the American Federation of Teachers claim that this type of regulation restricts academic freedom, legislators in Colorado, Georgia, Missouri, Michigan, Oklahoma, Ohio, California, and Utah have considered enacting different versions of the Academic Bill of Rights to protect students with conservative views and/or religious values.

I ask Andrew if he thinks that he will be at a disadvantage in the admissions process because of his religious beliefs. "It's not a big enough concern for me to worry about," he answers. "Nobody should be prejudiced against anybody for race, religion, or gender considering that every college takes federal funds. So I wouldn't put too much weight on that. I wasn't really thinking about it when I wrote my essays."

MARLENE

A few weeks after her visit to the University of Pennsylvania, the pressure of senior year courses, retaking the SATs, and the looming college application deadlines is really getting to Marlene. Already overwhelmed by all that she must accomplish in the upcoming weeks, she must now deal with a new and unexpected variable—her parents' expectations. "In a way, I regret visiting Penn and ever telling my parents about any of these places because now they're convinced that I'm going to get in," she says. "God forbid I say that I don't think I have a good chance of getting in because they think it's all in my head. They don't understand how competitive it is."

Besides the fact that Marlene is being courted by the University of Pennsylvania and other prestigious institutions, her parents have another reason to believe that she will have her pick of colleges. They recently attended a meeting at New Rochelle High School for Hispanic students, during which the school principal and faculty gave the audience some information about college and financial aid. At the end of the presentation, two students were formally distinguished based on the results of their PSATs from the National Hispanic Recognition Program. Marlene was one of the two honorees from among approximately 170 Hispanic students in her class.

Like most schools in the New York City metropolitan area, New Rochelle High School struggles with issues of racial inequity. Despite being the first Northern school district to be subjected to a judicial desegregation order by the United States Supreme Court in 1962, a well-documented academic achievement gap persists in the school system today. On the surface, the high school is diverse. Of the approximately three thousand students, 46 percent are white, 27 percent are African American, and 23 percent are Hispanic, and the school's auditorium and library are named after civil rights activists such as Whitney Young and Michael Schwerner. However, not all students are able to achieve at the same level. The classes themselves are often segregated, with the majority of white students in honors, while most students of color are tracked into nonhonors. Graduation rates are also significantly higher for white students, 97 percent of whom met the requirements for graduation—compared to only 84 percent of African American and 86 percent of Hispanic students—in the class of 2006. To their credit, the high school faculty and administration are taking steps to try to narrow the achievement gap at New Rochelle.

With her application deadlines looming, Marlene has finally decided to ask Mr. Morris, her AP Calculus teacher, who is also the head of the math/technology department at New Rochelle High School, for a recommendation. Mr. Morris was responsible for introducing the precalculus course that Marlene completed over the summer. "He's African American and came from a low-income household. So he can relate and really wants to create opportunities for minority students," she says.

Before asking Mr. Morris for a recommendation, Marlene thanked him for the opportunity to take the precalculus class in the summer. She feels grateful for the chance to advance to college-level math during her senior year of high school. "If it weren't for AP Calculus, I probably wouldn't be able to even consider more than half of the colleges on my list," she later says.

Mr. Morris is a handsome forty-something man with a commanding voice and a no-nonsense aura. He often talks with students about his philosophy of educational equity and his efforts to increase vehicles for underrepresented students to progress and thrive in higher education. He is a firm believer in second chances for students who want to learn.

"So I asked him if he would recommend me. He said that he would normally not do this, because I'm a senior and he didn't really know me that well until now, but it would be hypocritical if he didn't since he's trying to make the minority into a majority," Marlene says, noting her fortuitous good timing. Not only has she finally found someone to write her a recommendation, she is thrilled to have the head of the department advocate on her behalf.

After agreeing to support her college candidacy, Mr. Morris asked Marlene where she plans to apply. Modestly, she started listing her "safety schools"—schools at which she is likely to be accepted—like City College, SUNY Stony Brook, and Binghamton University. Upon hearing her list, he interrupted her to ask why she isn't considering any of the Ivies. Not wanting to sound out of her league, Marlene responded that she is considering several Ivy League schools but is still waiting to find out where she ranks in the class and to receive the results of her latest SAT.

"Then he told me the story of how he encouraged one of his students to apply to Columbia. The kid thought he had absolutely no chance of getting in. But he did," Marlene recounts. Her face lights up like a little girl's who has just received news that school is closed for a snow day.

AS THE HEAD of the math department, Mr. Morris's large office is divided by bookshelf partitions into smaller areas—a desk for his assistant and what looks like a makeshift conference room with a large round table in the center. He greets me with a hearty handshake and escorts me toward the back of the room. His personal desk is nicer, neater, and more tasteful than what you typically find in school offices. Sitting in front of his framed diplomas, Mr. Morris looks almost regal.

Mr. Morris gets right down to business. Having worked in mathematics education for twenty-one years, he has developed the pragmatism and perseverance of a true reformer. "I believe that education must become the first and foremost priority in the home. Through every venue, I have to get the message out there. If we sell education with the same fervor that we sell soda, we can do this," he says.

Mr. Morris does not coddle the students in his calculus class. He is not there to make friends; he is there to teach them the skills they need to make their lives better. "The opportunities for females and minorities are really not level," he explains. "They need to work a little harder, be a little more diligent, to prepare them to be successful in college, not just here. It can be a little painful. Sometimes a student might get a grade that they feel scares them, but I want the class to be a reflection of what it means to go to college. They need to have the skills to *stay* in college."

The teacher's hard-line approach is reminiscent of Jaime Escalante, who inspired the movie *Stand and Deliver,* which was based on the true story of a teacher who taught AP Calculus in a failing high-poverty-level school in Los Angeles. Of course, the challenges of teaching at New Rochelle High School pale in comparison, a point which Mr. Morris readily acknowledges. "I started as a substitute teacher and taught in the city. I've seen much worse. I've taught in areas where this chair is vacant because Juan got shot last night. I was attending about two funerals per year," he says, leaning forward over his desk.

Since coming to New Rochelle, Mr. Morris has been a champion of progressive curricular reform. He introduced the summer precalculus class primarily to give students who had been tracked into nonhonors courses an opportunity to advance. Of course, the class is open to all students, but he tries to reach out to talented students of color who might need an extra push. Marlene was one of the beneficiaries of this opportunity and is now doing well in his AP Calculus class.

Mr. Morris also fought to condense the ESL program from five to two years. He knows how crucial it is to accelerate the integration of English language learners into mainstream classes if they want to go on to college. And he works hard to recruit more faculty members of color to the math department and school district in general.

"Students should have role models who are reflections of themselves," Mr. Morris continues. "However, the teachers need to be *qualified.* If I opened up an all-black school, for example, I wouldn't have all black teachers because not only black teachers care about black kids. I've hired nonminorities who were more qualified so long as they believe that all students can learn."

Of the twenty-five faculty members in the math department,

three are Hispanic and Mr. Morris is the only African American. "I think we can and will do better," he says of his district's faculty diversity. "New Rochelle does what we can to bring qualified minority teachers in. It's not just me making these decisions. I think the people above me are supportive. But it's a constant struggle of fighting what's keeping the kids from learning. If we had the magic pill, we would write a book and call it a day."

· FIVE ·

"Waiting suuuuucks!"

LISA

I started rhythmic gymnastics as a young girl entranced by the flowing patterns of the ribbons and awed by the insane flexibility of the gymnasts. Having no natural flexibility and no exceptional talent, my parents whisked me off to a gym hoping to occupy their daughter for the summer. Summer came and went, but gymnastics stayed in my life. Knowing that I had finally found something I loved, I persisted. I allowed myself to be stretched and twisted in half because I knew I would be thankful later. Soon, everything began falling into place as I quickly climbed the ranks and became the 2001 Junior National Champion.

Even after reaching the senior division, I continued flying. But somewhere along the way, my heart began to lose interest. After attending two World Championships, not placing half as high as I wanted to, and being named second alternate at the 2003 Olympic trials, I began to not only tire of the sport, but to resent it. I hated being screamed at by my coach, not having a social life, and waking up each morning with every limb in my body screaming in pain. Most of all, I detested the fact that everything I was going through was worthless. Why should I spend five hours a day killing myself over a sport that nobody appreciated? Despite my desolation, I somehow managed to keep my second place rank.

However, this past February at the National re-ranking competition, I dropped down to fifth place. I was completely devastated. Only the top four gymnasts would be competing at Pacific Alliance Championships. As much as I had grown weary of rhythmic, I couldn't just give up a sport that had once given me so much joy. Moreover, I had goals: to win a National Championship, but ultimately, to represent the U.S. at the 2008 Olympics. I would lay awake at night wanting so much to rise above, but feeling helpless, hurting, because I was afraid to fail.

After much contemplation, I decided to finish the rest of the season and see how Nationals would go. I trained rigorously, pushing myself through unbelievable agony to jump higher, to stretch further; by the time Nationals rolled around, I had a renewed sense of self-assurance.

Warming up, my insecurities returned as I watched the current top four; they pranced boldly, assured that I was no longer competition. Adrenaline coursed through me in desire, in anger, but in confidence; I had to redeem myself. I threw my soul into the competition, re-living the pleasure of competing, all the while praying insanely. As I finished my last routine, I collapsed in weariness. All I could do now was wait for the judges' decision. But whatever my placing, I knew I had accomplished something even more important. I had re-discovered a passion and found the motivation to overcome my toughest self-imposed barrier. My perseverance had paid off; I was finally crowned the 2006 National Champion, bringing me one step closer to my Olympic dream.

Lisa's main college essay chronicles the ups and downs of the relentless training and ruthless competition that she has endured as a gymnast. She has just submitted the essay as part of her early action application to Yale and plans to use it in the rest of her applications as well. It is early November and the purplish-reddish streaks in Lisa's hair are fading into pink. She looks a little like a Harajuku Girl today, her tiny frame engulfed by a puffy white down jacket and a jumbo metallic gold purse draped over her shoulder. A retro black-and-white-polka-dotted scarf carefully tied around her hairline completes the hodgepodge ensemble. It's the kind of look you can get away with only in high school or on a runway. Lisa pulls it off.

To complement her application materials, Lisa created a scrapbook of articles and pictures of her gymnastics achievements for the admissions committees. The laminated booklet contains several profiles from various gymnastics magazines and a clip from an interview that she did with the local paper after winning Nationals. As the top American rhythmic gymnast, Lisa has no shortage of press coverage. She even has her own entry on Wikipedia, the wildly popular free online encyclopedia.

Lisa's teacher and counselor recommendations have also been sent off. "I'm pretty sure that my counselor wrote me a very good rec. He's been really supportive, especially with all the gymnastics stuff," she says. "I also think that my teachers will write nice things. I'm not too worried about the recs in general."

Lisa is gearing up for the 2007 World Cup of gymnastics. She will be traveling to Japan in a few weeks to compete. "It's going to be a very tough competition," she explains. "All the top Russians— everyone—will be there. The Soviets and Eastern Europeans always win. It's just like basketball with the Americans."

Since she placed first at Nationals last August, Lisa has her eyes focused on the ultimate prize—a chance to compete in the 2008

Olympics in Beijing. The upcoming World Cup in Japan will be an important stepping stone, and she has a lot to do before she leaves. In addition to her Yale application, Lisa must turn in the rest of her applications to her guidance counselor by December 1. Her final college list includes Harvard, Princeton, Stanford, Columbia, Northwestern, and the University of Michigan.

"Overall, I would guess that I have about a fifty percent chance of getting in early," Lisa says, like she's talking about the odds of her getting picked for a sports team or tickets to a sold-out concert. "I feel pretty good about it, but I don't want to get my hopes up." If she gets into Yale early, she plans to withdraw all her applications except for Harvard and Stanford because those are the only other colleges in which she would seriously consider enrolling. The competitor in her is still drawn to Harvard because it is such a powerhouse, but she also likes Stanford's more laid-back atmosphere.

The academic pressure and athletic training is starting to feel overwhelming for Lisa. "This is definitely the hardest year so far," she says. "I have so much homework. I used to be in bed by midnight, but now if I can get to bed by one thirty, that's good. It's tough 'cause I still have to wake up early for school and then do gymnastics for five hours in the afternoon."

Having contemplated the possibility for months, Lisa is now fairly certain that she will graduate from high school a semester early. After this semester, she will have enough credits to obtain her diploma, which will allow her to concentrate on gymnastics full time. "I don't think it's worth my health to try to do it all," she explains. Her parents and friends support Lisa's decision to dedicate herself to gymnastics training exclusively for the next few months.

The second semester of the senior year of high school has been designated as "party time" by most students. But Lisa doesn't seem to be bothered by having to miss out on this highly anticipated ritual. "I guess I could try to find someone to go to prom with," she says, as if she hasn't thought about it much. "We'll see."

FELIX

Unlike most sixteen-year-olds, Felix looks right at home driving around in a minivan. A dutiful tour guide, he navigates the sloping hills and nondescript windy roads searching out locations of significance in his hometown of Berwyn, Pennsylvania. The most remarkable thing about the scenery is how commonplace it all feels, full of Targets, Costcos, and Starbucks.

"This is where everyone goes to study," Felix says, pointing to a cookie-cutter public library. "And that's the Berwyn Fire Company," he says as we pass a quaint brick firehouse where he volunteers as an EMT. "I don't want them to see me 'cause I haven't been in recently," he says, slouching in the driver's seat while looking over his shoulder. "I've just had so much school stuff going on."

Realizing the difficulty of trying to capture "life in Berwyn" with a roadside tour, Felix begins to describe what goes on behind the scenes. "Our school has a huge mix of kids and there are lots of big parties," he says. "Conestoga was rated like the number-one drug school in some newspaper. I've heard of everything—the whole spectrum. It's not blatantly obvious but you hear about it." According to a 2003 survey of Pennsylvania youth, 57 percent of Conestoga seniors confessed to drinking alcohol, one third admitted smoking marijuana, 27 percent owned up to being drunk at school, and 16 percent confessed to selling drugs. Conestoga students reported much higher rates of drinking and drug use than their county or state peers.

Felix isn't much of a partier, however. "I mostly hang out at other people's houses or sometimes at the mall. But I don't usually go out a lot 'cause I have so much stuff to do, which is kind of sad," he confesses.

Felix also enjoys spending time with his family, especially his ten-year-old sister, Alexandra, whom he describes as funny, smart, and mature. "I think she's just more curious than most kids her age. She's seen more of the world," he says, his dimples deepening. In addition to being a voracious reader and movie buff, Alexandra also dances, swims, plays the violin, and loves lacrosse. "My parents joke that she should focus on lacrosse instead of studying to get into college," Felix laughs.

We head over to the Barnes & Noble café to meet up with Will, one of Felix's friends. "We're like the group that just enjoys everything and does lots of different stuff," he says as he steers the minivan into the strip mall parking lot. "We're not the druggies, not the sports group. We don't hang out with the marching band. What I like about our group is that each of us has friends in the other groups too."

Felix is well aware of his high school hierarchy, though he tries to maintain a mellow perspective. The yearbook editors just announced that he was voted Most Likely to Cure Cancer by the senior class. Unfazed by the accolade, he comments on the meaninglessness of superlatives and describes how one girl campaigned for Best Smile. "She just smiled at everyone and walked away," he says, arching his eyebrows. Felix seems unable to relate to people who clamor for attention.

Will, a skinny Asian American boy dressed in jeans and a light fall jacket, arrives at the bookstore ten minutes later, pulls up a chair, and joins us at the café table. The two teens immediately launch into a discussion about college applications—where everyone is applying, which kids are the most competitive, and who is getting an unfair advantage because of affirmative action or the fact that their parents happened to go to a particular school. According to their analysis, there are two primary Harvard heavyweight contenders in the senior class: Ben, "the perfect student," who graciously opted out of the Harvard rat race by deciding to apply early decision somewhere else at the last minute ("He realized that Harvard was what his parents wanted, not what he wanted,"

Felix says, seeming both impressed and relieved), and Susan, Felix's most fierce Harvard rival, who is also applying early action.

"We do all the same things except she's a girl," he says, shrugging his shoulders. "She's also Chinese, a section leader in band, a student council officer—I'm senator so that's one thing that's a little higher—but she has all the leadership stuff. Basically we're like exactly the same. She's like the girl version of me."

Will is not in direct competition with Felix. He's applying early decision to Cornell, but still seems to enjoy the Who's Gonna Get into Harvard? game. "I hope I get in," he says about his Cornell application. "But there are some things that I don't like about Cornell, like the weather and all the frats. It's a good school and everything, but I don't think I'll be devastated if I don't get in." He affectionately places a hand on Felix's shoulder and half-laughs at his friend. "I'm nothing like this guy."

"I know," Felix agrees. He is keenly aware of his intense infatuation with Harvard. "When you focus so much on one school it really sucks. Will likes to tease me about Harvard, like if I don't get in I'll kill myself."

NABIL

Nabil's body may be in Memphis but his mind is in a fantasy academic utopia. It is a world where virtuoso students choose from an endless list of demanding courses taught by gifted professors. This Dream U also has a juggling club. Nabil is teaching himself how to juggle, and he lights up like Steve Jobs announcing a groundbreaking invention when he talks about his new hobby. "I just got some more tennis balls from Wal-Mart today so that I can practice with five," he says with a wide-toothed grin. "After that, maybe seven. I've always thought how *awesome* it would be to learn how to juggle. It's just that lately I've had the extra down time to pick it up.

"Senior year is a drag," he says, shrugging his shoulders like a football player resigned to taking the field despite an impending loss. "I keep thinking of next year and how much fun it's gonna be. The new school, new people, challenging math courses." He pauses for a moment, lost in a daydream. "And the schedule! I keep thinking of next year, what math class I'll take if I go to Harvard or the University of Chicago, et cetera. Besides Math Analysis, maybe French, a writing seminar, and something else."

The early action deadline has come and gone, and Nabil is still tweaking his final list of schools. "I changed my mind about Boston University," he says. "The point is it's my decision and Dad's just giving me suggestions, not looking up the information." Having nailed down four colleges that he loves—Harvard, MIT, Princeton, and the University of Chicago—he is turning his attention to the search for a safety school.

Unlike most seniors who are staring down the barrel of college application deadlines, Nabil has a good deal of free time. He has already exhausted the math courses available to him at Cordova, so he decided to take Introduction to Probability Theory at the University of Memphis next semester. He'll have to leave school ten minutes early on Tuesdays and Thursdays to get there. "It's basically a statistics class with a Calc II prerequisite," he explains. "I think in math, more than probably for most other majors, preparation before college is very important. I just don't want to be behind."

When it comes to grooming himself for college, Nabil is like a marathon runner training for the big race. He practices every day, searching online course catalogs and reading up on math that he feels he should know. "I visit College Confidential to learn more about college and see if I can find anything useful," he says. College Confidential is an extremely popular Web site that is sponsored and edited by independent college admissions counselors. It includes articles on everything related to college admissions and financial aid, as well as discussion boards where students and admissions professionals post questions and answers. Many students display their grades and test scores to ask others "What are my chances?" of getting into various colleges. Of course, until they actually apply, no one can say for sure whether or not they will get in because admissions officers consider more than just the basic academic numbers.

In most countries, test scores and grades are sufficient criteria for admission to college. However, our nation's elite colleges also ask for interviews, letters of recommendation, and essays as part of their application process. This practice actually started in the late 1920s to prevent large percentages of Jewish students, who were starting to apply to these colleges in significant numbers, from enrolling in predominantly Christian institutions. Admissions officers probed into the "character" of each applicant for evidence of their background and religious beliefs. Harvard president Abbot Lawrence Lowell even had a confidential 15 percent quota for Jewish students. No such quota exists today. However, considering a student's character in addition to his or her academic credentials for college admissions remains an unusual practice, especially when compared with the vast majority of admissions policies at other universities around the world.

"The 'What are my chances?' threads always make me cringe a little inside," Nabil says. "Why post your stats for other people to evaluate? How much help can other people give you? I'm going to stop going there. It's making me more nervous."

I gently ask Nabil how he feels about his chances of getting into the colleges on his list. "I believe I have a very strong chance to get into the schools I'm applying to," Nabil replies in a steady voice, sounding convinced.

MARLENE

"There is no way I am going to get into any of my reach schools."

"Right now I feel like I have a ninety percent chance of getting into Harvard."

"In my four years of high school, I have never seen a kid that's not rich get into an Ivy."

With only a few weeks to go until the regular decision deadline, Marlene is on an emotional roller coaster, vacillating between peaks of overconfidence and valleys of intense insecurity. She is constantly updating and amending her college list, usually influenced by fear, longing, or pragmatism. Some of her confusion and uncertainty can be explained by the fact that she's trying to figure out the complexities of college admissions on her own. She gets information from college Web sites, discussion boards like College Confidential, and occasionally from other students in her honors and AP classes.

As is fairly typical of high-income suburban high schools, most of the counselors at New Rochelle High School are known for their college admissions savvy. From as early as ninth or tenth grade, they advise students on which standardized tests to take, how to enhance their extracurricular résumés, and strategies for getting into particular schools. Marlene's counselor works primarily with a particular subset of students at New Rochelle: Hispanics. Though she believes that Mrs. de Miranda means well, Marlene questions the quality of the counseling she receives compared to her non-Hispanic peers.

"I don't remember one time when she ever encouraged me to take an AP or honors class," Marlene says of her guidance counselor. "In fact, if I were to go into her office and say that I want to drop all my APs and honors she'd say 'okay' and take them off my schedule without asking why or anything."

Marlene is starting to take notice of the ways in which she feels students like her often get derailed from their ambitions. She describes sitting in her counselor's office on a recent afternoon when an ESL student came in, asking for information about applying to a four-year SUNY school. "She said something like, 'No, go to a two-year school first because you're not ready,'" Marlene recounts in frustration. "I mean, at least let her *try* to apply to the four-year schools."

Marlene has felt similarly discouraged. After reviewing her list of colleges, her counselor insisted that she add more safety schools (a not-so-subtle slight).

"Well, I can probably go to SUNY Stony Brook if nothing else works out," Marlene said. While SUNY Stony Brook is a fine institution, they admit close to half of the students who apply. She will almost certainly be accepted.

"Stony Brook is not that easy to get into," Mrs. de Miranda responded, scolding her. Marlene felt deflated but decided to ignore her counselor. She is still trying to get into the best colleges she can.

"She probably said that comment because Stony Brook is like the reach school for most of her students," Marlene later explains, her brow furrowed. "I feel like I know more about colleges than she does, any day."

According to Marlene, the putdowns did not end there. "She also said, 'Well, you know that if you weren't Hispanic, I would tell you to not even bother applying to half of the schools you're applying to.'" Marlene continues with her voice raised in protest. "I mean, I know it's true, but she doesn't have to remind me!"

Because she's Hispanic, Marlene is surrounded by people who assume that she doesn't have to work as hard for success because she will always have the affirmative action advantage. "I mean anytime I have a conversation with anyone at school, they always say, 'I'm sure you'll be fine' or 'Your application is completely different than mine.' That's why even if I do end up getting in—which is not going to happen, of course—I won't tell anyone who doesn't need to know. I wish I was sure I'd be fine! They all talk like they know what the hell they're saying, but they don't."

Though sometimes poorly executed, affirmative action programs are designed to promote and advance meritocracy. The United States is not the only country to practice affirmative action. Many other nations—including Germany, Brazil, South Africa, and Malaysia—have instituted similar types of policies for minorities who have historically been discriminated against.

Affirmative action was first introduced in the United States in 1965 as part of the civil rights movement. The policy stipulates that active measures be taken to ensure that women, African Americans, and other minorities enjoy the same opportunities for employment and education as white males. It was envisioned as a temporary remedy that would end once there was a level playing field for all Americans. Elite universities responded by recruiting and enrolling more black students.

Over the past three decades, a series of court cases have limited the scope of affirmative action policies. Affirmative action in university admissions was first challenged in the Supreme Court case *Regents of the University of California v. Bakke* in 1978. The plaintiff, Allan Bakke, sued the University of California at Davis for twice rejecting his medical school application, even though he had a better GPA and higher test scores than several minority students who had been admitted. With a narrow margin of five to four, the Court ruled that the practice of affirmative action was permissible, but strict racial quotas were found to be unconstitutional.

Justice Lewis Powell, a Harvard graduate, broke the Supreme Court tie in the *Bakke* case by siding with the rationale of his alma matter. Harvard filed a "friend of the court" brief advocating on behalf of considering race as a plus factor in college admissions. The university argued that racial diversity enhanced the academic and intellectual environment on campus and that affirmative action was necessary to recruit a diverse student body. Nevertheless, the *Bakke* ruling limited the impact of affirmative action by banning racial quotas and put the policy on the top of the list of national controversies. The ruling also established that student diversity had educational benefits in the eyes of the Supreme Court.

Diversity is now a buzzword used at all selective colleges, and evidence suggests that it does benefit students in several ways. Research demonstrates that students gain more from heterogeneous intellectual environments when they are forced to challenge and defend their beliefs. Diversity on college campuses also prepares students for an increasingly diverse society, and students who are exposed to diversity tend to live and work in more integrated communities than they would have otherwise. Long-term data on minority students who matriculate at predominantly white institutions under affirmative action programs shows that they tend to be more involved in civic life and charitable causes than their peers.

In many ways, framing affirmative action in terms of "diversity" rather than "merit" has led to widespread misconceptions about this practice, especially in regard to college admissions. A study using data from the University of California confirmed that the SAT loses its ability to predict academic performance in college if one takes into account a student's family income. In the most simple terms, this means that a poor student with a lower SAT score is just as likely to do well in college than a rich student with a higher SAT score. The reason for this is somewhat obvious: rich kids can afford SAT coaching (tutors or prep classes) while poor kids cannot. Unless colleges find some way to determine whether or not a student has been coached for the SAT (and how much or how good that coaching was) these scores do not represent a student's "merit." This is one of the reasons that Harvard initiated a new type of affirmative action that also takes a student's family income into account, giving a plus factor to applicants from low-income backgrounds.

Affirmative action in higher education is an undoubtedly controversial policy. The general public knows little about how or why it is implemented, which leads to a wealth of misinformation and distorted anecdotes that fester into a collective mythology about this closed-door practice. In the end, the students who benefit from affirmative action are usually forced to bear the burden of these misconceptions by being made to feel less deserving than their peers. Marlene typifies this pattern.

"Don't you think you're smart?" I ask her directly.

Marlene lowers her eyes and shrugs her shoulders. "Slightly. I feel like I haven't tried yet. I don't think of people as being smart or stupid, I think it's all about how much you work." Of course, this is a "smart girl" response. Lots of students study hard for Bs or Cs.

"Do you think you're as smart as the other kids who get into Ivy League schools?"

"Yeah, maybe," she answers, unconvincingly. "But if I actually got in, I'd feel guilty."

"LAST NIGHT, I GOT all my stuff together—my résumé, transcript, teacher evaluation forms, envelopes, et cetera—and organized them into two nice manila folders. So yay for that! I'm actually getting stuff done now!"

Marlene is jumping over hurdles that she once perceived as insurmountable. She recently received her class rank and was elated when it was confirmed that she qualified for a spot in the top 10 percent of her class. She also got the results of her second SAT—650 Math, 600 Critical Reading, and 650 Writing—a significant improvement over her first scores. To top it all off, Marlene has finally found another teacher to write a recommendation on her behalf. Dr. Gomez, her AP Spanish teacher from junior year, is the first teacher I have ever heard Marlene describe as being "really nice."

Despite the progress she has made, Marlene is still skeptical about her chances of getting into an Ivy League college. "When Dr. Gomez was skimming through the envelopes to see the schools I was applying to, I told her that before she thinks I'm crazy, I'm only applying because if I get in I'll get good financial aid. I always feel really embarrassed when I tell people that I'm applying to Ivies, so very few people know," she says.

Sensing Marlene's self-doubt, Dr. Gomez sought to empower her insecure student. She shared the story of her husband, who overcame various obstacles—including widely accepted low expectations—to become one of the very first Puerto Ricans to receive his Ph.D. "She's pro affirmative action and all that," Marlene says. "She also told me not to let anyone give me the whole affirmative action crap."

Later that day, Marlene ran into her friend Grace, who is on pins and needles, waiting for a response from the University of Pennsylvania, to which she applied early decision. Terrified of disappointing her imperious parents, Grace asked Marlene if she also felt pressured by her parents to get into a prestigious college. "I said not at all," Marlene recounts. "She was impressed that I work hard on my own, because most Asians—including herself, she said—only do well because their parents push them. That made me feel good about myself, that I am where I am on my own."

FELIX

G od, I love this place," Felix announces to no one in particular. Dressed in a brand-new Harvard Crimson sweatshirt, he is standing in the heart of Harvard Yard brimming with emotion. It is early December, and he knows that his early action application is sitting in the Admissions Office a few blocks away, waiting to be read. "If I don't get in, I can never wear this sweatshirt again," he jokes.

Felix has just finished playing piano for Professor Levin, a member of the Harvard music department whom he met during a summer program at Julliard. They kept in touch, and when Felix decided to apply early action to Harvard, he asked Professor Levin for a meeting. "It wasn't exactly an audition," Felix says. His pupils dilate with desire as he fidgets with his hands. "The Admissions Office doesn't really let professors advocate. He just sends in his recommendation and they decide. But he did say that he will do what he can." Though Professor Levin doesn't actually sit on the admissions committee, a positive evaluation from him would be a feather in Felix's cap. Besides demonstrating his exceptional musical talent, Professor Levin's endorsement could add another dimension to the supplementary essay that Felix has just submitted to Harvard.

"Oh wow, that thing is high!" At four-years old, my imagination was wild, and that night the black piano bench was obviously Mt. Everest. After minutes of hard struggle, I climbed atop the wooden bench but as soon as my eyes fell upon the gleaming 88 black and white keys, all thoughts of mountaineering exploits disappeared. "I wonder what they do," my inquisitive mind already at work, "What happens if I push—WOAH", and in seconds I was pounding away.

The music, the noise rather, drew my parents and the other guests to my debut performance of Loud Noises Op. 43 in G Minor. The proud parents they were, my mom and dad exclaimed that this was undoubtedly the sign of a piano prodigy simply awaiting nourishment. Years later, my ten year old self was trapped in my parents' "nourishment". I was no fan of practice and I wish I could say I truly was prodigal. I'm sure even my parents had moments in which they doubted the "sign", especially when they had to listen to the same annoying melody again and again. In the beginning years, I sat through my lessons in fear as my crazy Russian teacher cried for "EMOTION! Feel ze music tingle your heart!" Terror was certainly tingling my heart, but alas, no music.

On a trip to China at age 12, I biked around the streets of Shanghai, taking in the sights and smells of a vibrant city for the first time. I tried to explain the feeling of exhilaration to my parents that night but could find no words to describe the sensory overload. How does one describe pure emotion? At a loss for words, I could think of no other form of expression, and to my own surprise, began to hum a Chopin melody. It was then that I realized music was infinitely more than mere notes on a page, it was a medium through which complex ideas can be easily expressed, not through words but with notes.

Once, at a concert at Carnegie Hall, my family and I watched in amazement as Lang Lang bounced on a gleaming Steinway, his music reaching into every audience member's heart, and not letting go until the last chord. When he had finished, I sat stunned in my seat, how I wished to be up there one day! Two years later, I was. As a winner at the World Piano Competition, I was to perform on the greatest music stage in the world, on the very piano Lang Lang and so many other legends had played on. I sat in the hot spotlight, already dripping with sweat from the tuxedo, and suddenly the room became quiet. As my hands lifted, and the audience held their breath for that first chord, I realized that the dread and anxiety that I had felt throughout my years of learning were finally absent.

I thought of all the things I had learned from the piano; the perseverance, the diligence and preparation so required to prepare a tough repertoire. I had learned failure. So many times I sat with my eyes clenched praying that the name the judge was about to call was mine. So many times I let tears fall as the name called wasn't my own. My reverie was suddenly broken by the thunderous applause of the audience; this time was no failure. As I stood and took my bow and looked out across the appreciative audience, the piano taught me one last lesson, love. Through music, I felt the unifying force that brought the great Beethoven, Chopin, Mozart and others together, and finally understood the love and devotion my parents had given me. It is what I feel every time I hear a great piece of music, pick up a new book, debate politics or adorn the white coat in my research lab. It is an awe-inspiring feeling that the giants of music understood intimately and conveyed in their works of art, reaching out to not only tingle my heart but touch all who care to listen.

After he has finished playing for Professor Levin, Felix and I meet up in front of the John Harvard statue, which is known for being targeted by drunk Yale freshmen hoping to intimidate their rivals with chalk-graffiti insults before the annual Harvard-Yale football game. Felix wistfully surveys his surroundings like a hungry man looking in on someone else's Thanksgiving feast.

"I was at MIT all weekend," he says, "and the people were very *out there*."

"What do you mean?"

"Well, you know . . . the stereotype about the MIT kids . . . that they sit in their room and study? Well, *that's true*," he says. "I don't know if I'd fit in at that place. They're very focused on their studies, but the social life and parties are just *sad*. My friend said that since they all work so hard during the week, parties are really just there for you to get drunk and forget about life." Felix raises an eyebrow as if to ask, "Why on earth would anyone do that?"

"The good thing is that Conestoga really does prepare you for college-level work," he continues. "I was hanging out with this girl who lived in the dorm I was staying in. She worked till like three in the morning on five physics problems. I looked at them and they were pretty hard, but I was glad 'cause I could already do most of them—probably four out of five. It's cool 'cause you never really have that reference. You never really know if you're prepared. But

I guess all that work does really prepare you—even for something like MIT physics."

Felix focuses on staying positive for a few seconds before throwing his clenched fists in the air and screaming, *"God! Waiting just sucks!"* His words seem to hover in the frigid atmosphere along with his cloudy breath.

"I can't believe I have to open that e-mail in Hawaii. I'd just rather read it in the safety of my room. I'm old-fashioned like that. I'd rather have a letter that I can actually tear open in my room by myself. It sucks because my whole family is going to be there. I have to walk out and my parents are there, my grandparents, my great-aunt and uncle, cousins—"

Before I can attempt to console him, the raw anxiety of anticipation wells up inside him again and Felix cries out, *"Waiting suuuuucks!"* His last word comes out funny-sounding, kind of like a seal barking. We both start laughing.

"I'm serious," he says, still slightly amused. "It's like having sixteen years of goal-oriented tasks and now you have no goals. All my apps are in so I'm just *waiting.*"

"Do you have a good feeling about the outcome?" I ask.

"I think I have a good chance. . . . I hope I have a good chance. It seems that way compared to the kids from my school who got in last year. Now that all the apps are in, it's like no one wants to talk about colleges anymore. 'Cause once you start talking about it, it just chews you up inside. I turned on the TV so that I would stop thinking about it and there was some movie called *Harvard Man* on. That really sucked."

Felix lowers his head and shakes it from side to side to be purposefully melodramatic. "Oh Harvard. Harvard, Harvard, Harvard," he moans and lets out a long, audible sigh.

SIX

"Congratulations, you were rejected"

MARLENE

I almost had a nervous breakdown last night, so I'm staying home from school today to finish all this crap," Marlene explains. It is a cold bare-branched morning in early December, and Marlene is hoping to finish her applications this weekend so that she won't have to worry about them over winter break. "The worst was the 'Why Penn?' essay. I stayed up until two AM finishing it," she says. "*I better get into Penn.* Not because it's Penn, but because of all the work it takes to apply."

For a while, Marlene seemed to perpetually add and subtract colleges from her list, saying things like, "Northwestern is too far" or "I need more safety schools." With three weeks before applications are due, she has settled on Harvard, Yale, Dartmouth, Williams, the University of Pennsylvania, Brandeis, Colgate, SUNY Stony Brook, the University of Rochester, and Trinity College, a small private liberal arts college in Hartford, Connecticut. "It's so weird. I'm almost done, and I always thought that I'd be submitting on like December thirty-first," Marlene says, surprised by her own progress.

While applying to ten colleges may seem excessive, Marlene is part of a trend of students who are applying to more colleges than in the past. Researchers at UCLA found that about 18 percent of students applied to seven or more schools last year, compared with only 2 percent a generation ago. At $60 to $70 per application, applying to so many schools can be costly, but the colleges have waived their application fees for Marlene because she has been designated as a low-income student by her high school.

Marlene has been working on her essays for weeks. College essays are important, but most students tend to overestimate the role that they play in admissions decisions. Other parts of the application—grades, courses, SATs, recommendations, and extracurricular activities—have been earned or established months ago. The essays are the only blank slate left, and many students hope to compensate for weak spots in their applications by writing fantastic and memorable essays.

One of the biggest mistakes an applicant can make is to write about her passion for such-and-such, even though such-and-such never comes up again in her recommendations or on her list of activities. This raises suspicions that the student either is insincere or has been coached. While no topic is off-limits, it is also not a bad idea to avoid writing about common subjects, like sports or travel. Essays about sports tend to blend together because they talk about winning/losing, teamwork, or overcoming a setback—important themes that can become superficial when confined to the five-hundred-word limit. A fabulous family vacation is great, but having the opportunity to travel usually says more about the applicant's parents, and how much money they have, than about who the student is as a person.

The goal of the college essay should be to express an authentic voice that enhances the substance of the application as a whole. Admissions officers read these essays to determine whether or not an applicant would make a good classmate, community member, or friend. Marlene writes about her experiences as a Dominican American, how these two worlds intersect and how she navigates the divide between them.

As an eight-year-old I did not comprehend the mayhem going on around me. My parents were constantly watching the news and calling my relatives in the Dominican Republic. When my parents noticed the puzzled look on the faces of my sisters and me, they decided to sit us down and tell us the news. It turns out that due to political immigration circumstances, we would have to go on vacation to the Dominican Republic.

My family and I spent the next few weeks assiduously packing. I was exhilarated, but secretly wondered why we were leaving just as a new school year approached. When the day of departure finally arrived, I took a deep breath, embraced my favorite faded stuffed bunny Lucy, and boarded the plane.

Once we arrived to the airport in Puerto Plata, we were greeted by a local band playing traditional Dominican music, merengue. Until that moment, I had only heard it from my dad's stereo. As we drove to my grandmother's house I looked out the window with rapt admiration. Bumping down dirt roads, I saw vendors with fresh vegetables passing by my window. We were greeted by warm and friendly relatives most of whom I only knew through telephone calls and photographs. What I had heard so much about was now palpable.

Soon, I learned my parents had registered me in the third grade class of a nearby school. I immediately understood what was really going on—we had moved to the Dominican Republic, we were not on vacation.

I will never forget the first day in my third grade class. Even though I was accustomed to speaking Spanish at home, I was unable to read and write it. My teacher instructed the class to write the lesson in our notes. I anxiously followed her instructions, but had no clue what I was writing.

Four years passed and I grew accustomed to the way of life there. I loved to pass my afternoons sitting under a tree, talking casually with cousins and eating fresh mangos. Often my uncle taught me how to make yogurt in his small factory. I watched the seasons change as life moved on. But just as I was beginning to find my place, my parents resolved their immigration status and uprooted the family once more to return to the United States.

While in the Dominican Republic, I met and grew close to extended family. I learned not only a new way of life but about my roots. I returned to America a bit older, more mature and aware of the richness of my culture. I even had a greater appreciation for simple things such as not having to worry about the electricity going out. I came back with a greater sense of my customs, my family and the privileges I have as a Dominican American.

It has been six years since my family returned, and I vividly remember everything I relished while there. I always eagerly await the summers my family decides to go to the Dominican Republic to see the country and people I am so attached to. At the same time, I am glad that I can easily return to America that I equally love. Along with the privileges I have as a Dominican American, I am aware I have responsibilities. When I am in the Dominican Republic, I am considered American, and vice versa in the United States. I accept that it is my duty as a bi-cultural individual to inform and share with others, whether in the Dominican Republic or in America about the two cultures that I love so much. The two cultures that have made me who I am.

LISA

L isa goes through her routine on December 15 with only one thing on her mind. "All I can think about is the Yale decision. I had an econ test with simple addition, and for two plus four, I wrote *eight*," she reports with a giggle. After school, she runs the short distance home, dashing over mounds of snow and reflecting on the significance of the day.

For Lisa Wang, December 15 is packed with milestones. Not only will she receive the verdict on her early action application in a matter of minutes, she has just finished her last day of high school. Lisa is graduating a semester early to concentrate her full attention on gymnastics training.

"Our school comes back in session on the third of January, but I'll be leaving for Russia that day," she explains on her way home. "I'll be gone for two weeks, so by the time I get back I will just have to take all the tests I missed so that I don't end up with an 'incomplete' for my grade. So, yeah, ha ha. There goes my high school career." Lisa throws her little arms up in the air as a sarcastic commentary on the anticlimactic ending. Though she'll have to miss teenage rites of passage like prom and graduation, she isn't too bothered about giving up her final semester of high school to travel and train with the world's best gymnastics coaches.

Lisa's last performance at the World Cup competition in Japan was not what she had hoped. "I messed up pretty badly," she reports with a wince. "But it's all right. It just means that I have to go back to the gym and keep on working." Since her return from Japan, Lisa has been scrambling to catch up on the schoolwork she missed, coming home from gymnastics practice each night to "piles and piles" of homework. About a week ago, Lisa also had an interview with an alumnus from Yale, which has made her feel more optimistic about her chances of getting in early. "It ended up being great, so hopefully it'll help my app somewhat," she says.

Students who apply to college under early action programs can receive one of three responses: rejection, admission, or deferral. Rejection and admission are straightforward final answers. A deferral is a lukewarm *"We'll see."* Deferred candidates will be evaluated again with the rest of the students who apply under regular decision, though as many as 90 percent of deferred students are ultimately rejected in April.

Colleges typically defer up to a third of their early admission candidates, and they use this option for different reasons. In general, students who get deferred are considered to be strong but not excellent. In this case, admissions officers want to see how the student holds up in the context of a larger applicant pool. They may also want to give the applicant a little more time to mature and take his or her first semester senior grades into account. Because candidates who apply early must submit their applications in early November, they have not yet completed first semester of their senior year.

Sometimes, a candidate is deferred because admissions officers perceive that rejecting certain students outright, like the class valedictorian or a high-profile scholar/athlete, sends the wrong message to his or her high school. No college wants to be perceived as impossible to get into. Rejecting too many top students may discourage next year's crop of applicants, and a decline in applications is bad publicity in a world that measures the value of a college by its ranking in *U.S. News & World Report.*

A few years ago, the Ivy League colleges changed the way that admissions decisions would be announced by using the Internet to deliver the responses to candidates. Some other schools, such as Duke, Johns Hopkins, and the University of Chicago, also decided to notify students electronically. Applicants to these colleges no longer wait by the postbox for days on end, praying for the arrival of a fat envelope. Instead, they can now be found praying in front of a computer screen before they log on to a college's Web site to discover whether or not they have been accepted. In these cases, all the applicants to a particular college receive their decisions at the exact same time. A few days later, the lucky ones get traditional fat envelopes in the mail as a confirmation of their acceptance.

When she arrives home, Lisa is met at the door by her mother, who also spent the day consumed by the looming Yale decision. The two of them go directly to Lisa's white-walled room, where Lisa sits down in front of her desk to fire up her computer. Seconds later, her monitor comes to life with sparks of color flickering on the screen. Her mom leans over and hugs her.

"I'm nervous, you know, just *anxious,* like I want to know *now*," Lisa says as she logs onto the Yale Web site.

It takes a few minutes for the reality of what happens next to set in. A large picture of the Yale mascot, a wrinkled-face white bull-dog, appears on Lisa's computer screen along with big, bold writing that reads: CONGRATULATIONS LISA. WELCOME TO THE CLASS OF 2011.

Realizing that her daughter has just been accepted to Yale, Lisa's mother bursts into tears, but it takes Lisa a few minutes to comprehend the message. "I just saw this YouTube video where a student gets a message that says CONGRATULATIONS YOU WERE REJECTED," she explains. "I read the message like three times to make sure it didn't say CONGRATULATIONS YOU WERE REJECTED, and my mom was crying the whole time." Lisa shakes her head in disbelief. "My dad wasn't as emotional as my mom but he was really proud," she says.

Later that night, Lisa goes to a movie with a group of friends from school, most of whom are thoroughly depressed over college decisions. "Two people applied early to Harvard, another to Stanford, another to MIT, and another to Yale. They all got deferred," she explains. "So far, I haven't heard of anyone else who got in." Lisa reports the college admissions statistics like a news correspondent covering casualties in a war.

"I still don't believe that I got into Yale," Lisa says, sounding cheery yet dazed by her own good fortune. A few days later, her fat envelope arrives in the mail. Inside is a printed letter from the dean of admissions officially admitting her to the Yale class of 2011. In the lower right-hand corner of the formal document is a handwritten note. It says, "Congratulations! We were all so impressed with your application. Congratulations on the National Championship. Good luck! Go Bulldogs!"

ANDREW

Andrew wakes up on the morning of December 15 with a visceral feeling of hopeful confidence—he is someone who goes through life believing that things will work out for the best. Since Stanford is scheduled to release its decisions at 5 PM, Pacific Standard Time, Andrew knows that he will have to wait until 7 PM in Louisiana. "There's no point in worrying about it anyway," he tells himself, even though he spends most of his uneventful school day staring at the clock. He then heads over to his father's office to use the copy machine and work on the rest of his college and scholarship applications.

When the time comes to check online, Andrew's father is away from his desk, and he finds himself alone in an empty office. Taking advantage of the privacy, he settles into his father's executive desk chair like it is a prop in a movie about his life. He starts typing on the keyboard in front of him, putting gentle pressure on each plastic square: A-N-D-R-E-W. Everything around him seems to slow down except for the thump of his quick-beating heart as he prepares to move his right index finger over to the word ENTER. He lowers his finger onto the final key, takes a breath, and waits a few seconds.

Andrew reads a few sentences into the letter before realizing its intent. He got deferred.

Disappointed, Andrew walks out into the reception area to tell his father the news, and the two of them decide to call his mom from the car on the way home. "My dad was like, 'Oh well. You'll be okay.' My mom was a little, well, I wouldn't say *upset*, but you know how it is," he says, shrugging his shoulders.

By the time Andrew and his father arrive back at home, several of his friends have called, expecting to be showered with good news. He spends the next few hours on the phone, assuring everyone that he is fine. "I thought I was going to get in, and I didn't," he explains. "But it's all right. It's not the only college I'm applying to, and it *is* Stanford. I knew it wasn't guaranteed." It doesn't take long for Andrew to find out the tally of early admissions decisions for his classmates. No one got into Stanford early, and two other top students from Jesuit High have been turned away from Harvard and MIT.

"It's not like I have a poor résumé or anything," Andrew says. "I don't think it had to do with my grades. The 'Southern thing' was kind of talked about among my friends, like how Northern schools have a prejudice against Southern schools." Only about 8 percent of Stanford students hail from the Southeast, but when I questioned a representative from the Admissions Office, I was assured that these applicants are admitted at about the same rate as students from other parts of the country. Andrew's impression may be based on the fact that relatively fewer students from the South apply to schools like Stanford when compared with students from the Northeast and California, where most applicants to highly selective colleges are concentrated.

Even though his application will be reviewed again in a few months, Andrew is no longer optimistic about his chances of getting into Stanford. "They said in the letter that ten percent of deferred applicants get in," he continues. "I sort of feel like if they don't let you in early, they're probably not going to let you in regular." Andrew nods his head with uncertain resolution, like a game show contestant who just picked curtain number three.

FELIX

Felix spends most of December 15 in the clouds. In what he perceives to be a cruel twist of fate, he is stuck on a plane making its way from Philadelphia to Hawaii for a family vacation on the very day that Harvard is scheduled to announce the decisions for early action applicants. Having been barred from any cyber communication for the next several hours, Felix squirms in his confining airline seat like a child who must finish dinner before he is allowed to go outside to play. The anticipation is like a ticking bomb in the middle of his chest.

The long trip to Hawaii is broken up by a layover in San Francisco. As soon as he disembarks from the first leg of his flight, Felix runs madly through the airport with his father in tow, searching for an Internet terminal. They soon find a booth of computers. Felix sits down, enters his credit card number to pay for the time online, and pulls up a browser. "I swear it took me twice as long to log on because my hands were shaking so much and I couldn't type anything," he says and opens the e-mail.

Dear Mr. Felix Minxuan Zhang,

I am delighted to inform you that the Committee on Admissions has admitted you to the Class of 2011 under the Early Action program. Please accept my personal congratulations for your outstanding achievements.

In recent years, nearly twenty-three thousand students have applied for the sixteen hundred and seventy-five places in the freshman class. Faced with many more talented and highly qualified candidates than it has room to admit, the Admissions Committee has taken great care to choose individuals who present extraordinary academic, extracurricular and personal strengths. In making each admission decision, the Committee keeps in mind that the excellence of Harvard College depends most of all on the talent and promise of the people assembled here, particularly our students. In voting to offer you admission, the Committee has demonstrated its firm belief that you can make important contributions during your college years and beyond.

By early March, you will receive an invitation to visit Harvard from Saturday, April 21 to Monday, April 23. Our faculty and students have arranged a special welcome for you and we think the experience will be interesting and useful in making your final college choice. Of course, we would also be happy to have you visit at some other time and we hope you will make a special effort to do so if you will be unable to join us in April. . . .

You have until May 1 to respond to our offer. However, you may fill out and return the enclosed postcard or you may respond online in case you are able to inform us of your decision before May 1.

We very much hope that you will decide to attend Harvard, and we look forward to having you join us in September.

Yours sincerely,
William R. Fitzsimmons
Dean of Admissions and Financial Aid
Harvard College

Felix e-mails me from the San Francisco airport: "I GOT IN!!!!!!!!!!!!!!!!!!!!! Holy wow. I don't think it has fully set in yet. I keep re-reading the e-mail to make sure I didn't miss something or if there is some kind of catch. Whee!"

All he wants to do is jump up and down and scream, but because they are in public, Felix and his dad both end up doing what he describes as "a body spasm type thing and silent cheer." Elated and relieved, they find Felix's mother and sister, who are waiting at a nearby café. "I felt almost lightheaded walking back to my mom and sister," says Felix. "But my dad and I put on the 'deferred look' and told my mom that I was deferred. Then we both smiled and told the truth."

Felix's mom squeals at the top of her lungs when she hears the good news. The other patrons in the café turn around to investigate the commotion. "My son just got into Harvard," Danyi explains to the crowd as she tries to catch her breath. Right there in the airport, Felix receives a round of applause.

Felix uses the rest of his layover time to call a few friends and share the good news. They tell him that one of his classmates, Susan, was also admitted. His friend Andrew got deferred.

Later that night, the Zhangs celebrate Felix's Harvard acceptance with a gourmet dinner, followed by a worry-free vacation in Hawaii. "I'm so excited," he says, dragging out the word for several seconds. "It isn't even just getting into Harvard. It's just that feeling of relief and total release of pressure and weight. It's the feeling of just knowing somewhere wants you. Whew."

Though the agony of uncertainty has finally passed, Felix still has had to face one very minor tribulation. "My mom won't stop telling people, which is somewhat annoying at times," he complains. "It still sounds so weird when she says it." This new reality—Felix's official acceptance to the Harvard class of 2011—will take a while to sink in.

NABIL

Because he did not end up submitting his early action application to Harvard, Nabil was spared from finding out his fate in

December. Instead, he spends a carefree evening on December 15 at a Memphis restaurant called On the Border, where the Abdurehmans (minus one sick brother and their mother, who stayed home to look after him) are celebrating his sister's eleventh birthday.

In talking to his friends who applied early, Nabil has heard the word "deferred" today more times than he expected. But he is still optimistic about the future. "Two people I know, from White Station, got accepted to Harvard and Yale. It seems so much more feasible, so tangible, getting into Harvard now because people I know got into their top choice schools."

Nabil is almost done with his last fall semester of high school. And he can't wait. "I just can't bring myself to care as much as I used to, especially since I'm so close to leaving high school," he explains. "My grades have fallen a bit, especially in AP Government. It looks like I'll lose my current valedictorian position for number two, but so what? How much can it hurt to say I'm ranked two of about four hundred?"

Even if Nabil drops to second place, his class rank won't be recalculated until after the college application deadline, which means that the valedictorian/salutatorian debate is somewhat insignificant. As far as the colleges to which he is applying—Harvard, Princeton, MIT, Carnegie Mellon, and the University of Chicago—are concerned, Nabil is still the Cordova valedictorian. "Hopefully I'll have better luck with the admissions results than the applications themselves have gone," he says. "I lost my admissions ID for Carnegie Mellon, so I have to call them to send another one, and I didn't schedule an interview for MIT because the guy never got back to me." Though he is very bright, Nabil can be inattentive when it comes to deadlines. He has already put off applying to Harvard early and waits until the cutoff date to submit his regular decision applications. Fortunately, he is a good writer. Like Marlene, he writes about his bicultural heritage, recounting his trip to Ethiopia and the communication barriers he faced.

I broke down within the first week. I don't cry, but I did then. What was wrong with me? When I'd go and visit my family and their friends, I couldn't respond to their questions without incompetently stuttering an answer that inevitably turned out insufficient or requiring too much time and aid, despite my sincere efforts. Even Grandma laughed at me, although I knew she didn't mean to hurt me. In America people asked me where I came from. Here I was in Ethiopia and people still were asking me the same thing. What was I? Who was I? Who was this impostor that didn't know his culture, that couldn't even speak his own language and couldn't even communicate to his own family how much he loved them all. I couldn't tell Grandma, who carried me on her back when I was a baby, how much seeing her again after so long meant to me. I was nothing. No one cared what grade I was in, or how much I loved math back in the States. All they wanted was to be able to talk to me and I couldn't give them that. Here I was in my own hole of shame, feeling nasty and pretty disgusted with myself. But crying wouldn't help me, nor anyone else. I would be in Ethiopia for two months whatever happened. So I resolved to put aside my pride, ask questions as much as I could, and join the family. My speech was at a child's level, so I looked to children to practice with. I'd be over at the Rahji's (one of my over twenty cousins) house, drinking tea with him in our traditional murtos (cloth wrapped around the waist, extending the length of the legs) and a six year old boy would come with a sister of about the same age. I explained I'd like to practice with him (he didn't know English anyway). He soon asked me how to say some simple words like "fingernail," "ear," and "gums" as a sort of test. All but a couple evaded my recollection, and he promptly deemed me a fraud, a fake who "couldn't speak." This from a six year old. Aside from the whole awkwardness of trying to build and maintain such relations, I began hanging out more with friends my own age. In the process, I grew more acquainted with our traditional social gatherings.

In Ethiopia, guys meet differently than in America. A group of us would meet up at a host's house, where we all lie, half-propped up on pillows, in a circle or semi-circle, the better to see the everyone else. There would be tea, water, and coke to drink in the middle, along with snacks to munch on. Discussion varied from politics to family matters. I preferred to just sit and sip, listening to what they had to say and what words they said it with. Sometimes I'd ask what this word or that meant, and occasionally I was called upon to embarrass myself by participating in the discussion. My hands became a sort of second tongue with which I'd motion and mold images out of air to try to get my point across or to clarify what meaning or word I wished to convey. All the time I was learning Adaric (our cultural language), I tried what I could to read Amharic, the national language, too. At least half of what was written in the street was in Amharic, and it frustrated me to no end to not have any idea what any of it said. I gradually came to know many of the 200+ letters through studying and sounding out words on soda bottles, food packages, and anything else I could. Stumbling upon an English word in Amharic added to the humor and fun of deciphering the hieroglyphics; what would you think if you cautiously sounded out "La-one-duh-ree" (for "laundry") on a building to the side of the road?

Slowly, I began to realize how much better I was getting. Grandma stopped asking me to repeat what I said, stopped giving up and asking someone else. One day, when I was asked some question (I've since forgotten it, what's next stands out far more) and gave a response, my eldest aunt replied, "Did you hear him 'Min fida halla,' he said. Now he's learned [the language]." I did it. I was Ethiopian. They had accepted me.

MARLENE

Marlene monitors the results of her classmates' early applications like a bookie at the track. "MIT was zero for three, three
out of four got into Columbia," she reports. Of the three students who
got into Columbia, she describes one as "an extremely smart African
American" and explains that another one of the students is a legacy.

"I see a trend," Marlene declares the next day, after finding out
more information about her classmates' admissions decisions.
"Three out of six got into U Penn—a single legacy, a double legacy
plus brother, and a really smart African American, whose dad went
to Yale. For Brown, it was two out of three: a single legacy and a
triple legacy." Marlene uses the terms "single," "double," and "triple"
to refer to the number of family members who attended each university in order for the applicant to be considered a legacy. Her class
valedictorian (also a legacy) was accepted at Yale, though the two
students who applied early to Harvard with no familial connections were both deferred.

American colleges have always favored the children of alumni,
known as "legacies," while at prestigious universities abroad, where
an applicant's parents went to college is considered irrelevant.
Though legacy applicants are admitted at higher rates than non-
legacies at most schools, it is important to remember that graduates of selective colleges usually become the types of mothers and
fathers who invest early in their children's education, provide them
with academic resources, and encourage their intellectual growth.
Because of this, legacy candidates tend to exhibit the types of traits
that selective colleges find desirable. Children of alumni from Harvard, for example, actually have higher average SAT scores than
their classmates. In the vast majority of cases, a truly unexceptional
applicant will not get into a selective college just because he or she
may have a parent who went there.

Of course, not all legacies are created equal, especially where money and power are concerned. Daniel Golden, a Pulitzer Prize–winning journalist, recently investigated the role of preferential treatment in college admissions for his book *The Price of Admission: How America's Ruling Class Buys Its Way into Elite Colleges—And Who Gets Left Outside the Gates.* Golden, who spent six years researching this issue, unearths numerous examples of ways in which the underqualified children of wealthy alumni or major donors are given red-carpet treatment by colleges seeking to pad their endowments or heighten their profiles. Among other things, he describes how Princeton admitted the son of Senator Bill Frist, an alumnus whose family has contributed $25 million to the school, despite the fact that he received the lowest ranking on their academic scale; Brown courted the son of bigwig Michael Ovitz in spite of his poor scholastic record so that Ovitz's VIP friends, like Martin Scorsese and Dustin Hoffman, would make appearances at college functions; and Harvard finds creative ways to admit the underwhelming offspring of the university's most generous donors, whose names are included on a confidential "Z List," which is kept by the Admissions Office. Golden levels his most scathing criticism at Duke University by documenting cases in which the admissions committee's decisions to reject certain applicants were overturned by high-ranking administrators simply because their parents were capable of making massive financial contributions to the school.

To be fair, not all colleges favor wealthy applicants or children of alumni. California Institute of Technology (Cal Tech), Cooper Union, and Texas A&M give no preference to legacies in their admissions processes. It is also worth noting that relatively few students are regarded as "donor applicants" at elite colleges, considering that their parents must be able to fork over millions of dollars to make the cut. Still, Golden notes that the practice of applicants buying their way into prestigious universities is becoming increasingly common at many colleges, including Harvard, where the "Z List" of "well connected but often academically borderline applicants" has doubled since 2001.

Legacy preferences really frustrate Marlene. "The salutatorian got deferred from Wharton, and my Asian friend got rejected. What the hell?" she exclaims. Her friends without connections have almost all been turned away from their first-choice colleges.

JUST BEFORE THE New Year, Marlene invites me to her local Starbucks to meet her middle sister, Yvonne, who is home for Christmas vacation. The two sisters make very different first impressions. Yvonne is outgoing and assertive. She smiles while shaking my hand and brushes a long, brown curl away from her cheery face. Marlene, who is more quiet and reserved, sits next to her and clasps her hands together on the table. She lets Yvonne do more of the talking.

Yvonne is eager to discuss her first semester as a student at Elmira College, a small school about five hours north of New Rochelle, in upstate New York. "I love the fact that I have liberty away from home," she says, trying to ignore the ringing and beeping of her cell phone. "At first, I was afraid of not being able to make friends, but when I got there I realized that everyone was in the same situation." Though she seems happy with her choice for the most part, Yvonne struggled a bit in her classes this semester and was challenged to meet all the demands of her schoolwork. "I did have some academic trouble," she confesses, "but nothing serious." She plans to double-major in art and psychology but hasn't yet decided on a career path. "I might teach art or something. I'm not really sure."

Elmira College is not exactly high profile. "It kept popping up when I filled out college questionnaires, so I thought maybe I should check it out," Yvonne answers when I ask why she decided to enroll at this particular school. "I visited with my parents and really liked it because it's small. I graduated next to a *stranger* in high school and I really like the fact that at Elmira everyone knows you."

Yvonne knew that she wanted to go to a college with a more intimate academic environment. However, at the time, she had no idea that smaller schools—especially in rural settings in upstate New York—tend to be homogeneous. "There is *no* diversity there," she says. "When I first got there, some people didn't even know I was Hispanic by looking at me. They asked me, 'What are you?' like I was the first Hispanic that they met. I didn't think about it before enrolling, but now I'm pissed that the school doesn't do more to get minority students. We're from a low-income family, and I'm Hispanic, so they probably didn't even think I'd come." Yvonne widens her eyes at Marlene like she wants someone to back her up. Marlene quickly nods in affirmation of her sister.

When Yvonne arrived on campus, she tried to meet other students through the Hispanic Club. "But I was the only Hispanic girl there. And they only had activities for the Day of the Dead or ate tacos and burritos. Being Hispanic is not just Mexican. Next year, I want to run for president or vice president of the club so that I can incorporate other cultures."

I ask Yvonne if she has ever detected racism or discrimination on campus. "Nothing serious," she answers before launching into a story about a particular incident that bothered her. She tells me how her dorm sponsored an event for Halloween where students dressed up to welcome trick-or-treaters from the neighborhood. "At first, it was the stereotypical white family with cute little children," she explains. "But there are a lot of poor people living around the area and as the evening progressed, some of them started coming in without costumes to get free candy. A lot of people in my dorm *really* didn't like that. I felt that they were being kind of racist about it, and I gave the people plastic bags with candy myself."

Like many college students, Yvonne has been forced to make difficult decisions about financing her education. "When it came down to it, I was deciding between SUNY Albany and Elmira," she says, explaining how she made her college choice. "Even though

Albany would have been cheaper, I decided on Elmira because I didn't want to be a number. I'm not going to stop myself or settle for something that I don't like because I have to take out loans. I think the loans are worth it as long as I go to the college that I want." Yvonne estimates that she will graduate college with $72,000 in loans, about three times her family's annual income.

Marlene did not have the same reaction to college debt. "When I saw what Yvonne went through, I was like, 'Heck no. I'll just go to community college or something to avoid the loans,'" she says.

Though the two sisters each have their unique perspectives, they are both genuinely concerned about the other's well-being. Marlene worries that Yvonne will ultimately regret her decision to take on this financial burden, and Yvonne worries that Marlene is too concerned with getting into an Ivy League college.

"She associates college with personal value," Yvonne says of her sister. She then lowers her head and looks directly at Marlene, matching the intensity in her voice with the expression on her face. "A person's value is not determined by which college you go to as long as you go *somewhere* and make something of yourself," she exclaims. "I think you'd freak if you didn't get into the Ivies." Marlene does not argue. She squints her eyes and looks away as if to say, "I know you're right but get off my back."

Yvonne continues with her voice raised. "I go to Elmira. Am I *bad*?" Marlene lifts her eyebrows and nods up and down like an animated silent film comedienne. The two girls both start laughing.

"Seriously though," Yvonne persists. "We talk a lot about it— values and worth—I think she needs that."

"I don't even care where I go anymore," Marlene huffs. She drops her head down to the table in front of her and cradles it in the crook of her elbow. "Before, I used to freak out but now I don't even care."

· SEVEN ·

"This isn't supposed to be an endurance test"

ANDREW

Right before Christmas, Andrew and his parents were forced to relocate from their charming old Southern house to a nearby two-bedroom apartment so that the contractors could complete the renovation. The seemingly endless demand for new construction in an underpopulated city means that New Orleans residents are forced to wait for everything from roofs to gutters. But Andrew's mother, Carli, is determined to repair every crack, tear, and fissure in her family's beautiful home. She nurses it back to life like a loyal daughter tending to an ailing parent, fighting back sadness with strength and grit. The dust of construction and the toxicity of hundred-year-old plaster do not keep her from visiting the site almost every day.

Wearing a stylish black pantsuit and sleek high heels, Andrew's mother greets me on the front steps one morning, while she meets with yet another contractor. Tevis, a high school classmate of her husband's from Jesuit, is here to do the plaster. But he is in no condition to work today. His father has recently suffered a heart attack. And a few minutes ago, he found out that a close forty-one-year-old friend is in the hospital with severe meningitis. If things take a turn for the worse, his friend will leave behind a two-year-old daughter.

As soon as Tevis learns that I am from out of town, he really opens up, like he wants people outside of the city to understand what New Orleans residents are going through. "Here it is eighteen to twenty months after the hurricane, and we still have no idea what's going to happen," he says. "People my dad's age had a routine to do every day. They don't know what to do now. There are so many suicides and so many older people just dying of"—he pauses to find the right word—"broken hearts."

The post-Katrina death rate in New Orleans is alarmingly high. According to congressional testimony given by the director of the City of New Orleans Health Department in March 2007, the number of deaths in the first six months of 2006 was about 43 percent above the pre-Katrina death rate, even though the city's population had been cut in half. Though many of these people were suffering from "heartbreak," as Tevis calls it, their medical conditions may have been exacerbated by limited access to health care. Blue Cross Blue Shield reports a 72 percent decrease in the number of practicing physicians, and the Metropolitan Hospital Association estimates that there has been a 75 percent reduction in staffed hospital beds.

"The mentality of the city is that if we were to be hit by another storm, those who are able to get out won't stay here. The government is just not there to put us back together," Tevis continues. A survey conducted by the University of New Orleans Survey Research Center found that more than 20 percent of area residents suffer from "severe levels of stress and depression." Despite this trend, the city estimates that they have lost approximately nine out of ten practicing psychiatrists.

"If you were sick before the storm, the added stress has exacerbated the problem," Andrew's mom says with pain in her voice, "but we just have to pull through." Despite the hardships, New Orleanians are known for their perseverance. A recent survey of fifteen hundred residents found that although nine out of ten have suffered hardship as a result of Katrina, a whopping 70 percent of them remain "optimistic about the future of greater New Orleans."

The Tessier family came to Louisiana from southern France by way of Haiti in the late 1700s. They have been part of New Orleans "society" ever since. Andrew's sister, Elizabeth, and his mother were both debutantes, and his mother is about to become the president of an elite social club dedicated to "promoting the dignity, honor, character, and intellect of all that pertains to the interest and activities of women." Part of their work involves organizing events and parties, especially around Mardi Gras.

MARDI GRAS HAS been part of New Orleans' cultural fabric ever since 1699, when the first European settlers to reach the area named their camp at the mouth of the Mississippi Pointe du Mardi Gras, or Mardi Gras Point. The Carnival season falls between Christmas and Lent, as the early Christians incorporated the celebration from the Romans as a period of jollity and glee to precede the solemn days of Lent. "Mardi Gras literally means 'Fat Tuesday,' when you eat a lot, like the party before the fast," Andrew tells me one afternoon at a swanky new gelato shop uptown. "Two weekends before that is usually the first parade."

Mardi Gras in New Orleans is defined by parades and balls. The parades, which are organized according to various mythological, literary, and political themes, are held on city streets for all to see. "The oldest, prettiest ones still have wagons from a hundred years ago. Those are the best," Andrew says.

The parades are sponsored by private Carnival societies, called krewes, whose masked members throw beads or doubloons (aluminum coins imprinted with the krewe signature or emblem) from elaborate floats. Riding on a float is considered a significant honor, and Andrew's father rides on two of the most prominent ones. He prefers not to disclose the names of these organizations, as their membership is private.

New Orleans societies also sponsor Mardi Gras balls. In general, only invited guests may attend, especially the more elaborate balls, which, like the societies that host them, are designed to be exclusive. "The Rex Ball is massively famous," Andrew explains. "My parents went, and I got invited. But I didn't want to go because it's kind of an older ball, and I don't get to bring a date." The Rex Organization anoints the formal King of Carnival, based on his contribution to the city; his queen is selected from the young debutantes. All guests must bow to the royal court, a custom that made headlines in 1950 when the Duke and Duchess of York kneeled before Rex and his queen.

This year, Andrew will attend a posh ball that is geared toward the younger members of high society. He must be fitted for his formal mask and costume, which is made up of the traditional Mardi Gras colors—purple, green, and gold. "It's funny, they like staple you in," he says with a laugh. Each young man is allowed one date and seven "call outs," which are anonymous invitations that the boys send to the girls they like. "The balls are definitely skewed to the advantage of the guys," Andrew jokes about the eight-to-one female-to-male ratio. "You're masked so they don't know who you are. And once you dance with the lady you give them a little favor, like chocolates or something." After the ball, Andrew will change into a coat and tie to escort his date to the Queen's Supper, which is a more informal dance with a DJ and food.

"Have you ever seen a king cake?" Andrew asks, miming the cake's time-honored shape with his hands. The dessert—a traditional Mardi Gras delicacy—resembles an oversize doughnut and has a little plastic doll baked inside. "After the twelfth day of Christmas, the bakeries start making king cakes. As you get closer to Mardi Gras, you have king cake parties and someone always brings a king cake to class," Andrew explains. Whoever finds the doll is considered the "king" and must host the next party by buying another cake. It is estimated that more than 750,000 king cakes are consumed annually in New Orleans during the Carnival season.

"Mardi Gras is just the best," Andrew exclaims. "Everyone is in really good spirits and all the shops have special things to sell. It's just a lot of fun."

"WHAT DO YOU believe is the most important issue that will face your generation in the coming years?"

From among five possible essay topics, Andrew chose to answer this question in his application for the George Washington Scholarship at Washington and Lee University. His essay discusses the role of religion in twenty-first-century conflict. In it he writes:

I believe conflict in the 21st century will focus on religion. Since conflict poses the largest danger, the most important issue for my generation will be reconciling these theological differences to the masses.

In general, the common Christian views Islam as a radical faith that motivates a large portion of its followers to become at least fanatical and at most highly-motivated Jihadists. With news highlights oversimplifying complex religious issues, the common reader is presented with assumptions that all terrorists are Muslim and that Islam is, if not inherently evil, morally corrupt. Whether confronted with Islamic decrees to murder the Pope (because he quoted a 14th century historian criticizing Islam) or with Muslim terrorists bent on annihilating the West, the common man is bombarded with opinions and facts that seem to confirm Islam's radical violence. Countless Muslim terrorists have vowed to destroy the West and to forcibly convert all "heathen" non-Muslims, including the entire Christian faith. Even the people who believe that only a radical part of Islam is responsible for such violence seem to acquiesce that radicalism is not only rampant but also commonplace, considering the widespread violence throughout the entire Middle East. The violence in France revolving around Muslim youth and the controversy in England over Islamic practices (such as wearing veils) fuel the sentiment that Islam is invading Western culture and territory. These conflicts and disagreements push the masses and world leaders to believe that Islam is evil. Even before the September 11 Attacks, Western leaders have eyed Islam as particularly malignant. Even Winston Churchill once commented that "Mohammedanism is a militant and proselytizing faith."

Similarly, Muslims (mainly from the Middle East) have misconstrued views of the West and Christianity. The atrocities of the Crusades still remain vivid in the imagination of the Arabic Muslim population; and many believe America's War on Terror to be a continuation, especially after the invasion of Iraq. The rhetoric of European leaders on issues such as immigration (most poor immigrants are Muslim) presses the ideas of racism and creedism. Such incidents as the repression of the riots in France and the notorious Danish cartoons of Mohammed have radicalized the Muslims population, pushing some to use heavy rhetoric and even to accept violence as a means of redress. Such Islamic leaders as Mahmoud Ahmadinejad, the Iranian president, told Western leaders to "follow the path of God or vanish from the face of the Earth."

To reduce the inevitable bloodshed, my generation must resolve this misunderstanding. The leaders of both Christianity and Islam, in addition to the world leaders of the countries which support and harbor these religions, must convene and issue statements that emphasize the similarities between the religions and condemn the mutual violence. Both the Bible and the Qur'an depict episodes of violence and war, but both condemn it as a means to spread the faith—in the Qur'an 2:256 ("Let there be no compulsion in religion") and in Matthew 26:52 ("all who take the sword will perish by the sword"). Unfortunately, all communication has been twisted to date. However, we most hold out the hope that eventually we may better understand each other's religion and avoid conflict . . . we must as a collective whole push for better understanding and acceptance of both the differences and the similarities of these two great faiths. Should we fail, our generation will regret the missed opportunity to save potentially hundreds of thousands of human lives.

Based on this essay—plus his grades, test scores, recommendations, and extracurricular activities—Andrew has been selected as one of ninety-six finalists for the George Washington Scholarship, which ranges from a $2,000 scholarship to four years of full tuition, plus room and board. A few days after Mardi Gras, he sets out for an all-expense-paid trip to the Washington and Lee campus in Lexington, Virginia.

Washington and Lee is a prominent Southern university, first founded in 1749 as Augusta Academy and renamed Washington Academy about fifty years later when George Washington contributed a generous endowment to the fledgling school. In 1865, General Robert E. Lee was anointed as president of the university (then called Washington College), and served from the end of the Civil War until his death, when the school changed its name to Washington and Lee University in his honor. During Lee's time as president, he distinguished the institution by introducing practical undergraduate programs like business and journalism. He also introduced the university's beloved honor code, proclaiming, "We have but one rule, and it is that every student is a gentleman."

Andrew arrives on campus on the evening of Tuesday, February 27, and spends several hours mingling with faculty and meeting students before going to sleep in a private room in one of the dorms. "The other students who are here for the scholarship are definitely smart and friendly," he says. "I'm not like, 'Let me bow down and worship you,' but I've met some very interesting personalities and characters."

The following day is packed with interviews by students and faculty. Andrew dresses for the occasion in a coat and tie. He is scheduled to meet with the student panel first—five Washington and Lee students interview each potential scholarship candidate for about an hour. Andrew is impressed with the caliber of the questions, especially when one of the students asks him about his essay.

"You say in your essay that 'both the Bible and Qur'an depict episodes of violence and war, but both condemn it as a means to spread the faith,'" the interviewer notes. "What about the book of Matthew, Chapter 8, when Jesus says that he is not here to bring peace?"

Andrew enjoys being challenged, and even more so when he is prepared. He has read the book of Matthew several times and is familiar with the passage. "I think that quote is taken out of context," he responds to the student panel. "The point is that following the teachings of Christ is not an easy thing to do. It's not all flowers, hugs, and kisses. But just because it's not easy doesn't mean that it is violent."

The interviewers seem pleased with Andrew's thoughtfulness and command of the material. The rest of the meeting goes smoothly, and Andrew emerges with a deep respect for the students he met, saying, "They were really on top of it and prepared. I thought they asked really good questions and obviously did their research, which I thought was really impressive."

Andrew has several hours to kill before his faculty interview later that evening. He grabs a bite to eat with some of the other scholarship candidates and strolls around the manicured fifty-acre campus. Andrew admires the picturesque Colonial architecture and the Lee Chapel, which was built by the general in 1867. Lee and his family are buried in a crypt on the lower level.

Andrew is one of the last scholarship candidates to be interviewed by the three-person faculty panel, by which time they are somewhat exhausted from questioning scores of students. The meeting doesn't take long, and Andrew describes it as blasé. "They asked me what I wanted to major in like three times, and there were a couple of awkward silences," he says. "There's only so much I could say when they asked the same questions, but I understood that they were tired."

After breakfast the next morning, Andrew has a final group interview—three scholarship candidates conversing with a single admissions officer. As the only male student at the meeting, Andrew holds the door open for the two young women before entering the room. "I'm glad it worked out that way because I kind of wanted to go last," he admits. "You always want to be last, like in poker, because it gives you more time to think."

The admissions officer introduces himself and solicits some basic information about the students' backgrounds and ambitions. "What is your high school known for?" he asks the group. Andrew knows he has a great response to this question, especially when he hears the other candidates say things like "our football team" and "school spirit."

"My school is known for excellence," Andrew answers, sitting upright in his chair and looking directly at his interviewer. The other students appear unnerved, like they should have thought of saying something similar. "We're very traditional and proud of doing well," he continues. "For example, we say 'all tricks in forty-six' because that was the year that every single Jesuit sports team was undefeated in the state championships." The admissions officer is clearly pleased with this answer. The other candidates quickly try to amend theirs, but it is too late. Andrew stands out.

"I feel a little bad that I had the advantage of going last," he later tells me. "But I think I made a good impression."

After the interview, Andrew makes his way to the airport. "The campus visit really kind of put a different spin on my perspective," he says. "At first, I thought that the fact that the engineering department is so small would be a disadvantage, but after meeting the professors, I realized how much attention I would get as a student there. They have like four professors and ten engineering majors a year, which I think is an advantage. It would be great to get the scholarship, but I'm not sure if they will give it to two kids from the same family, since my sister already got one."

LISA

Colorado Springs, a mid-sized city about an hour south of Denver, is home to the United States Olympic Committee administration and the Olympic Training Center. The state-of-the-art athletic compound, opened in 1997, houses an 810,000-gallon pool, more than 113,000 square feet of sports training facilities, the largest indoor shooting center in the western hemisphere, an $8-million visitor center, and the U.S. Olympic Hall of Fame. The complex can accommodate up to 557 athletes and coaches at any given time with its housing, dining, and recreational facilities, and its auditorium seats 225 spectators. The best athletes in the United States will stop here at one point or another on their way to the Olympics.

The Olympic Training Center used to be an Air Force base, which becomes obvious upon arriving at the intimidating security gate. The boxy buildings inside are arranged in symmetrical rows with wraparound parking lots to accommodate the influx of spectators for various competitions and events. Signs are posted all around the property asking visitors to refrain from smoking in consideration of the athletes, like Lisa, who cannot afford to compromise any aspect of their fitness and well-being. To prevent the spread of germs, guests are encouraged to use the various hand-sanitizer stations mounted to the walls and pillars indoors.

At more than six thousand feet above sea level, the thin Colorado Springs air can cripple athletes who are sensitive to high elevation. Lisa has only three days to acclimate to the altitude before participating in the first major national gymnastics meet of 2007, the Rhythmic Challenge. The young women on the USA Rhythmic Gymnastics Team must perform four separate routines—rope, hoop, clubs, and ribbon—during this half-day event, which culminates in a reranking of the gymnasts. At stake is the first-place rank that Lisa achieved just a few months earlier at Nationals. She is now the gymnast to beat.

About a hundred people, mostly parents and teenage girls, settle into the bleacher seats at the far side of the colossal gymnasium on this mid-February Sunday afternoon. Each row of spectators is bookmarked by layers of winter clothes that have been removed once inside—piles of colorful Gore-Tex jackets, wool scarves, and flannel winter hats. A shadowy curtain divides the gleaming gymnasium in half, creating a backstage area for warm-up and downtime where about a dozen prepubescent figures jump and tumble in shimmering body-hugging leotards on the beige floor mats. With their overstated makeup and uniform hairdos, it is almost impossible to tell one girl from the next.

Lisa's parents, Ping and Cindy, are perched on the second row of bleachers closest to the judges' table. They blend in with the other parents in turtlenecks and sweaters, as does Lisa's ten-year-old brother, who keeps running in and out of the gym to talk on his cell phone or buy some candy. A few rows behind them sits a group of teenage girls. They smell like a potpourri of citrusy perfume and hair-care products.

"Is she nervous?" I ask Lisa's parents.

"*We're* nervous," Ping responds, and they both smile. Lisa must place in the top four to qualify for the upcoming international meets. A year ago, she was devastated when she came in fifth at this competition. However, her disappointing performance ultimately motivated her to work even harder.

Ping arranges to share video recording duties with the couple in the front row. "These are Ava's parents. We're good friends," he says, introducing the wholesome pair. Ava, a pretty girl with coppery hair, is the tallest member of the USA Rhythmic Gymnastics Team at five foot ten. Ava is also a senior and her mother tells me that she has applied to several prestigious colleges. Her first choice is Dartmouth, where she is a third-generation legacy.

At half past noon, the gymnasts emerge from backstage in a single-file line of bright smiles and glittering leotards. Fourteen girls, divided by age into "juniors" and "seniors," will compete this afternoon (the juniors, who are younger than fifteen, always perform first). The audience rises for the national anthem and turns to face a huge American flag hanging from the ceiling behind the judges' table. Looking lovely in a red-sequined leotard with glossy gold accents, Lisa mouths the tune, hand over heart. She is the smallest of all the girls.

Today's opening event is the rope. First up is a dainty white girl, who flips, leaps, skips, and hops to a classic Spanish beat, the kind you hear in dramatic bullfight scenes in the movies. The keyed-up audience erupts with applause each time she tosses and catches the rope, which resembles a small bungee cord.

The third contender is one of two African American girls in the group. Her compact, muscular physique is clad in fluorescent pink and neon green. Her first jumps are as mighty as the thumping bass of her accompanying big band music, but her strength soon begins to wane. Unable to concentrate, she gasps for breath and stammers through the rest of the routine. The music ends before she does. A few seconds later, she collapses and bursts into tears. Her coach runs out to escort her off the mat, hugging her for comfort as they make their way backstage.

"Did you see how out of breath she was?" Ava's mom whispers to the other parents with concern. "She only got here yesterday and hasn't had a chance to acclimate at all."

"She has asthma," Ping says. "The altitude is really hard on her."

The audience perks up as the first senior takes the stage. Dressed in a dazzling multicolored leotard, she steadies her ballerina figure and leaps into the air on beat to "The Flight of the Bumblebee," launching her first toss from between her toes. A few seconds later, she stumbles as her prop falls to the floor. There are significant deductions for dropping the rope, kind of like breaking your "baby" egg in Home Economics.

The next two gymnasts suffer the same fate. Both start off gracefully but quickly tire and eventually drop the rope at least once. Their labored breathing can be heard over the music as each routine ends in collapse. The girls stomp off backstage, visibly frustrated and disappointed by their performances.

"This isn't supposed to be an endurance test," Ava's father observes.

"Someone should decide whether this competition should be held at such high altitude," his wife agrees.

A group of Ping and Cindy's friends, who happen to live in Colorado Springs, enters the gymnasium. They greet them with quick hugs, and Ping hands the camera to Ava's father for a test run. Everyone knows that Lisa will be performing soon.

"Up next is Lisa Wang," says the announcer. The teenage girls behind us erupt into cheers.

"Go Lisa! Come on, Lees! Go Leeeesa!"

Lisa struts toward the mat in a shimmering scarlet leotard and matinee-idol red lipstick. Steadying herself for her debut, she digs her heels into the mat before leaping into the air on the first beat of a percussion-heavy rumba. High toss, double bend, leap, jump, toss, backbend, down on the mat, jump, roll. She is the best so far. With a strength that rivals her flexibility, her tosses and jumps are higher than the others'. She has perfected the art of making a difficult routine look easy by bringing fluidity and a great big smile to the challenging contortions. However, toward the end of her performance, Lisa seems to be a little rushed. Her only small flaw is finishing a few seconds late. The judges may penalize her for timing.

"That was okay," Ping says over the audience applause.

"It was the best so far," remarks another parent.

"Oh yes, it was the best so far, but she can do better."

After three more performances, the judges post their scores for the rope routines. Lisa comes in second place, trailing first place by only half a point. Ping pats Cindy on her knee, as if to reassure her that Lisa still has three more chances to take the lead.

The next event is the hoop, which requires even more precise timing than the previous event. The slightest miscalculation can result in the hoop rolling away, completely interrupting the flow of the performance. This happens to the second performer, whose hoop spins right off the mat. The third gymnast misses her first toss and never quite catches up. Both competitors look devastated.

"You've got to be perfect," says Ping, as the competition progresses. "There is nothing else you can do." I am struck by how sincerely he roots for each gymnast, as if he understands the intense pressure they are under. Despite the difficulty of every twist and bend and the hand-eye coordination required for the tosses, the magic of the sport is that every move must seem effortless—as if the human body was constructed for these contortions alone.

Several performances later, Lisa returns to the mat. Looking refined in a green and gold getup, she faces the judges on tiptoe and braces herself. A fast-paced classical beat comes on over the loudspeakers as she catches the first toss with her entire body, the hoop settling over her small torso like a coin rolling around on the floor. In the moments that follow, Lisa transforms the hoop into a jump rope, obstacle course tire, and a high-flying kite as she floats, twirls, and leaps across the room in every direction. The audience is silent, concentrating on the superhuman movements of the figure in front of them. Lisa makes her final catch with both knees planted firmly on the floor, reaching out over her toes in a backbend to grasp the hoop in her hand.

"That was *so good*, like *perfect*," exclaims one of the girls in the audience. Ping and Cindy smile at each other. Their friends gush and congratulate them.

"Look at Lisa's score," someone yells. Everyone gasps at the number—15.175 out of 20, the highest score of the day by far. Cindy covers her mouth as her friends take turns hugging her. Ping smiles and shakes his head from side to side, like he can't believe it.

"Isn't she pretty in her leotard? She looks just like a princess," a voice from the bleachers exclaims as Lisa's friend Ava walks on-stage a few performances later. Her parents lean forward in their seats. Ava's routine, which is set to classical music, starts off slow and polished. She looks like a ceramic figurine as she glides on the mat. Halfway through she misses a toss but quickly recovers. Then she misses again. The hoop rolls off the mat. Her father grunts; her mother averts her eyes like she has just witnessed a horrible car accident.

Cindy leans in to console Ava's mother, resting a small hand on her shoulder. "Almost," she whispers. "Almost perfect."

"That's why this sport is so heartbreaking," Ping whispers to me with pursed lips.

As the hoop competition draws to a close, the Wangs are greeted by several more friends. They are now surrounded by families, most of whom speak to each other in Chinese. The little kids play with small toys and coloring books as they settle in for the second half of the competition.

"*Welcome back, Lisa Wang.*" Lisa returns for the third event, where gymnasts must incorporate a ball or pair of small clubs into their routine. Now the front-runner in the competition, she is greeted by a roaring cheer as she strides toward the mat in shimmering red and gold. She flings her clubs up toward the heavens and bursts off the floor into a midair somersault on the first note of a tango, reaching both arms up upon landing as gravity drives the clubs toward her. Cindy holds her breath. Lisa makes the catch.

"Yes!" Cindy screams for the first time that day.

Lisa keeps going. Another flip, backbend, high toss, catch. Yes. One more leap, toss, catch. She ends by stretching her arms as far back as possible, as the clubs land gracefully in her hands. She throws her head forward with a huge smile, fitting for the flawless energetic routine.

"Oh my God. That was amazing," someone shouts.

Ava's dad leans over to Ping and whispers, "That was even better than hoop. Tremendous."

Several pairs of curious eyes emerge from behind the curtain to check out Lisa's score. With a 14.825, she ends up placing first in this event. Despite a smooth performance, polished routine, and high marks in the artistic category, Ava places only fourth. Her parents slump down in their bleacher seats and don't say a word.

Lisa's little brother returns for the final event: the ribbon. She is the second senior to perform. The crowd chants her name, as she is clearly the audience favorite. Her brother holds his cell phone up to the crowd, sending "Go Lisa!" cheers across the airwaves.

Lisa looks lovely and crisp in a simple black and white leotard. Her ribbon matches perfectly. Classical music starts to play as she nails the first toss. Throughout the rest of her performance, Lisa seems to morph into different animals. She pounces like a cat, sashays like a gazelle, and charms like a snake. The long silk ribbon floats along with her movements.

"It was artistic *and* emotional," someone comments after the routine has ended.

"She looked *beautiful*."

"She did so well. What a great day."

Lisa ranks second in the ribbon event. Ping does a quick calculation and announces that her score of 14.625 is enough for her to win first place in the competition. The Wangs jump up from their seats to hug each other and their friends. Their daughter has managed to hold on to her national title. Lisa is still the number-one rhythmic gymnast in the country.

"You know, she doesn't get too excited," Ping comments on how his daughter will likely react. "You don't really see her emotions except on the mat."

"LAST YEAR, I DID really badly at this competition," Lisa says. "I placed fifth and it determined everything. Usually altitude affects me a lot, but this year I didn't feel it that much. I'm so happy."

After posing for a team photo and being interviewed by a reporter, Lisa meets me at the recreational center across the Olympic training facility. Her stage makeup seems even more amplified in contrast with the simple track suit that she wears to the cafeteria. Nevertheless, her victorious glow radiates from underneath her pancake blush. Lisa doesn't talk much about the win, however. Years of near-misses have made her modest, and she knows she has a long road ahead if she wants to make the Olympics.

Since she graduated a semester early from Stevenson High School, Lisa has been living the life of a jet-setting gymnast, financed by the USA Rhythmic Gymnastics Team. She just got back from a ten-day trip to Russia, where she put in eight-hour days with top coaches at the Russian Olympic Training Center. She will return to Russia in a week for more intensive training before competing in a Grand Prix Competition in the Ukraine at the end of the month. Then it's back to Russia in early March for more training with top coaches.

Lisa complains a little about the grueling schedule. "I wake up at eight, do ballet from nine to eleven, have lunch, train from one to four, have dinner, and then train from six to nine. We get Sundays off, but I am so exhausted, I just sit in my room and don't move. On our one day off, we just want to sit and eat."

Despite her demanding practice schedule and international excursions, Lisa found time to arrange an admissions interview with a local Harvard alumnus. In late January, she got a call from a man who wanted to schedule the interview at 7:30 AM on a Saturday morning at a restaurant about forty-five minutes from her house. Though somewhat irritated by the inconvenient request, she had little choice but to agree. The following Saturday, she woke up at 6 AM to meet her Harvard interviewer as promised.

"When I got there, I asked the server if there was an elderly gentleman waiting for someone," she says. "He told me to look around, and the place was full of older men. I waited for *two hours* but the man never showed up. So I e-mailed him when I got home and he wrote back that he thought that the interview was next Saturday, even though he was the one who made the crazy appointment."

A week later, they met at 9 AM at a Starbucks near Lisa's house. Right off the bat, the gentleman asked her where else she had applied besides Harvard. When she told him that she had been accepted at Yale under their early action program, the conversation deteriorated into a Harvard versus Yale debate. Apparently, years ago, Lisa's interviewer had also been accepted at Yale but chose to matriculate at Harvard because he liked Cambridge more than New Haven. He spent most of the time putting Yale down rather than asking Lisa questions about herself or her Harvard candidacy. Some alumni interviewers can be overzealous when it comes to school pride, and us-versus-them interviews, like the one Lisa had, are not uncommon. Fortunately, admissions officers at top colleges are usually more concerned with recruiting the best applicants than with whether or not these students also applied to other schools. Since approximately 75 percent of students who are accepted to

Harvard eventually matriculate, the staff can assume that they have a good chance of getting whoever they decide they want. "It was a hassle, but whatever," she says of the experience. "I just hope it doesn't hurt my chances at Harvard."

NABIL

Every winter, hundreds of math-crazy teenagers from more than eighty different high schools congregate in Cambridge, Massachusetts, to compete in the annual Harvard-MIT Mathematics Tournament, or the HMMT for short. This is Nabil's second year at the HMMT, a daylong event organized by undergraduates, most of whom participated in lots of math competitions in high school. The coordinators, a group of Asian and white kids in oversize red HMMT T-shirts, congregate at the front of the MIT lecture hall for the final event of the afternoon, called the "guts round." Nabil recognizes a few of these subculture superstars from their past victories and an online mathematics discussion forum that he sometimes visits called The Art of Problem Solving.

The competitors are each after one of the soaring yellow-gold trophies displayed atop a table in the front of the room, lined up like wallflowers waiting to be asked to dance. The "guts round," is made up of two group competitions divided by difficulty and identified by the letters A or B. Students compete in teams, which are typically organized according to high school. Because Cordova High School is short on students with either the skill or interest to compete in the "A" competition, Nabil has joined up with some students he knows from other schools. He arranged for one of his teachers to sponsor the team.

Perched on the edge of his seat toward the back of the room, Nabil observes his opponents. The team from Thomas Jefferson High School for Science and Technology, a prestigious, selective magnet school in Virginia, is the team to beat. Teams from prominent boarding schools like Andover and Exeter, as well as Stuyvesant High School (an esteemed magnet school in New York City) are also major contenders for the top prize.

Two jumbo projection screens on either side of the lecture hall are set up to display the teams' scores. In a few moments, representatives from each team will scamper down the aisle ramps to retrieve the first problem, which is printed on small rectangular sheets of paper. They will then dash back to their groups, perform hectic calculations, and return their answers to the front of the room in exchange for the next problem. As the questions get progressively more difficult, the teams are eliminated if they submit incorrect answers. In this way, the group competition rewards both speed and accuracy.

The moderators instruct the teams to begin and the room erupts into the sort of organized chaos that is typically found on the trading floor of a stock market. Students run around "buying" and "selling" math problems. Nabil's cross-country running skills come in handy. He seems to be floating in his white Nikes as he submits and retrieves problems for his team. The competitors hunch over their desk chairs, scribbling with fervor.

"Sixty seconds," someone yells. Messengers dash to the front of the room to submit their answers for the last time. "Ten seconds . . . and stop. *Stop!*"

The tension evaporates, and the students applaud wholeheartedly. They smile and congratulate one another on a job well done. "I think we did a lot better than last year," Nabil says. His team scores a respectable 120 points, not enough to place but not too far behind the top score of 195.

"I LOVE IT HERE," Nabil exclaims during a post-competition debriefing from a bench near the exit of the lecture hall. "I haven't really had the chance to do anything with other math people before," he says. "I got onto the scene kind of late and I haven't had other people like me to encourage me."

Nabil relishes interacting with students who have similar interests—math and juggling are two things that many students at MIT do for fun. "Everyone here is so friendly, not at all cutthroat," he says. "One guy had like twelve jugglers in his bag. And I've met so many math campers—it makes me want to go even more." Nabil hopes to reunite with his new friends in a few months and plans to apply for math camp this summer in Maine.

Nabil is quite popular here. Now that the HMMT events have finished, he is persistently interrupted by other students looking to him for direction on where to go and what to do. After giving answers like, "Do whatever you want" and "Eat whatever you decide," he turns to me and explains, "I'm the only one of those guys who was here last year."

With almost no adult supervision—they saw their faculty sponsor for only a few hours at the competition—Nabil and his friends are staying by themselves at an MIT fraternity for the weekend. "The whole time we were out doing what we wanted to—visiting Harvard, going to the Au Bon Pain for breakfast, traveling back and forth through MIT as we pleased, not eating at specified times if we didn't want to," he gushes.

Nabil is optimistic that he will get the chance to return to Cambridge next September. A few weeks ago, he had an interview with a Harvard alumnus. After answering some questions about his résumé and talking about his connection to Ethiopia and interest in juggling, Nabil was fairly certain that he had impressed his interviewer. The man ended their conversation with three encouraging words about college: you'll have options. Nabil repeats this mantra—"I'll have options"—several times this afternoon, almost subconsciously.

The Harvard alumni interview wasn't the first for Nabil. He has also met with representatives from the University of Chicago and Princeton. The two women each had a distinctive perspective on the role of the college interview. "The Chicago interviewer left a better impression on me than the Princeton one," says Nabil. "The Princeton interviewer was nice and started asking me questions about myself from the start. It was very different from the Chicago one I had, where she told me she didn't like to think of it as an interview, but more of a chance for the prospective student to learn more about the college."

Something about how the Princeton interviewer emphasized his Ethiopian heritage made him uncomfortable. Nabil would have rather talked about his academic interests than about his ethnic background. "Not that it was the entire basis of the Princeton lady's interest in me, but it seemed like she thought it was so neat that my parents came from Ethiopia," he explains. "Of course, I also gave some other information about myself, like I intend on working for a Ph.D. in math—my answer to 'What are your goals?' or something like that. With the Chicago interviewer, I dropped that my parents came from Ethiopia—not planning to or anything—and she really didn't see it as important, or at least never brought it up again." Both interviewers complimented Nabil and indicated that they planned to recommend him.

"If I exude overconfidence or appear too happy, what else am I supposed to think?" he asks. Nabil has received lots of good news lately. A couple of weeks ago, he was selected as a National Merit finalist, which qualifies him for a $2,500 college scholarship, and recently received a letter from the University of Chicago saying that National Merit finalists are generally awarded half- or full-tuition merit scholarships. "Finalists are so wanted that they offer them plenty of scholarship money too," he says as a smile spreads over his face. "If nothing else, I can still go to Chicago. That's how I'm looking at it."

The next day, Nabil visits the Princeton campus on his way back home to Memphis. "It was definitely the most negative of my four college visits," he says. "But I saw it after the most fun weekend of my life in Boston, where I juggled and explored and visited and did math."

Nabil spends a night in his friend's dorm on the Princeton campus, where they stay up talking until 1 AM. The next day, he visits four different classes—two in math and two in computer science—and accompanies his friend to a Math Club meeting, where the members discuss number theory. In between, Nabil wanders around the charming campus but feels uninspired by his suburban surroundings.

"There isn't anything there except the school," he says. "There are some stores outside the campus, but that's it. There's nowhere to explore."

Visiting Princeton makes Nabil realize how much he loves losing himself in a city. Princeton is a fantastic school, but he is convinced that he belongs elsewhere. "I never realized that location mattered for me. I don't want to be somewhere in college where the only way I can go away to a real city is to take a five-minute train to a station with nothing in it, then have to switch to another train. Now Harvard and MIT are definitely my top two choices."

· EIGHT ·

"No rejections . . . yet :)"

MARLENE

If I can't get in to Rochester, there's no way I'm going to get into any of the Ivies," Marlene says. "It's basically all over for me." She still hasn't heard from the University of Rochester, even though three of her friends have already gotten in. I explain to her that it takes time to evaluate thousands of files and not all accepted students are notified so early. She's already convinced that she must have been rejected anyway.

There is a communal sense of uneasiness and dread hidden behind the daily routine at New Rochelle High School. The seniors are like corporate executives in the midst of company downsizing. They yearn for relief from the torment of uncertainty but fear the sucker punch of bad news.

Today, Marlene must present a persuasive speech for her Speech and Communications class, and she has chosen the hot-button topic of affirmative action. Even with her topic selection, she is hesitant to wander into the minefield of race. "Getting race involved in my speech would be way too complicated," she explains. "When a minority gets into a good school, everyone is respectful to their face, but when the person turns his or her back, it's a completely different story. When this African American girl got into Cornell early, these two guys said congratulations, but that same day one of them was like, 'She just got in because she's black,' and they both nodded."

Marlene stands in front of her upper-middle-class peers to present her argument. Reading from her notes, she begins, "Admission to U.S. colleges favors rich kids. To break the cycle, underprivileged applicants deserve special consideration." She points out the ways in which wealthy students are favored in the admissions process. She talks about the SAT, which gives an advantage to students who can afford test-prep services, and how well-off athletes often receive more generous scholarships than low-income students. She displays a political cartoon of President Bush to introduce the topic of legacies. In it, the president has his arm around his father's shoulder and argues against affirmative action by saying, "Why heck, some mediocre underachiever could have an unfair advantage because of race and circumstance, right, Dad?"

Not everyone finds the joke funny. When Marlene finishes her speech, she is confronted by one of her classmates, a legacy student who has been accepted early decision to the University of Pennsylvania. "I come from an upper-class family, and I never had a tutor for the SATs," the girl says, pausing for a moment. "Well, I guess my parents tutored me."

"That's my point," Marlene responds. "Low-income families have a completely different lifestyle. They can't equally compete for the same spot at an Ivy League school. I have totally lost hope."

MARLENE RUSHES HOME from school on March 18. She's read on her trusty source, the College Confidential Web site, that Brandeis has just sent applicants their decision letters. She may have given up hope of getting into the Ivy League, but she hasn't given up on Brandeis, her next favorite college.

Marlene's pulse quickens as she approaches her front door. She stares at the row of mailboxes on the first floor of her apartment building like one of them may contain a bomb. "Let's just get this over with," she tells herself, as she jams her small bronze key into the metal lock and yanks it toward her.

Damn it. The mailman must be late today. He's usually here by now.

Marlene figures that she might as well take a nap, but when she gets up to her fifth-floor apartment, she is too wound up to sleep. She flips on the TV and scrolls through the daytime programs. The next time she looks at the clock it is already 3:30 PM. She heads back downstairs to check again. As the elevator descends, her eyes fixate on the illuminated numbers of each passing floor. Four, three, two . . . the shiny doors part. *Please, please just let this work out,* she prays. She jerks the metallic mailbox door, which flings open like there's a jack-in-the-box inside.

Still nothing.

Desperate for a reprieve from her restlessness, Marlene makes a second attempt at an after-school nap. She kicks off her shoes, crawls into bed, and concentrates on shutting down her hyperactive mind. Soon she is enveloped by a peaceful darkness. Everything is black.

The apartment is quiet when Marlene opens her eyes again. She reaches for her cell phone to check the clock. It's 5 PM. She is suddenly convinced that the next time she opens the mailbox, she will find a letter from Brandeis. It is here, and there is nothing she can do to change that.

Bracing for the worst, Marlene heads back downstairs. In the elevator, she gives herself a mental pep talk. "If I don't get in, it will be okay," she tells herself. "I can always just go to Stony Brook." As she walks toward the mailboxes, the muscles in her face tense up. She slowly turns the key and peers into the cubby like a post-op patient peeling off surgical bandages.

Inside the mailbox is a great big fat envelope addressed to Ms. Marlene Fernandez with a prominent "Congratulations" printed underneath. *Yes! Thank God!* Marlene takes a long, deep breath. This is the first serene moment she has had in months.

Marlene decides to wait until she gets back upstairs to open the letter. The package feels weighty and significant in her hands as she rides the elevator up to the fifth floor. Sitting on the living room couch, she carefully opens the envelope and pulls out a navy blue folder with the Brandeis University emblem splashed across the front. Inside, she finds her acceptance letter.

Dear Marlene:

CONGRATULATIONS! It is my pleasure to offer you admission to Brandeis University and the Class of 2011. The Committee on Admissions was truly impressed with your personal and academic accomplishments. In particular, we found you to be an ideal fit with our campus environment and we are confident that you will excel here during your undergraduate years. We look forward to having you join the Brandeis community. . . .

Enclosed, you will find a host of information to help you begin your enrollment for the fall semester. To accept our offer of admission, we ask that you complete the Enrollment Form and return it, along with the non-refundable $500 University fee, in the envelope provided no later than May 1, 2007. You will also find information from the Office of Residence Life regarding your online housing form. Over the next few months you will receive additional information about Dining Services, Orientation, and Residential Life. Please be sure to pay close attention to these mailings and complete all forms in a timely manner to ensure your smooth transition to campus. . . .

Welcome to the Class of 2011!

Sincerely,
Gil J. Villanueva
Dean of Admissions

Marlene flips through the rest of the packet and discovers a letter from the Financial Aid Office. She wasn't expecting to get any information about financial aid this early and takes it as a good sign. After skimming the short introductory paragraph, her eyes dart toward the middle of the page. They widen in amazement. "Can this be right?" she asks herself.

Brandeis is offering Marlene $38,200 in financial aid for next year. Just to make sure, she rereads the columns of numbers: $27,000 is coming from an Alumni and Friends Scholarship. The government is paying for $6,000 in grants. She also has $1,700 in Work Study and $3,500 in Federal Perkins Loans.*

Now Marlene is really excited. "It's a really great package," she tells me over the phone a short time later. "It will cost me $14,000 total, which isn't bad at all."

About an hour later, Marlene greets her mother and oldest sister at the door to tell them the great news. She finds her mother's reaction underwhelming. "She said congratulations, but she basically has no idea what Brandeis is. I spent fifteen minutes trying to get her to pronounce the name," jokes Marlene. She then calls her sister Yvonne and her father, who happens to be visiting the Dominican Republic. Everyone is impressed and excited that Marlene got such a large scholarship.

---

* Perkins Loans are considered as part of financial aid because the government subsidizes the interest on this type of loan while a student is enrolled in school.

Marlene doesn't realize until a few weeks later that Brandeis is asking her to take out more than the $3,500 in loans each year. Though they are giving her $38,200 in financial aid, the cost of tuition, room, board, and fees for the coming academic year is $47,150. Even with her Perkins Loan, she comes up almost $9,000 short, which means that she will have to take out another loan to cover the gap. If she goes to Brandeis, Marlene will be more than $50,000 in debt by the time she graduates.

NABIL

It's Saturday morning, and Nabil is at cross-country practice as usual. But today is far from a normal day. The MIT admissions results will go online at noon, Eastern Standard Time, 11 AM in Memphis.

Nabil has arranged for his brother to call him on his cell phone when the time comes so that he can walk him through the process of accessing the MIT decision over the phone. Nabil also brought several tennis balls to practice today. He wants to break up his usual routine by juggling three balls while he runs. "That way, I will be able to say, 'I found out that I got into MIT after juggling at practice,'" he explains.

Nabil is pumped to begin this morning's six-mile run. As the clock starts, he puts one foot in front of the other and tosses the tennis balls in the air, jogging and juggling at the same time. The balls look like a roving solar system of fluorescent green planets orbiting around him as he runs. He couldn't care less that his teammates are staring at him. He keeps up the jogging and juggling for three miles and then carries the tennis balls, two in one hand and one in the other, for the rest of the distance.

In the past few weeks, Nabil has been outdoing himself on the field, often beating teammates who have always been the stars. It feels different to be pushing the pace of the pack. The experience gets him thinking about making the transition from student to professor. He imagines what it would be like to go from hearing about all these great teachers to becoming a teacher himself, guiding bright pupils as they solve difficult problem sets. Toward the end of the practice, Nabil finds himself conjuring the image of a commercial with Lance Armstrong he once saw. He hears the cyclist's voice pronouncing the ad's slogan in his head: "Why do we work hard? For victory? For glory? Or is it to build a foundation so that we can be someone else's?"

Nabil finishes his run ahead of schedule and decides to do his stretches in the back parking lot behind the school. He wants to be near his cell phone, which he positions on the roof of his car so he can keep his eye on it. He brings his right foot toward his lower back and holds the first stretch, pulling on his thigh muscle like a piece of taffy.

Keeping one eye on his cell phone, Nabil moves through the next steps of his post-workout routine. Why hasn't his brother called yet? Almost on cue, the small screen lights up. He flips open the phone and presses the receiver to his ear.

"Go to the MIT Web site," Nabil tells his brother. He walks him through the process of logging in, making the directions as clear as possible to avoid any missteps that might prolong the wait time. It takes only a few minutes. His brother enters the password and clicks on the SUBMIT button.

The next thing Nabil hears is an earsplitting scream. "You're in. You're in," his brother shrieks. In the background, his other siblings cheer and yell "Congratulations!" into the phone.

Nabil does not know what to do. "Okay, I got into college," he thinks. "Now what?" As he drives home from practice, Nabil has the strangest feeling—he feels perfectly normal.

By the time he gets to his house, Nabil's parents have already told their friends and family in Boston, Philadelphia, Texas, and

Ethiopia, where one of his uncles even recognizes MIT as "a good school where scientists are trained." The communal excitement amplifies Nabil's gratification.

"Everything suddenly seems more realistic now," he says. *"I got into MIT."*

VERY FEW STUDENTS at Cordova High School even bother to apply to a college as selective as MIT. On Monday, Nabil shocks some of his teachers when he tells them that he got accepted. Of course, others gush that they knew he could do it, especially his cross-country coach, who assures Nabil that his recommendations "wrote themselves." He hesitates to tell only one person, his English teacher, who recently gave him two detentions for tardiness and seems particularly disappointed that he is not doing his best. "I know she'll be very happy for me, but it will make her expect more of me, so I'm going to wait to tell her," he explains.

After getting into MIT, Nabil can't help but feel like school is over, even though it is only March. Each day drags out. He feels even more distant from his classmates. "Doing the math thing pretty much separates me from everyone else at school," he says. "I'm usually the only one from my school to qualify for the math competitions. Eventually, it just adds up and I feel alone."

Nabil is constantly reminiscing about all the fun he had at the Harvard-MIT Math Tournament and imagining what it will be like to be a student in Cambridge. "I think being around people like me is what's most important," he says of the community. He keeps noticing little things that he loves, like an online picture of an MIT campus street sign that says NERD X-ING and when the hosts of NPR's *Car Talk* joke around about the fact that they went to MIT.

Nabil has a week and a half to savor his MIT acceptance before he hears from the other colleges. "My attitude now is 'Forget Princeton, Chicago, and Carnegie Mellon. The question is do I want to go to Harvard or MIT?'" he says. "Even though I thought Harvard was my first choice for a long time, I'm leaning toward MIT. My dad thinks MIT would be a better fit, too."

To hear Nabil tell it, MIT students seem to have more fun doing things they enjoy, while Harvard students can be rich elitists. Still, he understands that his pro-MIT bias may be influenced by the fact that he has spent more time there. Before making any final decisions, Nabil plans to visit both schools in April, when the campuses will host fun-filled weekends designed to entice admitted students. "I expect to get into Harvard but I almost wish I'm wrong so my decision will be that much easier," he says.

MARLENE

Marlene was not expecting anything significant in the mail. But the day after she got into Brandeis, she received another fat envelope, this one from the University of Rochester. She had already assumed that they had rejected her. Holding the fat envelope in her hand, she feels great to be proven wrong.

The University of Rochester is awarding Marlene a $10,000 merit scholarship. To determine the rest of her financial aid package, they include an additional form, which asks for more detailed information about her family's expenses like rent, groceries, and cable. "I'm assuming they're asking more questions since I have such huge need," she says. "I doubt they'll give me nearly enough." Since Marlene would much rather go to Brandeis anyway, she decides to ignore the extra paperwork and just decline the University of Rochester's offer.

Later that day, she gets a call from someone in the Trinity College Admissions Office. She has been accepted and her admissions packet will be arriving shortly. Marlene thanks the person on the other end of the phone and hangs up. She starts to feel like a driver hitting all the green lights.

"This keeps me hopeful," Marlene writes in an e-mail that evening. "No rejections . . . yet :)"

ANDREW

There are only a few things that connect the eight colleges of the Ivy League. Mostly, they compete against one another on the athletic field and in recruiting the finest students. They also collaborate on certain admissions policies, which is why they all have the same application and notification deadlines. This year, the Ivies have agreed to electronically notify students of their admissions decisions on March 29. The Duke Admissions Office gets a slight head start by posting its admissions results exactly one day before the Ivies post theirs.

On the evening of March 28, Andrew is in Baton Rouge for the Louisiana Mu Alpha Theta State Convention. The two-day math tournament is held in a Holiday Inn, where he arrives along with about fifty contenders from Jesuit High School. The boys all wear royal blue T-shirts in place of their traditional school uniforms. A few months ago, they chose "The Grapes of Math" as their theme for 2007. The phrase is printed on the back of each shirt above an illustration of various mathematical symbols embedded in a bunch of grapes.

After a brief introduction, the Jesuit contingent joins the thousand other students from across the state, and they all assemble into four-person teams for the first round of competition. The rules stipulate that every team include students with a range of mathematical ability who go by the Greek letters of mu, alpha, or theta. The mus are taking calculus, the alphas take trigonometry, and the thetas know geometry and algebra. There are 125 assigned math problems. In the next few hours, each team calculates and theorizes as many answers as it can.

"We completely destroyed the competition in the first round, which was awesome," Andrew says. "All the calculus questions were ridiculously easy, at least for us. They gave a lot of integral problems, and our teacher is great at teaching integrals." By the end of the night, his team is in first place with a thirty-point lead.

The competition concludes around 11 PM, and Andrew remembers that he needs to find a computer to check the Duke decisions. He heads to the hotel's Business Center but the only computer is occupied by a student working on a paper for school. "We're all nerds here," he jokes and decides to check if one of his friends brought a laptop.

As he exits the elevator on the fourth floor, where the boys from Jesuit are staying, Andrew keeps his eyes out for a familiar face. He runs into two of his friends who also applied to Duke.

Andrew is shocked when he hears that neither of them got in. *How is this possible?* he wonders. They are both terrific students, and one of them won the Nationals in chess. "He is just as good of a student as me—also up for valedictorian—so I'm really surprised," says Andrew.

All this time, Andrew had been confident that a top student from Jesuit would definitely get into Duke. Now he's not so sure. His friends are both nearby as he logs onto the Internet from a laptop on the desk in the corner of their hotel room. It's awkward, but Andrew is too absorbed in finding out the status of his application to worry about it.

"Congratulations," says one of the boys when he finds out that Andrew has been accepted.

Andrew thanks his buddy and tries to downplay his excitement. "I couldn't really say anything because I knew that they didn't want to talk about it," he later explains. "I didn't want to seem like I was rubbing it in their faces." Nevertheless, with an acceptance to Duke and the lead in the math tournament, Andrew goes to bed feeling like a hitter on a hot streak.

. . .

THE NEXT MORNING, Andrew sits in a hotel conference room, staring at a piece of blank paper on the table in front of him and waiting for instructions. He is about to compete against the finest math students in the state for the Louisiana Mu Alpha Theta Scholarship. The high scorer on this difficult exam will get $500 for college.

The proctor signals for students to begin. Andrew flips the test over and thumbs through the pages. There are eighteen problems— way too many to answer in the time given. He skims through them and starts with the ones he can do fastest. By the end, he has finished twelve problems and even finds a few "fun" ones. Nine of his answers turn out to be correct, which is not enough to win the scholarship but enough for Andrew to feel satisfied with his performance.

Andrew spends the rest of the morning and most of the afternoon solving math problems, but the impending results of his Ivy League applications are never far from his thoughts. At lunch, he realizes that he forgot his password for the U Penn Web site at home. He calls his parents and asks them to send the password as a text message.

The general competition ends around 4 PM, the same time that the Ivy League decisions are posted online. Andrew's team is in first place with a comfortable ninety-point lead. But there is no time to savor the accomplishment. He has only thirty minutes before he must report back for the play-off round in which the top four teams will compete.

Andrew runs upstairs to check his friend's laptop. He jams the plastic room key in the lock and fiddles with the doorknob, waiting for the magnetic code to register. A green light about the size of a Tic Tac flashes above the handle. He swings open the door, plants himself at the desk, and taps his feet on the paisley carpet as he powers up the computer. Once online, he goes right to his e-mail account. Harvard sends e-mails rather than having students log on to a separate Web site.

It's hard to believe, but there it is, just sitting in his in-box. With his right index finger resting on the mouse, Andrew moves the small flashing arrow across the computer screen to the words OFFICE OF UNDERGRADUATE ADMISSIONS AND FINANCIAL AID in big bold typeface. *Click.*

Dear Mr. Frank Andrew Tessier, Jr.,

I am very sorry to inform you that it is not possible to offer you admission to the Class of 2011. I wish I were writing to report a different decision, but the competition was so rigorous this year that there were many outstanding young men and women to whom we could not offer places in the class.

Nearly twenty-three thousand students, a record number, applied to the entering class. The great majority of the applicants could certainly have been successful here academically, and most candidates presented strong personal and extracurricular credentials as well. The Committee was, therefore, faced with the necessity of choosing a class from a great many more talented and highly qualified students than it had room to admit.

We wish it were possible for us to admit more of our fine applicants, and we understand how difficult the college application process can be for students and their families. While the Committee conducted its deliberations with the utmost care, we know that no one can predict with certainty what an individual will accomplish during college or beyond. Past experience suggests that the particular college a student attends is far less important than what the student does to develop his or her strengths and talents over the next four years.

We very much appreciate the interest you have shown in Harvard College. We hope that you will accept the best wishes of the Committee for success in all your future endeavors.

Sincerely,
William R. Fitzsimmons
Dean of Admissions and Financial Aid
Harvard College

The rejection is a letdown but not a surprise. "I kind of think that with Harvard, you either get in by chance or if you have something that's really unique that no one else has," he says. "I am disappointed but I can't change it. So that's that." Andrew has no time to check his other Ivy League applications because he must report back to the tournament for the play-off round. Although he feels a little shaky standing up from the computer, he decides to push the bad news out of his mind and heads downstairs.

Andrew doesn't tell anyone about not getting into Harvard. Instead, he resolves to direct his energy toward winning the competition. Over the next two hours, his team answers as many problems as they can. But the play-off questions are much more difficult, and they struggle for the first time all day. They know that their lead is dwindling, but they won't find out their final score until tomorrow.

Around 6:45 PM, Andrew goes back upstairs to check on the rest of his applications. The sting of the Harvard decision dilutes his eagerness, and he feels less secure about his chances of getting into an Ivy League college. Andrew can feel his heart beating fast against his ribcage as he brings up the Web browser and types in the address for the Princeton University Undergraduate Admissions Office. He presses ENTER and waits for the screen to change.

Andrew is waitlisted at Princeton.

In general, colleges keep waitlists for the same reason that airlines overbook flights—it is difficult to accurately estimate how many people will turn up to claim their spots. If fewer students than expected decide to enroll, colleges can admit their "second choice" applicants.

Creating a waitlist also helps a college to preserve a desirable public image. Waitlisting a student who has done everything "right" can be a way to soften the blow of rejection, even though this student has little to no chance of ever getting accepted. Colleges want to be seen by the public as both selective and accessible (hard to get into for everyone else, but easy for me). Students will apply only if they think they have a chance, albeit small, of getting in.

Because of the increase in talented applicants, waitlists have been growing in recent years, according to the National Association for College Admission Counseling. The most selective colleges each waitlist more than a thousand students. The list decreases significantly as most students enroll at other schools. Those who are left usually receive a final decision by May or June, but few, if any, students are eventually admitted. Last year, Princeton did not admit a single student from their waitlist.

Being on a waitlist isn't like taking a number at the bakery. College waitlists are not ranked. If spots open up, admissions officers review all waitlisted applicants, taking into account each student's senior year grades. They also consider institutional needs, like increasing the size of the music department or making sure they have enough students from Nebraska. A student's desire to enroll is important. To use the airline analogy, people who make the most noise have the best chance of getting on the plane. This is also one of the few times when admissions officers get to advocate for particular students whom they really like.

Andrew understands that getting waitlisted at Princeton will likely amount to a rejection. "I'm definitely bummed, because now it's zero for two for the Ivies," he says. "Maybe I didn't have as good of a shot as I thought I did."

As he contemplates the situation, Andrew receives a text message on his phone from his parents. It's the code to log on to the U Penn admissions Web site—his last chance at an Ivy League acceptance. He types in the password like he is following a recipe, looking back and forth between the keyboard and his cell phone to make sure he gets it right. It takes a few seconds for the computer to verify his information and release the decision.

Yes! He got into the University of Pennsylvania.

Andrew goes back downstairs to find two of his friends who had gotten into U Penn early decision. They high five and hug, saying things like, "It would be so awesome to go to school together" and "You really should come with us next year."

A little while later, Andrew calls his parents to tell them the Ivy League decisions. "I think my mom is a little bummed out about Harvard. She's more bummed out than I am," he says.

LISA

It is hard to keep track of time when you are crisscrossing the globe for gymnastics competitions. Lisa is officially on the road to the 2008 Olympics. She is so disoriented that she doesn't realize that today is the day that Harvard announces who will be part of the class of 2011.

Now in top form, Lisa is getting noticed by all the right people. She delivered her best international performances to date in the Grand Prix competition in Russia and the World Cup competition in the Ukraine, where she placed 25, one of the highest rankings ever for an American gymnast. She just returned from Europe a few days ago and is waiting for her upcoming travel itinerary from the USA Gymnastics Federation. She begins the morning like normal. She wakes up early; eats her usual breakfast of eggs, fruit, and juice; and heads to the gym for her regular five-hour training session.

As usual, Lisa's mother is waiting for her in the parking lot of her gym after practice. Lisa opens the passenger-side door of the family's black minivan and slides in with her gym bag. They even notice the significance of the date until they get back home.

"It was really weird," Lisa says. "All of the sudden, I remembered 'Oh yeah, Harvard decisions come out today.'" Since she got into Yale back in December, Lisa hasn't thought much about college, especially because she knows she will defer her enrollment for a year to concentrate on gymnastics full-time. Her sights are set on the Olympics.

After tossing her gym bag on the floor, Lisa heads straight to her computer. As she waits for the system to load, she wonders whether or not she will have time for a visit to Cambridge before she leaves for Europe in less than two weeks. She was hoping to go to Yale for their admitted student weekend anyway, so maybe she can squeeze in the trip.

Lisa opens her Web browser and notices her mother lingering by the doorway. "Good luck," she says from across the room. They smile at each other as Lisa clicks on the e-mail from the Office of Admissions and Financial Aid. The e-mail seems ambiguous at first but Lisa soon understands the message.

Dear Ms. Lisa Wang,

I am writing to inform you that the Committee on Admissions and Financial Aid cannot at this time make a final decision on your application for a place in next year's entering class. However, because of your outstanding achievements and promise, the Committee has voted to place your name on a waiting list of men and women for whom we hope places may become available later. . . .

The number of students to be admitted from our waiting list will depend entirely on the number of students who decline our offer of admission. That number has varied greatly from year to year. In some recent years, we have admitted over one hundred candidates. In other years, it has not been possible to admit anyone from the waiting list. . . .

We hope you will decide to remain a candidate. Over the years, some of our very best students have been admitted from our waiting list. . . .

Sincerely,
William R. Fitzsimmons
Dean of Admissions and Financial Aid
Harvard College

"I got waitlisted," Lisa informs her mother, who runs over to see the evidence. They are both stunned. Her mother reads the e-mail again and then leans over the back of Lisa's chair to embrace her daughter from behind. The disappointment hits Lisa like a fallen tree branch on a windy afternoon.

"Rejection is never good," Lisa says. "Now I'm just questioning everything, wondering what I did wrong. Maybe I would have done better without the interview." She is convinced that telling her Harvard alumni interviewer that she was accepted early to Yale had a highly negative impact on her application.

While it is difficult to speculate on any specific part of a student's application, it is unlikely that Harvard based their decision solely on Lisa's alumni interview. Only in rare circumstances—like if a student made a racist remark or offensive comment—could an alumni interview possibly make or break an admissions decision. It's doubtful that the Harvard staff would turn down Lisa just because her interviewer reported that she also got into Yale.

Lisa e-mails me the next day with good news: "I got into Stanford!!!!!!!!!!!!!!!!!!!! YAYY! hahaha. I don't know why but it makes me really, really happy. At least I know 2 other phenomenal schools want me!!"

She now has two weeks before she must return to Europe for gymnastics. In the meantime, Lisa has to decide which college is right for her.

NABIL

After MIT, the other colleges I applied to can only be anticlimactic," Nabil says. Even so, he heads to the library after his class at the University of Memphis on March 29 to meet up with a friend and check the rest of the decisions.

Nabil scans through the messages in his in-box. There it is—an e-mail from the Harvard Office of Admissions and Financial Aid. He notices that he also has a message from the University of Chicago. This e-mail comes as a surprise, as he wasn't sure when he would hear from Chicago.

Nabil doesn't debate which school is more important. He clicks on the Harvard e-mail first. Despite his affection for MIT, he wanted to go to Harvard from the beginning and still might choose to enroll there.

Nabil reads a few sentences before realizing that he has been put on the Harvard waitlist. He was expecting to get in and wonders why they didn't accept him. Maybe he would have gotten in if he had applied early. There's nothing he can do about it now, though, so he scrolls through the messages in his in-box and opens the e-mail from the University of Chicago.

Dear Mr. Abdurehman,

I am pleased to inform you that you have been admitted to the University of Chicago, Class of 2011. Congratulations! You should be proud of the accomplishments and promise that led to your selection.

We feel a particularly strong responsibility to admit students who are not only qualified but who are ready to continue the crucial business of educating themselves. You have been se-lected by our faculty and admissions counselors because you recognize the pleasure—the absolute joy—to be found in active, creative learning. Our decision was not based on numbers but on your achievements and your words, a difficult determination to make but one that gives proper honor to the University and to you.

You have the chance to be part of a school with a glorious his-tory and an exciting present. We look to you to help us grow, to grow with us, and to be part of a tradition that elevates us all.

Yours truly,
Theodore A. O'Neill
Dean of Admissions

P.S. A letter of admission and accompanying information have been sent through the mail.

P.P.S. We have prepared a Web site for admitted students where you can reply to your offer of admission, sign up for campus visit programs, and communicate with your classmates through a blog and bulletin boards. We invite you to log in with your Uncom-mon username and password at thickenvelope.uchicago.edu.

Nabil was pretty sure that he would be accepted to the Univer-sity of Chicago, but he feels gratified to see the letter in print. Now it's time to check on Princeton, a school he's less certain about. He would rather go to MIT anyway, so it almost doesn't matter what the e-mail says, he tells himself.

The first thing Nabil sees when he logs onto the Princeton Web site is their oversize logo with the school emblem and a large pic-ture of an orange and black tiger, the school mascot. He reads:

CONGRATULATIONS!

The committee and I are pleased to offer you admission to the Princeton Class of 2011. Earlier today we mailed you a letter of admission and a folder of information, including details for admitted students who would like to visit campus in the coming weeks. If you applied for financial aid, a message from the Financial Office is included below. You will find more extensive information about your financial aid award in the mailing you will receive.

If you have any questions about Princeton's academic program, residential life, or a particular interest, please let us know and we will help you get the answers. To learn more about the April Hosting program, and to register, please go to http://www. princeton.edu/aprilhosting/.

Thank you for applying. We are delighted to be offering you a place in next year's freshman class at Princeton.

Congratulations again.
Janet Lavin Rapelye
Dean of Admission

"I can't believe it," Nabil tells me after reading the letter. "Princeton is offering me a $31,000 scholarship. It's just so *huge*!" He thinks back to all the skeptics who questioned how he could afford the colleges on his list and hopes that MIT's financial aid package will be comparable.

"Amazing or not, I was actually relieved that I didn't get into Harvard," Nabil says about an hour after receiving their response. It would have been hard to justify going to MIT over Harvard, even though he believes that this is where he will be most happy. "It's more important to be at a place you love than to go to the college that's the most prestigious," he professes.

Nabil's fat envelopes arrive at his house a few days later. He is accepted at his safety school, Carnegie Mellon, and finds out that the University of Chicago has chosen him as a College Honor Scholar, which comes with a full-tuition merit scholarship, about $35,000 each year. Nabil is one of only twenty students selected for this award from the 10,408 who applied in 2007. "Everyone's happy for me and believes I deserve it," he says. I've never seen him so fulfilled before. He beams like someone whose long-shot horse just crossed the finish line first.

Nabil is still set on going to MIT. There's only one thing stopping him from saying yes immediately—he hasn't gotten his financial aid package from them. His fat envelope from MIT included a letter requesting additional tax forms from his father before they can calculate his award. "I just called to tell them that the one form they said we were missing didn't apply to us," he says. "Chicago's asking us to pay $15,000 and Princeton is asking for $16,000. Even if MIT asks that we pay $25,000—which they really can't, can they?—I still don't see me turning them down because I like it there so much. I just think I fit in there."

MARLENE

Marlene has been fairly composed for most of the day. But when the last school bell rings, with four more hours until the Ivy League decisions are posted, she knows there's no way she can just go home and hang out. She needs to be distracted. As much as she hated having to wait months for the verdicts, there is still that chance of everything working out. In a few hours, this portion of her life will come to an end. She will know her options once and for all.

Marlene decides to go to a local diner with her friend Carolin. They choose a booth next to a jukebox stocked with Bon Jovi and Prince songs but don't bother making any selections. Even though she's seen the enormous menu countless times, Marlene reads through the entire thing, considering every entree from pancakes to pickled herring. She settles on the pizza burger, a hamburger with mozzarella cheese and tomato sauce.

"What?" Marlene asks Carolin several times throughout their conversation. Carolin graduated from New Rochelle last year and is a freshman at Westchester Community College. Though it feels good to be with someone who is not obsessed with the college rat race, Marlene is too distracted to concentrate on the discussion. She can't stop staring at the fluorescent clock on the wall above the cash register. The waitress puts an oversized plate with a pizza burger and fries in front of her, but she is too nervous to eat. The fries feel dry and mushy in her mouth so she pushes them around on the plate, drowning them in ketchup just for fun.

Marlene gets back to her apartment around 4:30 PM. No one is home, except for her father, who is taking a nap in his room. She slips into the house unnoticed and logs on to the computer in the living room. "I'm getting so many instant messages," she says. "Everyone, of course, assumes that I'm getting in, so they aren't asking *if* I got in but *where*." She ignores most of the messages. Until she knows the outcome, she wants to talk only to Carolin and her sister Yvonne.

By 5 PM, the Harvard e-mail still hasn't arrived. Marlene tries to log on to the U Penn, Yale, and Dartmouth Web sites, but they are overloaded with requests from thousands of applicants attempting to access their admissions decisions at the same time. She keeps trying. Yale is the first Web site to let her through. It's a rejection.

She tells her sister about it over Instant Messenger. "It's just one school, it's no big deal," she writes, remaining optimistic. Another friend, a student at Dartmouth, told her that he didn't get into Yale either. Anyway, she still has three more schools to check.

Marlene goes back to the U Penn Web site and this time is able to log on. As she types in her password, she remembers how much she loved the campus when she visited. She imagines how amazing it would feel to get in and how great it would be to go there. *Come on. Come on. Let this work out.*

It is not good news. Marlene is rejected. Tears well up in her big brown eyes. She tries to fight them off, pull herself together, and check the next Web site. But something inside is already defeated.

All the instant messages from curious friends that pop up on her screen just seem to be mocking her as she logs on to the Dartmouth server. The tears come down harder when she reads that they wait-listed her.

Since there's nothing from Harvard in her in-box, Marlene shuts down the computer. Her cell phone starts ringing but the last thing she wants to do is talk to anyone. She turns it off, runs into her room, and locks the door. Marlene throws herself on her bed and buries her head in her pillow.

Half an hour later, Marlene emerges from her room and goes toward the computer. "I might as well just confirm that I got rejected," she says. Her prediction is verified when she opens the e-mail in her in-box. Harvard rejected her.

Marlene locks herself in her room. The tears, gulps, and moans that have been building up inside of her for months come gushing out. There's no reason to hold it in anymore; there are no more bright sides to look at or spirits to boost. She decides to keep the news from her parents for now. She isn't ready to face them yet. They'll just feel sorry for her, which will only make it worse.

Late that evening, she starts to return a few messages. "All these 'I'm sorry's' make me feel like someone just died," she says. She avoids the computer for the rest of the night and doesn't go to school the next day.

· NINE ·

"I have an Asian fan club"

ANDREW

Andrew's mother is waiting for him when he gets home from school on April 3. "You got a letter from Washington and Lee," she says, pointing to the one envelope he's been waiting for, which is sitting on the dining room table. The business-size envelope looks nothing like the enormous packages that Andrew got from the other colleges, which isn't a good sign. "It's not like everything is riding on this," he reminds himself as he picks it up.

Andrew was disappointed when he found out that he didn't get into Stanford a few days ago, but he is resolved to move forward. He still got into most of the colleges that he applied to, including the University of Pennsylvania, Duke, Vanderbilt, the University of Virginia, and Johns Hopkins, and he got a full scholarship to Louisiana State. He also decided to remain on the waitlist for Princeton just in case. The only thing holding him back from making any major college decisions is whether or not he got the Washington and Lee scholarship. "I don't know if the fact that they already gave a scholarship to my sister will work against me," he says. "They might not want to give two scholarships to the same family."

Andrew opens the envelope from Washington and Lee and finds several pieces of paper inside, each of them folded separately. He pulls out the first page and begins reading as his mother quietly watches from twenty feet away, until she realizes that her presence is probably making him nervous and decides to slip out of the room. The letter informs him that he got into Washington and Lee, but there's no mention of the scholarship. Andrew shrugs his shoulders and unfolds the next page, which asks students to respond to the offer of admission by May 1. "All right, I definitely didn't get it," Andrew thinks to himself and opens the final letter. It must be some information about campus housing or something like that.

Dear Andrew,

   Congratulations! On behalf of the George Washington Honor Scholarship Committee of Washington and Lee University . . . I am pleased to inform you that you have been the designated winner of a $44,170 George Washington Honor Scholarship which covers the cost of tuition and fees, as well as standard room and board. . . .

   This scholarship will be renewable for each year of undergraduate work at Washington and Lee, provided you maintain a grade point average of 3.0. Other scholarships or resources that you receive will not decrease your George Washington Honor Scholarship unless, taken as a whole, all of your scholarships, prizes et cetera, including the Honor Scholarship, exceed Washington and Lee's annual standard cost of attendance ($47,300 in 2007–08). . . .

   Again, my sincere congratulations on your impressive record. Please contact me if I can provide further information on the George Washington Honor Scholarship, or if I can be of assistance to you in any other way. I feel you would make an invaluable addition to this campus community and hope you will join us as a member of the Class of 2011.

Sincerely,
Erin Hutchinson
Senior Assistant Director of Admissions
and Honor Scholarship Coordinator

"Look!" Andrew exclaims, calling his mother back into the room and holding out the paper in his hand for her to see. She realizes it must be good news and runs over to hug him. Only 25 of the 4,215 students who applied this year were offered a full-tuition scholarship. Her son is one of them.

Andrew feels like he just won the lottery, which is not far off considering the size of his scholarship. "I can't believe I just got two hundred thousand dollars for college, and the award goes up with tuition every year," he says. "On top of that, I can use my seven hundred fifty dollars from the National Merit Scholarship for books and stuff." He decides to rule out all the other colleges except for U Penn. He's already been to Washington and Lee, so he makes arrangements to visit Philadelphia a few days later.

ANDREW DOES A DOUBLE take while walking across the University of Pennsylvania campus. Somewhere between the Admissions Office and the library, he notices a group of girls sitting around in a circle. Normally, he wouldn't stop to ogle but this time he just can't help but stare. Each of the girls has covered her face in green paint.

"Hey, what's up?" asks Andrew, not wanting to be rude. They've probably noticed him gawking, so he might as well say hi. The girls don't respond. Maybe they didn't hear him.

"How's it going?" he asks again. This time, they make an exaggerated effort to ignore him, purposely looking in every direction but his. Andrew wonders what he did wrong. Are they mad at him for staring? Is he standing too close? Does he have a big "loser" sign on his back? He feels like a senior citizen at a rock concert. He has no idea what is going on.

"I wish I could talk to the guy in the blue sweatshirt," one of the girls says to her friend after what feels like eons of awkward silence. "Too bad we're *pledging,* and we can't talk to anyone." Andrew feels relieved to be clued in. The silliness of the hazing ritual makes him laugh.

April is known as one of the busiest months in the admissions calendar. Now that the decisions have been announced, campuses all over the country are once again rolling out the red carpet to attract students. To keep their yield up, colleges host activity-filled recruiting events throughout the month of April to convince admitted students to enroll. The itinerary usually includes things like campus tours, introductions to professors, free meals, and club-sponsored parties. Students generally have until May 1 to choose where they will be next year.

Andrew arrives in Philadelphia on the morning of April 6. Rather than stay in one of the hotels recommended on the college's Web site, he hooked up with the Kite and Key Society, a service organization on campus, through the Internet to see if someone might agree to host him. They arranged for him to stay with a transfer student named Jay, who lives in a high-rise dorm with rooms that are laid out like apartments. After meeting up at the Admissions Office, Jay helps Andrew drop his stuff off in his dorm room and then goes off to do some schoolwork. Andrew decides to explore the campus on his own for a few hours. "I want to get a feel for the place and talk to people to see what it's like," he says.

Walking around the University of Pennsylvania is like wearing earplugs on a noisy, crowded plane. The tranquillity of old oak

trees, Gothic stone towers, and stronghold arches makes it is easy
to forget about the raucous city just outside the campus gates. Andrew enjoys wandering around, especially when he gets to Locust
Avenue, where many student organizations—from hip-hop dance
clubs to Habitat for Humanity—have set up recruitment and fund-
raising tables. They sell things like T-shirts and tickets to support
their various causes.

After a few hours, Andrew finds Jay, and the two of them go to
the Admissions Office to pick up another prospective student who
is also bunking with them tonight. "It was interesting to sleep in a
dorm," Andrew says. "We stayed up until two or three in the morning, just talking about everything. It was totally different from the
admissions officer-y perspective."

The next morning, Andrew takes the Penn Previews campus
tour, which he describes as "kind of boring, mainly because I had
already walked around so much." Afterward, all the prospective
students are assigned to have lunch with several faculty members
from the individual departments to which they applied. Andrew
eats with an engineering professor who asks him which colleges
he is considering. The professor is highly impressed when Andrew
tells him about the Washington and Lee Scholarship. "I could tell
that he was sort of thinking that I should probably take the scholarship and save hundreds of thousands of dollars. He knows how
expensive U Penn is," Andrew reports.

Halfway through the lunch, Andrew and the professor are joined
by a female student in the Management and Technology Program,
an interdisciplinary program cosponsored by Penn Engineering
and the Wharton School of Business. The Management and Technology Program is one of the most selective undergraduate programs in the country, though a representative of the university tells
me that they refuse to disclose the exact number of applications
they receive for the program because they don't want potential candidates to be "too focused on numbers." A receptionist unofficially

reports that they accepted about sixty applicants from the four hundred students who applied in 2006–2007.

The young woman gushes about the opportunities she's had as a Management and Technology student and how she is looking forward to her investment banking job next year. "Are you kidding me?" Andrew responds when she tells him that she'll be working more than a hundred hours a week next year. This is the second future investment banker that he has met during the visit, and he can't fathom why someone would take a job with such brutal hours. "I want to live, not just work," he says. "I enjoy business a little, and investment banking sounds kind of cool, but those hours really turn me off. That sort of program just isn't for me."

After lunch, Andrew takes a tour of the engineering department and sits in on a five-person student panel, which he describes as "interesting and frank." They talk about classes, social life, and university policies. "U Penn is a very 'preprofessional' school," Andrew observes. "The classes aren't given just for their own sake; they are to prepare you for the real world." Though he wants to become an engineer, he is more drawn to a liberal arts environment, where students receive a broad education in many different subjects.

Around three in the afternoon, Andrew hops in a cab to the airport. The trip gave him exactly what he needed—a real sense of what it would be like to be a student at the University of Pennsylvania. The next day, we have a long phone conversation about his college decisions.

"Penn's a really good school," Andrew says. "The campus is beautiful and the people were really smart. But I'm not in *love* with it. Of course, the money thing is major, so W and L seems like the most well-rounded choice. The professors are competent and engaging. Plus, they have no TAs. I want to go to the best college that makes sense."

Andrew decides to accept the George Washington Scholarship at Washington and Lee University. Though Princeton took thirty students from the waitlist this year, Andrew finds out a few weeks later that he did not get in. "Yeah, I'd like to go to Princeton and everything, but I'm happy where I am. And I have a full scholarship," he says.

MARLENE

The week after the college decisions are announced, I meet up with Marlene at our regular Starbucks. She looks like she's just returned from a long weekend in the country. When I ask her how she's handling the rejections, she rolls her eyes and says, "Thursday was just horrible. I wasn't expecting to get in, but my family had like no clue what was going on. I finally told my mom on Friday. She got a little teary-eyed, but then she went on to say that she's proud of me, yada, yada." Marlene seems almost embarrassed for having taken the whole thing so seriously. "I was sad and all, but I'm over that stage. Every time someone says 'I'm sorry' when they hear that I didn't get in, I'm like, 'Why are you sorry? No one died.'"

In the past few days, Marlene found out that she has been waitlisted at Williams College and accepted to Colgate. For next year, Colgate is offering her $46,155 in financial aid (including $1,500 in Perkins Loans) to cover their $48,055 cost of attendance. "They're only expecting me to contribute $1,900 extra, which is *amazing*," she exclaims. If Marlene goes to Colgate, she'll graduate with about $14,000 in debt.

"I'm honestly shocked that Colgate gave me so much," Marlene says. "But I still think I'll like Brandeis better. I don't know about my financial aid award for Trinity yet, but at least the major waiting is over." She stretches out the "r" at the end of the word "over" and catalogs the outcome of her college applications, holding up a finger each time she mentions the name of a school. "Accepted—Brandeis, U Rochester, Trinity, Colgate, Stony Brook. Waitlisted—

Dartmouth, Williams. Rejected—Harvard, Yale, Penn." Marlene's eyes widen like she's taking in a panoramic view. She cocks her head and says, "Not too bad."

Several days later, I get an e-mail from Marlene with "I am the biggest idiot ever" in the subject line. She just received her financial aid award from Trinity, and it is basically the equivalent of a full ride. They are offering her $45,700 in grants to cover the $45,864 cost of attendance, which means that she could easily make up the gap by taking a part-time or summer job. The only problem is that Marlene has already declined her acceptance. She had assumed that Trinity wasn't going to give her any money because she hadn't received their financial aid award until just now.

I advise Marlene to try calling the Admissions Office to explain the situation and ask them to disregard her reply. Since the May 1 deadline hasn't passed, most colleges are willing to be flexible, especially if a student has a good reason for making such a mistake. The next day, Marlene gets in touch with a Trinity College official, who assures her that she can have a few more weeks to consider the college. She just has to send him an e-mail explaining what happened so that he has a record of the misunderstanding. Marlene makes plans to go up to Hartford to see the Trinity campus with her parents.

LISA

I will just disappear from the face of the western hemisphere," Lisa jokes. She has accepted the Russian Gymnastics Federation's invitation to train in Moscow at least until the World Cup competition in September. Not only that, but the USA Gymnastics Federation is financing all of her training and travel expenses. The only problem is that her hectic schedule allows her only a little more than a week to decide between Stanford and Yale before she heads to Europe for the upcoming round of training and competitions.

Over the next few months, Lisa will take part in international Grand Prix and World Cup competitions in Spain, Portugal, Belarus, the Czech Republic, Israel, and Brazil. All this travel is not without its downside. "I'm kinda sad I'll be missing my senior prom and high school graduation, and all the yearbook signing things," she explains. "But when I'm handed an opportunity like this, I just can't turn it down."

After spending the morning of April 7 at gymnastics practice, Lisa and her family head to downtown Chicago, where I meet up with them at a luncheon for admitted students sponsored by the Yale alumni club. Lisa's parents, Ping and Cindy, greet me warmly as I enter the restaurant, which is more like a glorified sports bar with most of the patrons watching baseball on several flat-panel monitors mounted on the walls. The Yale students are gathered in the back section of the restaurant eating pizza and drinking soda from a buffet table. The event looks kind of like a children's birthday party with kids on one side of the room and parents on the other.

Lisa is chatting with several students in a corner, so I sit down next to Ping and Cindy. They are both more dressed up than usual. Ping has donned an elegant blazer, and this is the first time I've ever seen Cindy wearing makeup. As we talk, they casually glance over at Lisa, checking to see if she is making friends, like it's her first day of kindergarten.

There have been many changes since the last time I saw the Wangs at the Olympic Training Center in Colorado Springs. They are moving to Princeton, New Jersey, over the summer as Ping is being transferred to an office in New York City. They're looking forward to the move. They already have some friends there and enjoy the community, plus Princeton also has a good school system in which they will enroll Lisa's younger brother. Ping and Cindy both confess that they really want Lisa to choose Yale over Stanford because it is so much closer to their new house on the East Coast. They are disappointed that Harvard is not an option for her as well.

After the luncheon, Lisa and I find somewhere more intimate to talk. This is our last opportunity to speak in person for the next few months. "I probably won't even be back in the States until next July," she explains. "It's really stressful because I'm still wavering between Yale and Stanford. I didn't expect to be so conflicted."

We head over to a hip coffeehouse a few blocks away and end up being served organic tea by a woman wearing a mod shift dress, plentiful tattoos, and lots of piercings. It's the kind of place they don't have in Lisa's suburban hometown. But with her purple-streaked hair and canvas shoulder bag, she seems to fit right in with the students typing on their laptops and talking about things like whether or not Barack Obama should run for president.

About two weeks have gone by since Lisa was accepted to Stanford, and she still hasn't decided if she wants to go there or to Yale. She spends most of our conversation comparing the two colleges, saying things like, "Yale seems more focused on undergrads while Stanford seems like it might be more graduate school oriented," and "Stanford has a big sports program so you probably get more of the jock culture," and "The thing I like about Yale is the residential college system. Stanford is more sprawling."

Yale is courting Lisa like a suitor trying to dance with the homecoming queen. In the past few days alone, she has received phone calls from two alumni, her interviewer and a more recent graduate who also went to Stevenson High School. She also got a call from the admissions officer who reviewed her file and wrote the note of congratulations on her acceptance letter. This is especially impressive because, in my experience, admissions officers do not personally call students. "At the moment, I feel like Yale did more to reach out to me, and Stanford is more of an institution," Lisa says. Naturally, all the attention from Yale left a favorable impression, but she is still not completely convinced that she should go there over Stanford.

Stanford has one particular advantage in Lisa's eyes. "I feel like I got into Stanford purely on my own merit," she explains. "With

Harvard and Yale, I sent in a supplement with all my gymnastics clips and stuff, but Stanford specifically said no supplements, so I just did the regular application. All they knew about my gymnastics was what I wrote in my essays." Of course, an admissions officer could still figure out the nature of Lisa's athletic achievements based on her résumé, even without the supplement. Either way, neither Yale nor Stanford would base their admissions decision solely on gymnastics. Lisa has the academic talent to justify any college acceptance, but even top students always question why they got in and others didn't.

Though Lisa's schedule is packed before she leaves for Europe, I encourage her to visit Stanford and Yale. "This is important," I say. "You have earned the right to make an informed decision about your college education."

A few days later, Lisa e-mails me with her itinerary. On Thursday, April 12, she will arrive at Stanford at 8 PM, where she'll spend a little more than a day before leaving on an 11:30 PM. flight the next night. She'll get back to Chicago at 5:20 AM on Saturday and go to gymnastics at noon, after which she'll sleep a little and pack for her trip to Spain. On Monday, April 16, she'll go to practice in the morning, fly to New York City around 6 PM, take the train to New Haven, and get to Yale around midnight. She'll spend Tuesday on the Yale campus and take the train back to LaGuardia Airport for an 8 PM flight to Chicago, from where she'll depart the following afternoon to compete in Spain.

"I was really lucky that I could squeeze everything in," she writes. "Now, I just have to hope that all the flights will go smoothly!"

THE NEXT TIME I talk to Lisa, she is waiting to catch a plane back to Chicago from New York. With only two hours of sleep in the past two days, her voice is hoarse and she has caught a cold. She is coughing and sniffling on the other end of the phone as she describes her whirlwind campus visits.

"Everything went wrong on the trip to Yale," Lisa explains. "Today was just a really, really bad day. It rained the whole time and I was so exhausted." Lisa's plane to New York City was delayed so she didn't get in until 1 AM. Her father picked her up, and she slept for about an hour at the apartment that his company is renting for him in the city. The two of them took the 5:30 AM train up to New Haven and were standing in front of the Yale Admissions Office when it opened that morning.

"The admissions officer who was soliciting me shook my hand and said, 'Yours was one of the first applications that I read, and I was really impressed,' which made me feel really good," Lisa says.

After collecting her registration packet, Lisa and her father went to the dean's address to admitted students, which was followed by a student panel on diversity. Afterward, they toured the residential colleges and dining halls before getting on a train back to New York. "I'm just so tired right now, and I felt like I didn't really get enough time on the campus," she continues, her voice cracking from her congestion.

I ask how the trip to Stanford went. "Stanford was really nice," Lisa answers. "I had a great host and great weather. But I think after everything, I feel like with my interests and extracurriculars Yale is a better fit." After the Olympics, Lisa intends to study politics and journalism, so she wants to be close to Washington, D.C.

"Also, both my parents really want me to go to Yale, so you know," she continues. "Plus, even if I went to Stanford, I feel like the majority of people will stay in California, and I'll probably end up on the East Coast."

"So you're decided on Yale?" I ask.

"Yeah, I think so," she answers.

"Are you happy with your decision?"

"Yeah, but I'm too tired to think right now," Lisa says and lets out a weak chuckle. I wish her safe travels, and we say good-bye.

MARLENE

On the afternoon of April 18, Marlene's parents both drive her to midtown Manhattan, where she boards a bus headed to the Brandeis campus in Waltham, Massachusetts. There is a lot riding on this visit. "I would have applied to completely different schools if I could do it over again," she says. "I realized that I really do not want to be at an all-white college in the middle of nowhere." Her new resolution means that she has already ruled out two of her college options, Colgate University and the University of Rochester. She also has little interest in Dartmouth or Williams, even if they do take her off the waitlist.

Last weekend, Marlene and her parents visited Trinity College in Hartford, Connecticut. "I hated it, so it's off my list," she declares. "It's in the middle of the ghetto and it's all white people. I really, really hope that I like Brandeis because it's kind of like my only option."

Marlene arrives at the Brandeis campus around 8 PM and is greeted by a friend of hers, Dana, who graduated from New Rochelle High School last year. Dana and her best friend have agreed to host five girls, including Marlene, for the night. Marlene walks over to the dorm with the rest of the gang. The accommodations are comfortable, and everyone seems excited to meet the admitted students.

Named for the late Supreme Court Justice Louis Brandeis, Brandeis University was founded by the American Jewish community as a nonsectarian university in 1948. Admission is selective. Brandeis rejected about two thirds of the applicants who applied this year. Minority students make up about 12 percent of the student body, though Marlene feels comfortable being on a campus where the majority of students are Jewish. "It's kind of like New Rochelle," she jokes.

After dinner and an ice cream social, Marlene, her friend Dana, and the other four prospective students stay up until 2 AM, playing cards, eating pizza, and getting to know one another. She feels groggy when she wakes up the next morning at 8 AM to attend the president's address and tour the campus, which is nice, but not as spectacular as some of the American Colonial colleges like Yale and the University of Pennsylvania. Most of the square brick dorms were built in the 1960s and '70s, and the uninspired architecture makes them look dated. Some buildings are more impressive, however, like Unsen Castle, which resembles a Gothic tower, and the Rose Art Museum, which holds an impressive collection of paintings in a clean, modern space. Students hang out and play music at Cholmondeley's, a coffeehouse known on campus as Chum's, which is said to be the inspiration for Central Perk on *Friends*. The show's creators are both Brandeis alums.

During lunch, Marlene ends up sitting next to an administrator who works with the minority and first-generation college students on campus. "He was really nice and I talked to him about going premed because that's what I'm thinking of doing now," she says. After lunch, she goes to a biochemistry class, which she really enjoys, followed by a preprofessional health panel where "they talk about how Brandeis was above average for med school acceptances and stuff like that," she explains. Marlene also sits in on an anthropology course before picking her stuff up from Dana's dorm room and heading back on the bus to New York City.

"The thing I liked most about Brandeis was the people," Marlene says after the visit. "They were genuinely nice. Like if I was looking for a building or whatever, I didn't have to ask anyone. People just came up to me and asked if I needed directions. I'm definitely going to go there."

With the college admissions process behind her, I ask Marlene how she feels about the ordeal. "I do believe everything happens for a reason. I'm very excited about going to Brandeis, and I know I'll be happy there."

FELIX

At 7 AM on April 20, Felix and his friend Susan board a plane in Philadelphia and fly up to Cambridge, Massachusetts, to attend Harvard's Pre-Frosh Weekend for the class of 2011. At the same time, Americans are still mourning the tragic killing of thirty-two people on the Virginia Tech campus less than a week earlier. Outside of the cafés around town, the words "VT in our hearts, in our minds" are written in pink letters on small sidewalk chalkboards as a reminder of the calamity.

Felix and Susan are among the very first prospective students to turn up on the Harvard campus for the events. They head straight to the Admissions Office to register and meet their hosts for the weekend.

"What high school are you from?" asks the receptionist when they arrive.

"Conestoga High School," they respond in unison. Felix immediately follows up by saying, "Jinx. I won."

"We have been competitive since the fifth grade," Felix explains later that day when the three of us meet for coffee at the Au Bon Pain in Harvard Square. "I call her the female version of me." He cocks his head at Susan. "That's a compliment." She returns a knowing smile.

During registration, Felix ran into Erin Fehn, the admissions officer who had interviewed him months before. "Right when I gave my name, she remembered me before I remembered her," he says. "That was really cool." Felix and Susan are loaded up with colossal packets of maps, schedules, and flyers to guide them through the weekend's agenda. They are both being hosted by seniors, who will graduate in a few months. Felix isn't too impressed with his host's accommodations. "Maybe I'm too picky about the dorms, but I thought it was too industrial and the rooms weren't that nice."

"Felix's host is a neurobiology major, which I'm considering, and mine is a government major, which he's considering," his friend Susan explains. Both she and Felix are dressed in jeans and a sweatshirt; hers displays the Conestoga High School logo, while Felix is wearing a brand-new Harvard sweatshirt. "I also want to get one of those blazers that where you open it up, it's all crimson inside. It's just so elitist and preppy that I want it," he jokes.

Felix and Susan spend the morning walking around campus, visiting Harvard's regal libraries and eating lunch in Annenberg Hall, the freshman refectory that looks like the set of a *Harry Potter* movie. After lunch, they kill time playing chess outside of the Au Bon Pain in Harvard Square, where a memorable scene from *Good Will Hunting* was shot. The organized events—things like a student-run fashion show, a rap concert, a comedy show, and several parties—are scheduled for later tonight.

Looking over the itinerary and brochures, Felix waxes philosophic about the second semester of his senior year in high school. "I'm chilling out for the first time in my life, really," he says. "I'll come home with no homework and just sit there. I'm kind of like a lame duck congressman. It's kind of like I can't wait to leave but I also don't want to leave."

In a few weeks, Felix will begin a monthlong internship for which he will receive high school credit. Conestoga seniors are permitted to leave campus for a "culminating project," as long as they have completed the paperwork and prerequisites for internships, apprenticeships, and other activities. Felix will work for the Foreign Policy Research Institute in Philadelphia, a prestigious foreign relations think tank whose research interests include the war on terrorism, South Asian nuclear proliferation, U.S. relations with China and Russia, and issues pertaining to development in the Middle East. "I wanted my internship to mean something," he says.

Felix sighs as he looks around at all the students coming and going around Harvard Square. His acceptance has not offered the absolute personal fulfillment that he had expected. "I definitely thought that getting into Harvard was like the most important thing ever," he reminisces. "But once I got in, it was like okay. It's a hurdle that everyone has to go over. Once you're over, you're over." Though he's excited about his future here, Felix has had some doubts about Harvard. "Before, it was all about classes and academics, but senior year I've been going to a lot more parties and socializing and that stuff became more important."

"How are your friends reacting to the 'H bomb'?" I ask. The "H bomb" is a snooty term used by Harvard students to describe their alma mater ("dropping the H Bomb" refers to the act of telling others that you are enrolled at the university). I remember how strange it was when I first told people that I was going to Harvard. Many of them have strong reactions, expecting you to be exceptionally intelligent, incredibly stuck-up, or a combination of the two.

"People definitely treat you differently, which is why I never wear any Harvard clothes, unlike this guy," Susan says, pointing to Felix. "There's a difference between getting into Penn State and wearing a sweatshirt every day and getting into Harvard and wearing one. People think you're snobby or elitist."

"Yeah, some people get all weirded out by it, but what can you do?" Felix responds with a shrug of his shoulders.

Administrators at Conestoga High School have tried to curb some of the academic rivalry among students by changing the way that they flaunt college acceptances on the prominent "College Board." Starting this year, the tacks on the large map will not display the students' names, only the colleges where they are enrolled. "People were really upset," explains Felix. "Lots of people look forward to looking at the map every year. Our school is all about fame and recognition."

Such a competitive high school environment often breeds resentment of students like Felix and Susan, who have achieved a high degree of measurable academic success. After she got into

Harvard early, Susan withdrew all of her other college applications. Felix, however, still applied regular decision to Yale and MIT and was accepted to both. "No offense, but everyone thinks applying to MIT was kind of unnecessary because you can cross-register there if you go to Harvard," Susan tells him. "People were mad. There was definitely a backlash about that."

Even though Felix fell in love with Harvard, he applied to Yale and MIT because of his parents' encouragement and the fact that he wanted to keep his options open. Some of his classmates who were also applying to these schools felt threatened by this. They assumed that they would likely be compared to Felix. This fear is somewhat unfounded. While it is true that colleges are looking for the best students, they do not have quotas for the number of applicants that they will accept from a particular high school, nor do they directly compare applicants from the same school. However, they do consider variables like a student's class rank, which may promote the misconception that one student can "take" another student's place.

"Half of the kids were like, 'It's no big deal,' but some others were pissed," Felix responds to Susan's observation. "One person called me an asshole. I just said, 'Hi, good morning.' She responded like that and then told me that it's completely inappropriate if you get into Harvard to apply to Yale."

"She had the hardest time with colleges though," Susan replies.

"If I had a friend who got into Yale and then applied to Harvard and MIT, I wouldn't care at all," Felix says.

Susan agrees. "Misery loves company. People will talk about where they didn't get in more than where they did," she observes. "When my friends didn't get in to where they wanted to go, I couldn't find the words to console them. They didn't really want to hear that from me anyway. But it's so ridiculous!"

"It. Is. Ridiculous," Felix declares. "Like the juniors—" His voice trails off. He and Susan both roll their eyes.

"Oh my God. It's not even the juniors, it's like the *freshmen,*" Susan exclaims. "There are some freshmen who know everything about us because we got into Harvard. One time, I was coming out of the bathroom at school, and there was this little Asian girl yelling my name. I was like, 'Who are you?'"

"I have an Asian fan club," Felix says, half-kidding. He thinks back to when he first got into Harvard months ago. "Right after the college decisions came out it was the biggest gossip fest *ever.* After I got back from Hawaii, I was in school and heard this one kid go, 'That's Felix Zhang!' like I was some kind of celebrity."

Susan nods. "One sophomore e-mailed me and said, 'I can't tell you who, but my friend wants to know your class schedule from sophomore to senior year.' It was *so ridiculous,*" she says. "I'm happy that I got in, but it's different when people start analyzing what I did to get there."

"My biggest concern is that they'll all burn out 'cause they're trying to go above and beyond, like staying up until one AM," says Felix. "It's totally just this culture's fault and our school's not helping. I think it's the media hype too."

Felix laughs when I remind him how anxious he was just a few months ago and how badly he wanted to go to Harvard. "I guess I was consumed with it too. But it's really getting worse. I thought *I* was bad but the younger kids are just *freaking out.*"

Even administrators at Harvard have expressed public unease about the toll that lifelong college-prep and overgrooming can take on students. Harvard now officially encourages applicants to slow down and take time off between finishing high school and entering college, though only 4 percent of entering students accept the advice. This suggestion is posted on the Harvard admissions Web site in a message titled, "Time Out or Burn Out for the Next Generation," which acknowledges that selective colleges are perceived to contribute to the cultural pandemic of student anxiety. However, the authors stop short of accepting responsibility. They write:

Many of us are concerned that the pressures on today's students seem far more intense than those placed on previous generations. College admission—the chance to position oneself for "success" through the acquisition of the "right" college degree—looms large for increasing numbers of students. Particularly because selective colleges are perceived to be part of the problem, we want to do everything possible to help the students we enroll make the most of their opportunities, avoiding the much-reported "burnout" phenomenon that can keep them from reaching their full potential.

Of course, the quest for college admission is only one aspect of a much larger syndrome driving many students today. Stories about the latest twenty-something multimillionaires, the astronomical salaries for athletes and pop-music stars, and the often staggering compensation packages for CEOs only stimulate the frenzied search for the brass ring. More than ever, students (and their parents) seek to emulate those who win the "top prizes" and the accompanying disproportionate rewards.

As I watch Felix reflect on his experiences with college admissions, I am struck by how much he's changed from the anxious overachiever I first met back in August. "When I was applying to Harvard, I don't think it was for the right reasons. It was more for the name," he admits. "But I've thought about my different options, and there are just so many academic and social opportunities here. So I think I'm choosing Harvard for the right reasons now. *I think.*"

· TEN ·

"It's okay if you need to stop by a metaphorical gas station and get directions"

MARLENE

A week before her high school graduation, Marlene is like a
backpacker enjoying the first warm shower she's had in days.
Now that the mud and dirt are gone, and the journey behind her,
she is able to appreciate all that she has gained. "I'm really glad I'm
almost done," she says. "But I guess I'm also grateful that I got to go
to New Rochelle High School. Sometimes I wonder how I would've
turned out if my family had never moved here, you know?" She
nods and smiles at the occasional passerby as we walk down the
yellow and gray hallways of her high school one afternoon. The
walls, which just a few weeks ago were filled with fliers announcing
club meetings and SAT deadlines, are mostly empty.

Marlene's senior prom was held a few days ago, and she decided
that she couldn't really afford to go. "It basically came down to
either prom or getting a laptop for college and the laptop had prior-

ity," she explains. "Both my sisters got to go to theirs but I guess all three of us had different circumstances." The New Rochelle prom was held at the Copacabana in New York City, which meant that the tickets were extremely expensive. Marlene sighs before dictating the costs. "The tickets were like one hundred twenty dollars, then the limo would've been around one hundred seventy-five dollars, then there's the dress, hair, nails, after-prom parties, et cetera. So, yeah, unnecessary hassle."

Instead of letting the evening pass unnoticed, Marlene and some friends had made plans to go out to dinner in the city and then meet up with some of their classmates after the prom. The plans ended up getting canceled, however, when one of her friends had to back out to attend her prefreshman orientation at Queens College, a four-year school about forty-five minutes from New Rochelle. "I was okay with it until around five PM later that day. I saw some of the seniors where I live all dressed up and taking pictures outside our building," Marlene recounts.

Her sister Yvonne noticed that Marlene was a little bummed out, watching the others get ready for prom night. So she and her boyfriend took Marlene and her friend Carolin out for dinner at a local Mexican restaurant. "I was feeling a little regretful, but after that night, I didn't care. I talked to some people that went, and they said it was just okay," Marlene says.

Marlene has mixed emotions about her classmates. "I guess I just don't feel connected to most of them," she explains as we descend the concrete stairwell. "I'll keep in touch with some people but a lot of the friendships were superficial."

"Do you think you'll keep in touch with any of your teachers?" I ask.

"Not really. Maybe some teachers from ninth grade"—she pauses— "and Mr. Morris, and my Spanish teacher from this year."

We linger in the main entrance of New Rochelle High School, surrounded by trophy cases and flags from different countries around the world, which are supposed to symbolize the diversity of the student body. "New Rochelle High School is a huge public school and extremely diverse, but it can get really shady," Marlene comments, taking in her surroundings. "For instance, in the yearbook, there's a section entitled 'On the Run,' which is basically two pages dedicated to pictures of seniors and their cars. How unnecessary is that?"

I ask Marlene how she feels now that it's all over. "I don't regret applying to so many schools, or applying to all the schools that eventually rejected me," she replies. She ended up not getting in off the waitlist to either Dartmouth or Williams. "I honestly don't think that I would have been mentally ready to attend an Ivy League school, even though I really, really wanted to get into one."

The only concern still weighing on Marlene is the cost of going to Brandeis. Ironically, it was Yvonne who encouraged her to choose a less expensive school instead of taking on a hefty student loan burden. Sometime around spring break, Yvonne decided not to return to Elmira College. Without the academic support she needed, she was struggling in her classes and decided it just wasn't worth it. She'll be transferring to Westchester Community College next year and later on to a four-year college to finish her degree. Unfortunately, she has about $18,000 in loans from Elmira for this year alone.

"I feel like I truly and genuinely love Brandeis, but at the same time, I sometimes feel like I should have gone to Colgate or Trinity because of the money thing, especially since Elmira didn't end up working out for my sister," Marlene says.

"I remember the first time I met you, I said I wouldn't go to a school if I have to take out more than twenty thousand dollars total in loans," Marlene continues, shaking her head. "Look at me. I'm going to the school that gave me the least amount of money. Ugh. I think the fact that Elmira didn't work out for my sister still made me more cautious about what I was going to do in the end. I know that Brandeis's retention rate is ninety-six percent. That was the first thing I checked."

Marlene gets quiet for a moment before finishing, "I never told you, but after I decided to enroll at Brandeis and my sister decided to come home next year, I went through a period where I was seriously, seriously, seriously considering just going to Westchester Community College and then transferring because it would be *so much cheaper.* But of course I changed my mind back to Brandeis because I'm honestly ready to leave New Rochelle." She looks around the atrium and then focuses her gaze on the trophy cases as the corners of her mouth curl up.

"Now that I'm done with the whole thing, I feel like I truly comprehend how it all works and whatnot. I remember when I was in ninth, tenth, and maybe even eleventh grade, I had no idea how college worked, like what's the difference between an associate's, bachelor's, and master's degree, or what order you would get them in. I would go to Mrs. de Miranda or some other adult to try to get them to explain it to me, but I guess they never really understood what I was asking or something. So it's good in a sense, because now I know how graduate schools work and that I have time to do whatever I want to do."

Marlene has earned her achievements and confidence. "I love, love, love Brandeis," she gushes. "I know I have a lot of potential and I know I'll do great, graduate in four years, and then move on to greater things. Who knows? Maybe one day I'll own a nice big house here in New Rochelle or Scarsdale." She laughs like she can't believe the words that just came out of her mouth.

"You see," she says. "I'm more positive now."

ANDREW

B en looks so handsome—and so mature!" exclaims a blond-haired mother in a powder blue sundress as she kisses her friend on the cheek, leaving behind a faint mauve imprint.

"Thank you," the woman responds in a soft Southern accent. "I just can't believe the boys are graduating." Her diamond earrings sparkle from underneath her flaxen bob as she shakes her head from side to side.

A mostly female crowd is gathered outside the Pontchartrain Center in Kenner, Louisiana, greeting each other with lean-in hugs and compliments. They appear to be waiting for their husbands, who are trapped in a seemingly endless line of sedans, to park their cars and return to the building. The graduation ceremony for the Jesuit High School class of 2007 is scheduled to begin twenty minutes from now, at 8 PM sharp. This is Jesuit's 160th commencement, and every detail of the ritual has been planned in accordance with tradition.

Jesuit places a premium on punctuality. The ceremony is supposed to last exactly one hour. This morning, Andrew and his classmates had to practice for twice as long to ensure promptness. "That is Jesuit," he explains, "regimented, on time, and a ton of emphasis on ceremony." The teachers even have an office pool of bets on how long the graduation will last. Most of the wagers hover around fifty-five minutes.

The Pontchartrain Center is a newly constructed offbeat seventy-thousand-square-foot building with an events calendar that includes everything from the Great Southern Gun & Knife Trade Show to a performance by the Jefferson Ballet Dance Review. The main atrium is a series of glass gables with metal trusses and rafters that give the facility a very modern look. A young man with a military haircut and formal cadet uniform supervises the distribution of graduation programs from a dais in the center hall. Parents, grandparents, siblings, and friends thumb through the glossy twenty pages, pointing out names that they recognize as they shuffle into the auditorium.

The most prominent accent on the unadorned stage is a massive royal blue curtain backdrop. There are five empty leather chairs in the center and a wooden podium in the right corner behind a simple flower arrangement. With no reserved seats for graduates, it is unclear how they will enter or where they will sit.

It takes about ten minutes for the fashionable audience to fill most of the 3,500 seats. The men are dressed in modified versions of the Brooks Brothers' sports coat and tie ensemble, though I notice several dapper seersucker suits in the crowd. For the most part, the women wear Ann Taylor–type print dresses or pastel pantsuits and carry clutch purses to match their high-heeled sandals. Every toe looks perfectly polished in colors that would have names like Cotton Candy or Milky Way.

At exactly 8 PM, the entire auditorium suddenly goes as dark as a movie theater, except for the dim stage lights and the soft glow of video camera viewfinders sprinkled around the room. The suddenness makes it seem like there might have been a power outage, and several audience members look confused. Seconds later, the blue backdrop on the stage is slowly raised to reveal two rows of bleachers on which 270 tuxedo-clad graduates sit upright with their hands resting on their knees. The display looks like an art exhibit of perfectly uniform black-and-white figurines in fixed positions. It is an amazing sight.

The brass band starts to play "Pomp and Circumstance" over the applause and camera flashes. Faculty members march into the auditorium and sit in the first few rows. The president then asks everyone to rise for the national anthem and convocation prayer, which is led by one of the Jesuit priests in full garb. The boys stand at attention and sing softly, hands over their hearts. They then cross themselves in unison and lower their heads in prayer.

The president presents two awards for leadership before introducing the class valedictorians, who he describes as "the ten students with the highest overall academic averages." One by one, the boys descend from the bleachers to collect their polished plaques. Andrew is toward the end of the group. He stands as his name is called, strides down the aisle, and crosses the stage with a stoic expression on his face. He accepts his award with one hand and shakes the priest's hand with the other. A photographer snaps the exchange. Andrew returns to his seat.

One of the valedictorians—the young man with the highest numerical average in the senior year—gives a brief address. He uses a metaphor of a butterfly that emerges from its cocoon with underdeveloped wings and says, "Jesuit has prepared us for the obstacles we'll face as we continue to learn and grow." He also mentions how the school has rebuilt itself in such a short time after the "unbelievable interruption from normalcy" that was Hurricane Katrina.

It is time for the awarding of diplomas. The president asks the audience to respect the sanctity of the occasion by reserving their applause until each row of graduates has received their degrees. "Shouting and other noise-making is not in keeping with the dignity of this formal ceremony, and anyone who behaves otherwise will be escorted from the premises," he warns.

The degrees are awarded in order of achievement. There are two types of diplomas, "accelerated" and "college prep," and each of these has four categories of degree recipients: summa cum laude, magna cum laude, cum laude, and successful completion. Attendants carry the leather-bound documents in small stacks from backstage and hand them to the presenters.

The first row of graduates rises simultaneously. They look like waddling penguins, side-stepping toward the aisle without turning their backs to the audience. When his name is announced, the graduate strides across the stage to collect his diploma, flashes a smile for the photographer, and promptly returns to his position in the bleachers. In accordance with the instructions, the audience politely acknowledges the entire row after the last student in line has received his degree, at which point the next row of graduates stands in unison to repeat the procedure. The orderly ceremony moves quickly. The last boy to receive his diploma gets a subdued standing ovation from the crowd.

"Everyone wants to be your friend when you're on top," the president declares in his address to the graduates, which comes after the awarding of degrees. "The storms of 2005 challenged us, and we found out who our real friends are." He then goes on to touch on the themes of gratitude and patience, saying, "Greater achievement comes with deferred gratification. Society decays when people defer to instant gratification . . . be vigilant in guarding against self-entitlement. Where entitlement lives without truth, the perpetrators are seen as victims and the victims as evildoers." The president ends his address with a prayer and the band begins to play the Jesuit alma mater.

"We did it," a father whispers to his wife, resting his arm on her shoulder. She reaches over and squeezes his elbow as they smile at each other.

Everyone claps along as the band transitions to the Jesuit fight song, which signifies the conclusion of the convocation ceremonies. The audience begins to make their way out of the auditorium and the curtain closes on the graduates. The fight song ends with the words:

Jesuit High, our Alma Mater
Hear thy sons thy name proclaim to ev'ry ear.
We pledge our lives to thee
Our love, our trust and loyalty.

The entire graduation clocks in at under an hour. The teacher who guessed fifty-six minutes and thirty seconds wins the office pool.

NABIL

Can you change your glove?" Nabil asks the dark-skinned woman behind the Subway counter. There is a hint of recognition in the smile that she offers in return. Perhaps she understands that, as a practicing Muslim, Nabil wants to avoid contaminating his six-inch tuna-fish sub with any trace of nonhalal meat products.

It is the day before Nabil's high school graduation, and his mother and a few of her friends are busily preparing refreshments for a gathering of their nearest and dearest (one cousin is even flying in from California) later this evening. By all accounts he has finished high school with a bang, having just received a $750 All-Star Award from the Commercial Appeal, a Memphis newspaper, in recognition for his accomplishments in math. The honorees were profiled in the paper and invited to attend a formal banquet in the Grand Ballroom of the famous Peabody Hotel.

Tomorrow, Nabil will deliver the Cordova High School valedictory address to approximately four hundred members of the class of 2007. In between bites of Cheetos, he describes the contents of his five-hundred-word speech. "We worked hard to get to where we are, but we still don't know everything. There's always so much to learn, so keep working hard, doing what you've been doing, and good luck in the future," he says.

Leaning back in the green booth, with his long legs extended and crossed underneath the table, the maturity that Nabil has gained this year shows up on his face. His distinguished cheekbones are as sharp as the crease of a soldier's trousers, and he looks like he has grown an inch or two in the past nine months. Perhaps these are the physical signs of the wisdom that can be gained by weathering disappointment. A little more than two weeks ago, Nabil had what he calls "the worst day ever," though he manages a hearty chuckle after uttering the description.

Nabil had submitted his financial aid applications to colleges back in March, several weeks after the February 1 deadline. In most cases, the delay did not turn out to be a problem. Harvard waitlisted him anyway, Chicago offered him a full-tuition merit-based scholarship, and Princeton notified him of their generous financial aid offer ($31,000 in grants and $2,000 in work study) when he was accepted. Nabil didn't even bother completing the financial aid forms for Carnegie Mellon, which ended up not mattering after he was accepted to other schools that he was more interested in attending. As of early April, the only remaining monetary question mark was MIT, which also happened to be the college of his dreams.

When he was accepted to MIT, Nabil received a notice in his fat envelope asking him to submit his father's W-2 tax form. So he called up the Financial Aid Office to explain that his father does not receive this form because he is self-employed. He was grateful when the voice on the other end of the line told him not to worry about the forms. He thought the matter had been settled.

A few weeks later, Nabil left for MIT's Campus Preview Weekend. When he arrived on campus, he received another unsettling notice from the Financial Aid Office. Now they were asking for six additional financial forms to complete his application.

For the first time, Nabil started to worry. He knew that he had only two weeks to sort this out before the May 1 deadline, when he would have to make a final decision and communicate his enrollment plans to the colleges. Not wanting to delay, he headed over to the Financial Aid Office, but they held firm in their insistence that he could not receive financial aid without submitting these six forms. Nabil spent the rest of the weekend checking in with his dad between prefreshmen activities like student panels and receptions. A few days after he got back to Memphis, he and his father were finally able to send the detailed financial aid forms to MIT.

By mid-April, after his second visit to Cambridge in two months, Nabil was convinced that MIT was the perfect place for him. He had researched the courses that he wanted to take, connected with other future students, and started making plans to join the Juggling Club or maybe try out for the cross-country team. Nabil was even willing to go to MIT over Princeton if it cost him a little more.

But how much more could it cost?

A week or so later, Nabil still hadn't received notice of his financial aid award. He called the Financial Aid Office again. They told him not to worry, they had all his paperwork and would notify him on Monday, April 31 (the day before the deadline). Nabil pushed any concern he had out of his mind. However, April 31 came and went without word.

By the morning of May 1, Nabil still had no idea how much it would cost him to attend MIT. To top it all off, his final exam for his Introduction to Probability Theory class at the University of Memphis was also scheduled for that afternoon. Because of his back-to-back course schedule that morning, the only time he would have to check in with the MIT Financial Aid Office was literally on the way to the exam. Holding his breath and silently praying, he dialed the number from the road.

It wasn't good news. The financial aid officer informed Nabil that MIT expected his parents to contribute $43,000 to his education each year, despite their annual income of $80,000 for a family of seven—including four children under the age of eighteen. Nabil demanded to know how this number was derived. How could the university possibly ask his parents to part with half of their annual income to cover a single child's college tuition?

It was explained to him that MIT considers his father's stake in the gas stations at which he works as an "asset," even though he does not own any commercial property outright. Nabil knew he could never ask his father to sell his business or take out a second mortgage to pay for college, especially when he had so many less expensive options.

After hearing the news from MIT, Nabil forced himself to continue the drive to the University of Memphis for his final exam. Afterward, he sped to his father's gas station to deliver the distressing news. Nobody knew what to do. In a last-ditch effort, they called both Princeton and MIT to negotiate for more time. Nabil was told that although a drastic adjustment to his financial aid award was unlikely, MIT would extend the enrollment deadline another week to review the offer. Princeton, however, would not budge.

Nabil felt as though he had no choice. He shrugged his shoulders and headed to the post office to send off his response cards to the colleges that had accepted him. He will be a member of the Princeton University class of 2011.

"I wasn't crying or anything," Nabil says of his reaction to the turn of events. He lowers his head and concentrates on picking his cuticles, which I had never seen him do before. "It was more just the unexpectedness of it. It was so late. The way I was looking at it, I just thought I would be going to MIT for the past month or so. I guess it was just more about switching gears. If I knew I was going to have to go to Princeton, it wouldn't have been a problem."

Almost two thirds of MIT students received financial aid in 2006. The average award was $27,800 in loans and grants to cover the cost of attendance, which for last year was approximately $46,350. The following information is provided to applicants on their Web site:

> The amount of financial aid for which an undergraduate is eligible is determined by the family's financial situation. Using information provided by the family on the Free Application for Federal Student Aid (FAFSA) form and the College Scholarship Service (CSS) PROFILE form, MIT establishes dollar amounts for the parents' and the student's contributions. In addition, all aid recipients are expected to meet a portion of their need through a loan, part-time job, or both. This "self-help" component is set annually ($5,500 for 2006–2007). The balance is met with MIT scholarships—grants from endowed scholarship, gift, and Institute funds. This policy assures each student a reasonable loan, and provides an equitable distribution of grant funds.

Most people think that financial aid is readily available to needy students and that there is a straightforward process of getting it.

In this scenario, "financial aid officer X" punches some numbers into a computer and out comes the amount that a family is able to contribute toward higher education. This number is then subtracted from the college's sticker price and the balance represents the amount of the financial aid award.

Of course, getting financial aid for college is not this simple. For starters, students run out of luck when colleges run out of money. It is important to meet financial aid deadlines because most colleges have a fixed budget for need-based scholarships. In general, awards tend to be most generous at the beginning of the process. Some colleges also give priority to applicants with strong academic credentials as an incentive to attract these candidates.

One of the biggest variables in the amount of financial aid awarded to a particular student is how the college considers parental assets. Some colleges, like Princeton, look only at the family's annual income and savings when calculating their expected contribution for higher education. Others, like MIT, may scrutinize assets (whether or not parents own their house, a business, or other properties). They may also ask for more detailed information from those who are self-employed. In reviewing the details of expenditures and earnings, financial aid officers may determine that the family has more money available for college than the income they report to the federal government, which sometimes gives additional leeway for expenses associated with running a business (travel, entertaining clients, or expensive office supplies like computers). Though subject to extensive regulations, financial aid is not an exact science, which explains the vast difference between the awards that Nabil received from Princeton and MIT.

Financial aid officers are not all the same. Savvy professionals may be able to find ways to award students more money, just like good accountants can get their clients big tax refunds. Applications that land on the desk of someone who is inexperienced, overworked, or overbudget may be at a disadvantage in the process.

Also, because financial aid officers tend to hear many more complaints from disgruntled parents than compliments from satisfied customers, being courteous never hurts.

Nabil is now focused on moving forward and preparing for next fall at Princeton. "Don't check me under 'suicidal' or anything," he jokes. "I'm still looking forward to next year. I know it will be great."

Because Princeton often sponsors trips to New York City and Philadelphia for students, he's no longer worried about feeling isolated. He's also looking forward to taking classes with top math professors and exploring possibilities for doing undergraduate research. "The Princeton math department has a daily teatime in the math lounge, where students can get to know teachers better," he reports.

Now that classes are over, Nabil will have about three months off before he heads to college. Though he got into topnotch colleges, he did not get into math camp. "The application was due on May 1, the problems came out mid-January, and I didn't start writing up my work until late April," he explains. "I knew I waited too long to finally send in my solutions." Instead he'll start looking for a summer job and will continue to daydream about college life.

"There are so many different options," he says. "You don't know where a path will lead, so you can only look forward."

FAMILY AND FRIENDS of the Cordova High School class of 2007 laugh as they walk by a navy blue Dodge pickup truck in the parking lot of the Mid-South Coliseum with the words "Sexy Senior" and "High School Freedom" scrawled across the dirty front windshield. They make their way through the front entrance of the arena in polyester pantsuits, cotton polos, and nylon summer dresses, passing several security guards and a concession stand stocked with class of 2007 memorabilia. Once inside, a pretty Sandra Bullock type distributes graduation programs. They will soon become paper fans in the stuffy heat of the stadium, which has the faint odor of stale beer.

The Mid-South Coliseum was once a major center of cultural activity, but these days the twelve-thousand-seat arena hosts only seventy events a year, including the circus, jury duty summons, and graduations for high schools like Cordova. The center show ground, which is now tiled with cardboard, has previously functioned as a basketball court and an ice skating rink. This stage once welcomed Elvis and the Beatles, who played one of their final American performances here in 1966, when the cost of admission was only $5.50 per ticket.

A giant old electronic scoreboard featuring ads for Coca-Cola and Dr Pepper hangs from the coliseum's rounded roof, which is missing quite a few ceiling tiles. Cordova graduates will soon march underneath the dim billboard and down a provisional center aisle that has been carved out between about fifteen horizontal rows of red folding chairs. They face a makeshift high-rise platform stage draped in green, the school's color. It holds several additional folding chairs for distinguished guests, a podium for speakers, and a couple of long rectangular tables on which the students' diplomas are stacked high. A green and white felt flag with the school's logo dangles from the table, touching one of the potted ferns arranged in front.

The members of the Cordova marching band, who are dressed all in black, begin to play the traditional graduation song "Pomp and Circumstance." Graduates emerge in two separate lines from the backstage area, which probably served as the home and visitor locker rooms in the days when the Mid-South Coliseum was an athletics arena. Boys and girls proceed down the walkway in pairs (the boys wear black and the girls wear green robes), marching to the da-da-da beat of the music.

Nabil is one of the first students to appear. Adorned with extra tassels for various academic distinctions, like class valedictorian and honors society, he struts down the aisle and assumes his place onstage with the other student honorees. He then surveys the thousands of people in the stands, relishing the moment.

"Whew! Go Melissa," yells a group of smiling girls with elaborately braided hair and sparkling eye shadow. An extended family jumps up and cheers "Go Tia!" Everyone applauds for one particularly creative student with foot-long arrow stubs glued to the top of his graduation cap. Other members of the crowd scream names like Maaaatt, Beckyyyy, and Jaaaay-son as camera flashes sparkle around the stadium.

As the final members of the graduating class trickle in, the audience folds down the cushions on their flip seats, which are upholstered in a ratty red carpet material with lots of stains. Everyone is seated. The first speaker is the senior class president, an African American girl with straight shoulder-length hair, who talks about changes to the school dress code and encourages graduates to remember events like pep rallies, Winter Fest, and the class trip to Orlando, Florida, each of which she describes as "a blast." Next up is the salutatorian, Ben, who was a teammate of Nabil's on *Knowledge Bowl*. He talks about his own challenges in high school, like joining the cross-country team junior year. "I walked in an out-of-shape nerd and walked out a slightly less out-of-shape nerd," he jokes and ends his address with a quote from the band Semisonic. "Every new beginning is some other beginning's end."

Nabil's co-valedictorian, an Asian girl who is too small for her oversize green gown, follows Ben. She begins with a parable about seedlings that eventually "snap, crackle, and pop" out of their shells and take root in the metaphoric soil of Cordova High. She sums up her sentiments with the popular Robert Frost quote "Two roads diverged in a wood and I, I took the one less traveled by."

Nabil is the last student to address his fellow graduates. He is introduced as having excelled in ten AP courses and completed additional math classes at the University of Memphis. An audible "ooo" echoes around the stadium when the announcer says, "We wish him luck at Princeton next year." Nabil receives the loudest applause of all the class speakers and walks up to the podium with a wide grin. He speaks in a commanding and purposeful voice.

I would like to start off by welcoming all the parents and teachers, friends and family, ladies and gentlemen, and fellow classmates to the graduation ceremony for our Cordova class of 2007. If I may start off with a quote:

> 'Twas brillig, and the slithy toves
> Did gyre and gimble in the wabe.
> All mimsy were the borogroves
> And the mome raths outgrabe.

—LEWIS CARROLL, "JABBERWOCKY"

Do you understand that quote? Because I don't. And that's perfectly okay, to not know, to be clueless, to get lost and have to find your way back to safety, whether in a math problem or the school hallways or on the highway. It's okay if you need to stop by a metaphorical gas station and get directions. We all do occasionally, don't we? Do you know where you're going to be, what you're going to do in ten years? How about just five? And would we even want to know? For myself, surprise me.

I always find it funny when I think about James Stockdale, the Vice Presidential candidate who rhetorically asked in a debate, "Who am I? Why am I here?" Me, I ask why we go to school. To learn, of course. Why do we learn? Inevitably, the more we learn, the more we realize how little we know. And this in an age when there's so much to learn we can't possibly know it all. There was always so much at Cordova High that I bet for most of us what we most remember wasn't, couldn't be taught in the classrooms. In the end, how much did our grades matter? Long after we forget our GPAs, we'll still remember our classes, and how boring that one insert-class-name-here was or just how useful taking Speech turned out to be (for me at least). All these years of work weren't for nothing, but we must realize it's not this destination that we have worked toward, but the experience of having worked, of having pushed ourselves. The beat goes on, as the saying goes, and tomorrow, we still have our lives to continue. What have I learned? Aside from the academics, I've had to juggle between cross-country, track, Knowledge Bowl, and several different clubs these four years. This huge juggling act was all in preparation for the immensely difficult "real world" to come that people keep talking about, and that I keep dreading.

Yes, we are the Cordova Class of 2007, but none of us made it here all alone. Some of us have tutored others, or been the tutorees, or gotten missed homework assignments from someone else, or whatever. Although we are all of one class, I don't pretend to know all of your names; the relationships we've built between us are tighter among some than others. Our individual backgrounds include many different countries around the world and also many different languages. Despite all these differences, what we do have in common is the opportunities Cordova High afforded us and how we learned from them, whether in the school or on the field or wherever.

Some of us will be going to the same college, to close colleges, to colleges scattered across the country, or to other countries for the military. As valedictorian, I'm supposed to say "good-bye," at least linguistically, to all of you who are going on to do so many things and who helped make our class what it is today. But how can I? I don't know what the future contains for me, or for any of you, or where and when, if ever, our paths should find themselves crossing at the most unexpected time. All I can do is, as for myself, hope that each of you will do well, and take care of yourselves by making wise choices. With that wish in mind, I say to you, good luck.

How to Use "How To" Books

If you or someone you love is in the thick of the Fat Envelope Frenzy, you are probably looking for quality information about college admissions and financial aid to get you through the process. With so many topical books and Web sites, how do you decipher the good from the bad? It can be helpful to think of books about college admissions as belonging to one of four different categories: encyclopedic guides, students' perspectives, "how to," and big-picture.

Nearly everyone is familiar with the first category of college admissions books. Encyclopedic guides are those big, fat, floppy publications that provide a little information about a lot of colleges. Fiske and Peterson both publish fine examples of books in this genre each year. These guides are most useful in the beginning stages of the college application process as they provide the basic information on the landscape of schools and various admissions requirements. Like many reference books, it probably makes more sense to use these guides at the library rather than invest in buying them.

The second type of college admissions book is a helpful complement to the first. These books are written from the students' perspective, usually by editors who administer thousands of surveys on hundreds of different campuses. It's important to get some information from real college students, who tend to be refreshingly frank, especially because they don't work for these schools. Books such as *The Students' Guide to Colleges: The Definitive Guide to America's Top 100 Schools Written by the Real Experts—the Students Who Attend Them* by Jordan Goldman and Colleen Buyers or the Princeton Review's *Best 366 Colleges* can provide insight into things like class sizes, dorm life, and students' interaction with faculty on campuses across the country. As with the first category, these books can be easily referenced in the library.

After getting basic information about colleges and their students, most applicants will probably want to know more about what it takes to get into the schools they like. Enter the third category— the "how to" book. These books are designed to give advice on how to gain an advantage in the college admissions process and usually contain the words "insider," "truth," "getting in" or a combination of the three. This category includes seductive titles like *Rock Hard Apps*, *A Is for Admission*, and *What It Really Takes to Get into Ivy League and Other Highly Selective Colleges.*

Though some are better than others, "how to" books are predicated on an inherently false premise: the idea that a one-size-fits-all strategy will work for every student at every college at every point in time. Never take blanket advice like "Avoid writing your essay about community service" or "Send in extra teacher recommendations even if the college doesn't ask for them" as if it were gospel. Plenty of students who write about community service or submit no more than the required materials get into top colleges each year.

Look at the author's credentials before selecting any "how to" book. People who have actually read and evaluated college applications probably have something useful to say about the process; those who describe themselves as "packagers" or whose experience is confined to working only with high school students might not understand how college admissions offices really make decisions. *The New Rules of College Admissions: Ten Former Admissions Officers Reveal What It Takes to Get into College Today* by Stephen Kramer and Michael London is a good example of the former.

A popular subcategory of "how to" books only deals with a particular part of the application—the college essay. To be worthwhile, a book dedicated to writing the college essay should have something insightful to say about good writing in general. *On Writing the College Application Essay* by Harry Bauld is probably one of the few books in this category that might be worth owning (or taking out of the library). Many college essay books are comprised almost entirely of examples of "successful" essays, like *100 Successful College Application Essays,* published by the Harvard Independent, or *50 Successful Harvard Application Essays,* compiled by the Harvard Crimson. If you're the kind of person who finds samples helpful, you can probably get all the material you need by browsing through these books.

Books that fall into the fourth category, the big-picture books, are probably the least used and the most useful. These books tackle complex themes and provide systemic information about the history, climate, and context of selective college admissions. They are usually written by respected academics or journalists and present factual information gleaned from solid research. Historical works like Jerome Krabel's *The Chosen: The Hidden History of Admission and Exclusion at Harvard, Yale, and Princeton* and Nicholas Lemann's *The Big Test: The Secret History of the American Meritocracy* tell the story of how college admissions staples like the college essay or the SAT evolved over time. *The Gatekeepers* by Jacques

Steinberg follows a Wesleyan admissions officer through a single application cycle and presents an insightful account of the various forces at play in the actual process of selecting a class. *The Early Admissions Game: Joining the Elite* by Christopher Avery, Andrew Fairbanks, and Richard Zeckhauser and *The Price of Admission: How America's Ruling Class Buys Its Way into Elite Colleges—and Who Gets Left Outside the Gates* by Daniel Golden both present well-researched, fact-based exposés of the ways in which certain groups of students benefit from the closed-door admissions policies of selective colleges. Big-picture books like these are essential for anyone who wants to really understand how the system works.

In my opinion, the Internet is the best place to go for free, useful information about financial aid. Avoid anything written by private student lenders, like Sallie Mae or Chase, who are notorious for using misleading information about college financing to lure naïve students into taking out high-priced private loans. Stick to government or reputable nonprofit organizations when getting information about financial aid. Look for Web sites that end in .org or .gov, such as FinAid! (www.finaid.org), the U.S. Department of Education (studentaid.ed.gov), and the National Association of Student Financial Aid Administrators (www.nasfaa.org), each of which offers useful information about the types of financial aid available, including criteria for eligibility, deadlines, and applications.

Of course, it's always good to talk to other people about college admissions and financial aid as well. Visit different campuses, sit in on information sessions, and don't be afraid to ask tough questions. Call financial aid counselors if you need more information about deadlines or criteria. Speak to college students about their experiences with admissions, financial aid, academics, social life, or anything else you want to know. You might be surprised by how much good information you can get by simply asking for it.

· ACKNOWLEDGMENTS ·

Words cannot express my deep gratitude to Andrew, Felix, Lisa, Marlene, and Nabil for sharing their stories for this book. I can only hope that the high esteem with which I hold each one of them comes across in the telling. I would also like to thank their parents, siblings, friends, teachers, and counselors for their contributions to and support of this project.

I am incredibly grateful to my parents, Wende and Arnie, and my husband, Josh, for the hours they spent reading dozens of drafts, encouraging me to keep going when I felt frustrated, and putting up with me while under the stress of tight deadlines and sleepless nights. There is no way that I could have gotten through this process without them. I also want to thank the rest of my family, especially Shari, Jonathan, Joe, Aunt Linda, Uncle Rick, Linda, Eddie, Arlene, Jay, Andrew, and Grandma Kate. Grandma Sally deserves a special thank you for being the first to read my completed manuscript and always telling me the truth. I love you all.

I am fortunate to have so many amazing friends who supported me throughout this endeavor. Thanks to Noah Brosowsky, Kristina Hagstrom, Chris Van Ginhoven, Tim Holm, Betsy Devine, Julie Vultaggio, and Nahoko Kawakyu-O'Connor for reading various drafts and incarnations of this book in their spare time. Major props go out to the members of my writers' group, the Crucial Minutiaeists—Courtney Martin, Cristina Pippa, Daniel May, Ethan Todras-Whitehill, Felice Belle, Florian Duijsens, Jennifer Gandin Le, Kimberlee Auerbach, Theo Gangi, and especially Kate Torgovnick, the best writing partner, editor, shrink, and cheerleader ever.

This book would never exist without my extraordinary agent, Tracy Brown, a sincere advocate and endless champion who always believed in its message. I am incredibly grateful to my amazing editors, David Roth-Ey and Jeanette Perez, whose thoughtfulness and devotion to this book made the writing process truly collaborative. Thank you also to the wonderful people at HarperCollins for their stellar copyedits, jacket design, marketing strategies, and everything else that went into making this work available to the public.

Last, I would like to acknowledge all the amazing teachers and mentors who believed and invested in me. Thank you to Professors Bridget Terry Long, Gary Orfield, Robert Schwartz, Chris Avery, and Julie Reuben, who have given of themselves so freely throughout the course of my graduate studies at the Harvard Graduate School of Education. Thank you to Karla Jackson-Brewer, Katie Orenstein, Robin Stern, and the rest of the Woodhull community, especially Naomi Wolf for not only telling me that I could do it but showing me how. To Karl Furstenberg and the rest of the Dartmouth Admissions Office, I remain eternally grateful for taking me in and lighting this fire in me. It is the mark of a true education.

· SELECTED BIBLIOGRAPHY ·

"Adlai E. Stevenson High School: Information Resources." http://district125.
k12.il.us (accessed September 24, 2007).

Aratani, Lori. "Overachieving Students Hear a New Message: Lighten Up;
Schools, Parents Seek to Dial Back Academic Demands." *The Washington
Post*, February 6, 2007, p. A01.

Avery, Christopher, Andrew Fairbanks, and Richard Zeckhauser. *The Early
Admissions Game*. Cambridge, Mass.: Harvard University Press, 2003.

Avery, Christopher, Caroline Minter Hoxby, Clement Jackson, Kaitlin Burek,
Glenn Pope, and Mridula Raman. "Cost Should Be No Barrier: An Evaluation of the First Year of Harvard's Financial Aid Initiative." NBER Working Paper No. W12029 (February 2006). Available at SSRN: http://ssrn.
com/abstract=883078.

Baker, Gerard. "Go Directly to Yale." *The Times* (London), January 4, 2007, p. 4.

Borin, Jeannie. "Applying to College: No Easy Task." collegerecruiter.com
(March 27, 2007). http://www.collegerecruiter.com/admissionscounselors/
archives/2006/11/applying_to_college_no_easy_ta.php (accessed September 24, 2007).

Bowen, William G., and Derek Curtis Bok. *The Shape of the River: Long-Term
Consequences of Considering Race in College and University Admissions*.
Princeton, N.J.: Princeton University Press, 1998.

Bowen, William G., Martin A. Kurzweil, and Eugene M. Tobin. *Equity and Excellence in American Higher Education.* Charlottesville, Va.: The University of Virginia Press, 2005.

Bowen, William G., and J. L. Shulman. *The Game of Life: College Sports and Educational Values.* Princeton, N.J.: Princeton University Press, 2001.

Brandeis University. "Information and Resources." http://www.brandeis.edu/ (accessed September 25, 2007).

Carroll, Kate. "Rejected Applicant Alleges Bias Against Asians." *The Daily Princetonian,* November 13, 2006, http://www.dailyprincetonian.com/ archives/2006/11/13/news/16544.shtml (accessed September 24, 2007).

Channing Bete Company. "2003 Pennsylvania Youth Survey Report." http:// www.pccd.state.pa.us/pccd/lib/pccd/stats/payouthsurvey/2003_pa_ youth_survey_report.pdf (accessed September 25, 2007).

Chinni, Dante. "Heaven's Gate: Will Gaining Admission to One of the Nation's Elite Colleges Guarantee a Prosperous Future—or Just a Mountain of Debt?" *The Washington Post,* April 2, 2006, p. W10.

"City of Berwyn, Pennsylvania: Information Resources." http://www.berwyn pennsylvania.com (accessed September 24, 2007).

"City of Memphis, Tennessee: Information Resources." http://www.cityof memphis.org/framework.aspx?page=1 (accessed September 24, 2007).

City of New Orleans Official Tourism Web site. http://www.neworleans online.com (accessed September 24, 2007).

"City of New Rochelle, New York: Information Resources." http://www.new rochelleny.com (accessed September 24, 2007).

Cohen, Arthur M. *The Shaping of American Higher Education: Emergence and Growth of the Contemporary System.* San Francisco: Jossey-Bass Publishers, 1998.

College Board. "Trends in College Pricing 2006." http://www.collegeboard. com/prod_downloads/press/cost06/trends_college_pricing_06.pdf (accessed September 24, 2007).

College Board. "Trends in Student Aid 2006." http://www.collegeboard.com/ prod_downloads/press/cost06/trends_aid_06.pdf (accessed September 24, 2007).

"College's New Financial Aid Initiative Keeps Yield Near 80%." *Harvard University Gazette,* May 20, 2004, http://www.hno.harvard.edu/gazette/ 2004/05.20/03-yield.html (accessed September 24, 2007).

"Conestoga High School Profile 2006–2007." http://www.tesd.k12.pa.us/stoga/profile.pdf (accessed September 24, 2007).

"Cordova High School: Information Resources." http://www.memphis-schools.k12.tn.us/schools/cordova.hs/ (accessed September 24, 2007).

Cornwell, Rupert. "Nowhere Does Privilege Thrive So Well in the 'Classless' US Than in the Classroom; Out of America It's Meant to Be the Land of Opportunity. But Getting into a Top College Is Far Easier If Daddy Went There." *Independent on Sunday* (London), October 1, 2006, p. 54.

Correspondents of *The New York Times*. *Class Matters*. New York: Henry Holt, 2005.

DeNavas-Walt, Carmen, Bernadette D. Proctor, and Cheryl Hill Lee. U.S. Census Bureau, Current Population Reports, P60–231. *Income, Poverty, and Health Insurance Coverage in the United States: 2005*. Washington, D.C.: U.S. Government Printing Office, 2006.

Dillon, Sam. "A Great Year for Ivy League Colleges but Not So Good for Applicants to Them." *The New York Times*, April 4, 2007, p. B7.

Ehrenberg, Ronald, Liang Zhang, and Jared Levin. "Crafting a Class: The Tradeoff Between Merit Scholarships and Enrolling Lower-Income Students." *Review of Higher Education* 29, no. 2 (2006): 195–211.

Espenshade, Thomas J., and Chang Y Chung. "The Opportunity Cost of Admissions Preferences at Elite Universities." *Social Science Quarterly* 86, no. 2 (June 2005): 293–305.

Espenshade, Thomas J., Chang Y. Chung, and Joan L. Walling. "Admissions Preferences for Minority Students, Athletes, and Legacies at Elite Universities." *Social Science Quarterly* 85, no. 5 (December 2004): 1422–1446.

Farrell, Elizabeth. "Following Harvard's Lead, 2 Ivies Make Changes to Help Needy Students." *The Chronicle of Higher Education*, September 29, 2006, p. A44.

Fears, Darryl. "In Diversity Push, Top Universities Enrolling More Black Immigrants; Critics Say Effort Favors Elite Foreigners, Leaves Out Americans." *The Washington Post*, March 6, 2007, p. A02.

Finder, Alan. "Ivy League Admissions Crunch Brings New Cachet to Next Tier." *The New York Times*, May 16, 2007, p. A1.

Fischer, Karin. "Elite Colleges Lag in Serving the Needy. *The Chronicle of Higher Education*, May 12, 2006, p. A1.

Fitzsimmons, William, Marlyn McGrath Lewis, and Charles Ducey. "Time Out or Burn Out for the Next Generation." Harvard College Admissions Office Web site (2001), http://www.admissions.college.harvard.edu/prospective/applying/time_off/timeoff.html (accessed September 25, 2007).

Geiser, Saul, with Roger Studley. "UC and the SAT: Predictive Validity and Differential Impact of the SAT I and SAT II at the University of California." University of California Office of the President Web site (October 29, 2001), http://www.ucop.edu/sas/research/researchandplanning/pdf/sat_study.pdf (accessed September 24, 2007).

———. "Additional Findings on UC and the SAT." University of California Office of the President Web site (2002), http://www.ucop.edu/news/sat/resaddendfinal.pdf (accessed September 24, 2007).

Golden, Daniel. *The Price of Admission: How America's Ruling Class Buys Its Way Into Elite Colleges—and Who Gets Left Outside the Gates.* New York: Crown, 2006.

———. "The Z-list Is the New A-list: Why Being a Harvard Alumnus of Modest Means Can Hurt Your Child's Admissions Prospects." *02138*, Premier Issue, http://www.02138mag.com/magazine/article/826–3.html (accessed August 28, 2007).

Gordon, Larry. "College Hopefuls Living in Limbo; As Wait Lists Grow at Some Popular Schools, More Applicants Are Holding Out for a Chance to Fill Rare Open Slots." *Los Angeles Times*, May 10, 2007, p. B1.

Gose, Ben. "How to Keep from Application Overload." *The Boston Globe*, June 14, 2004, p. D1.

Gurin, Patricia. "New Research on the Benefits of Diversity in College and Beyond." Diversity Digest Web site (September 1999), http://www.umes.edu/hr/diversity_files/page0001.html (accessed September 24, 2007).

Harper, Jennifer. "Study Suggests Strategies for Ivy League Wannabes." *The Washington Times*, June 5, 2006, p. A09.

"Harvard University Summer School: Information and Resources." Harvard Summer School Web site, http://www.summer.harvard.edu (accessed September 25, 2007).

Higher Education Research Institute. "The American Freshman Forty-Year Trends: 1966–2006." (2006), http://www.gseis.ucla.edu/heri/PDFs/pubs/briefs/40yrTrendsResearchBrief.pdf (accessed September 24, 2007).

"History of the Common Application." https://www.commonapp.org/CommonApp/History.aspx (accessed September 25, 2007).

Jaschik, Scott. "Advanced Yes, Placement No." *Inside Higher Ed* (February 20, 2006), http://www.insidehighered.com/news/2006/02/20/ap (accessed February 21, 2007).

——. "Poison Ivy." *Economist* (September 21, 2006), http://www.economist.com/world/na/displaystory.cfm?story_id=7945858 (accessed September 20, 2007).

——. "Silver Spoon Admissions." *Inside Higher Ed* (September 5, 2006), http://www.insidehighered.com/news/2006/09/05/admit (accessed September 20, 2007).

"Jesuit High School, New Orleans: Information Resources." http://www.jesuitnola.org/about/aboutindex.htm (accessed September 24, 2007).

Karabel, Jerome. *The Chosen: The Hidden History of Admission and Exclusion at Harvard, Yale, and Princeton*. Boston: Houghton Mifflin, 2005.

——. "The New College Try." *The New York Times,* September 24, 2007, http://www.nytimes.com/2007/09/24/opinion/24karabel.html?em&ex=1190865600&en=d076d1cdb3289fea&ei=5087%0A (accessed September 25, 2007).

Kittay, Jeffrey. "The Ivy Curtain; How Meritocracy in Higher Education Arose from a System Built to Keep WASPs in and Jews Out." *The Washington Post*, October 30, 2005, p. T03.

Klein, Julia M. "Merit's Demerits." *The Chronicle of Higher Education*, November 4, 2005, p. B12 .

Kurtz, Howard. "College Faculties a Most Liberal Lot, Study Finds. *Washington Post*, March 29, 2005, p. C01.

Lau, Tatiana. "Legacy Study Raises Questions About Policy." *The Daily Princetonian*, March 29, 2007, http://www.dailyprincetonian.com/archives/2007/03/29/news/17854.shtml (accessed September 24, 2007).

Lin-Liu, Jen. "China's 'Harvard Girl': A College Student Has Become an Example for a New Style of Raising Children. *The Chronicle of Higher Education*, May 30, 2003, p. A40.

Marklein, Mary Beth. "Advanced Coursework: An 'Arms Race' Among Students." *USA Today*, March 21, 2006, p. 2D.

Mathematical Association of America. "American Mathematical Competitions: Information and Resources." http://www.unl.edu/amc (accessed September 24, 2007).

McCauley, Mary Beth. "Within the Ivy League, a Shift to the Right on Abortion?" *The Christian Science Monitor*, January 25, 2005, p. 12.

Megalli, Mark. "So Your Dad Went to Harvard: Now What About the Lower

Board Scores of White Legacies?" *The Journal of Blacks in Higher Education* 7 (Spring 1995): 71–73.

"Mid-South Coliseum: Information and Resources." http://www.midsouth coliseum.com (accessed September 25, 2007).

"Naked Hypocrisy: The Nationwide System of Affirmative Action for Whites." *The Journal of Blacks in Higher Education* 18 (Winter 1997–1998), http://links.jstor.org/sici?sici=10773711%28199724%2F199824%290%3A18%3C 40%3ANHTNSO%3E2.0.CO%3B2-O (accessed September 23, 2007).

"National Hurricane Center: Information Resources." http://www.nhc.noaa. gov (accessed September 25, 2007).

"National Merit Scholarship Corporation: Information Resources." http:// www.nationalmerit.org (accessed September 24, 2007).

"New Rochelle High School Homepage: Information Resources." http://nrhs. nred.org/home.aspx (accessed September 24, 2007).

"Phillips Academy Andover Homepage: Information Resources." http:// www.andover.edu (accessed September 24, 2007).

"Pontchartrain Center: Information and Resources." http://www.pontchar traincenter.com/site14.php (accessed September 25, 2007).

"Princeton University Costs and Financial Aid." Princeton University Undergraduate Admissions Web site, http://www.princeton.edu/admission/ financialaid (accessed September 25, 2007).

Robertson, Laura. "Ivy League Campuses Experience Spiritual Awakening" (2007), http://www.cbn.com/cbnnews/news/051117a.aspx (accessed August 29, 2007).

Sacks, Peter. "How Colleges Perpetuate Inequality." *The Chronicle of Higher Education*, January 12, 2007, p. B9.

Sanoff, Alvin P. "College Applications Take Off." *USA Today*, February 13, 2006, http://www.usatoday.com/news/education/2006–02–13-college-applications_x.htm (accessed September 25, 2007).

Schmidt, Peter. "Academe's Hispanic Future." *The Chronicle of Higher Education*, November 28, 2003, p. 8.

Schmidt, Peter, and Jeffrey R. Young. "MIT and Princeton Open 2 Summer Programs to Students of All Races." *The Chronicle of Higher Education*, February 21, 2003, p. A31.

Schwartz, Barry. "Why the Best Schools Can't Pick the Best Kids—and Vice Versa." *Los Angeles Times*, March 18, 2007, p. M1.

Shea, Christopher. "Victim of Success? Are Asian-American Students Discriminated Against in College Admissions?" *Boston Globe*, November 26, 2006, p. C3.

Silber, John. "In and Out." *Boston Globe*, October 30, 2005, p. E6.

Stephens, Kevin U. Testimony of Dr. Kevin U. Stephens, Sr., M.D., J.D. U.S. House of Representatives Committee on Energy and Commerce: Post Katrina Health Care: Continuing and Immediate Needs in the New Orleans Region, March 13, 2007.

Students for Academic Freedom. "Academic Bill of Rights." (2004), http://www. studentsforacademicfreedom.org/abor.html (accessed September 24, 2007).

Terenzini, Patrick T., Alberto F. Cabrera, Carol L. Colbeck, Stefani A. Bjorklund, and John M. Parente. "Racial and Ethnic Diversity in the Classroom: Does It Promote Student Learning?" *The Journal of Blacks in Higher Education* 72, no. 5 (September/October 2001): 509–531.

Thelin, John R. *A History of American Higher Education*. Baltimore and London: The Johns Hopkins University Press, 2004.

"The Harvard-MIT Mathematics Tournament: Information and Resources." http://web.mit.edu/hmmt/www (accessed September 25, 2007).

"The Rejects." *02138* 1 (May/June 2007): 96.

Tierney, William G. *The Changing Landscape of Higher Education: The Future of College Admission*. Washington, D.C.: National Association for College Admission Counseling, 2004.

"Top Colleges Show Record Rejection Rate." *Financial Times* (London), March 29, 2007, The Americas, p. 9.

"U.S. Olympic Training Center—Colorado Springs: Information and Resources." United States Olympic Committee Web site, http://www.usoc. org/12181_19096.htm (accessed September 25, 2007).

Viadero, Debra. "Advanced Hype—Studies Say AP Enrollment Doesn't Necessarily Ensure College Success." *Teacher Magazine* 17, no. 6 (May 1, 2006): 12.

"Village of Lincolnshire, Illinois: Information Resources." http://www.village. lincolnshire.il.us (accessed September 24, 2007).

Walters, Joanna. "Education: 'Any Black Student Will Do': A Disturbing Report Shows Some African Americans Are Being Squeezed Out of the US University Population." *The Guardian* (London), May 29, 2007, p. 12.

Washburn, Jennifer. *University Inc.: The Corporate Corruption of Higher Education*. New York: Basic Books, 2004.

"Washington and Lee University History." Washington and Lee University Web site, http://www1.wlu.edu/x22.xml (accessed September 25, 2007).